A Complete Guide to
PROVINCIAL and NATIONAL
Park Campgrounds

Camping
British Columbia

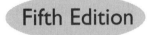

Fifth Edition

Jayne Seagrave

Heritage
House

HERITAGE HOUSE PUBLISHING CO. LTD.
#108 – 17665 66A Avenue
Surrey, BC V3S 2A7

Library and Archives Canada Cataloguing in Publication
Seagrave, Jayne, 1961-
    Camping British Columbia: a complete
guide to provincial and national park campgrounds.—5th ed.

Previously published as: Provincial and National Park campgrounds
    in British Columbia.
ISBN 1-894384-88-1

    1. Camp sites, facilities, etc.—British Columbia—Guidebooks. 2. Provincial parks and reserves—British Columbia—Guidebooks. 3. National parks and reserves—British Columbia—Guidebooks. 4. Outdoor recreation—British Columbia—Guidebooks. 5. British Columbia—Guidebooks. I. Title. II. Title: Camping British Columbia.

FC3813.S42 2005   796.54'09711

First edition 1997, second edition 1998, third edition 2001, fourth edition 2004

Edited by Karla Decker and Brenda Martin
Book design by Nancy St.Gelais and Darlene Nickull
Cover design by Frances Hunter
Front cover photo of Goldpan Provincial Park by Chris Cheadle/BritishColumbiaPhotos.com
Back cover photos by Jayne Seagrave
All interior photos provided by the author except p. 50, G. Wood.
Printed in Canada

Heritage House acknowledges the financial support for its publishing program from the Government of Canada through the Book Publishing Industry Development Program (BPIDP), Canada Council for the Arts, and the British Columbia Arts Council.

The Canada Council | Le Conseil des Arts
for the Arts | du Canada

BRITISH COLUMBIA
ARTS COUNCIL
Supported by the Province of British Columbia

ACKNOWLEDGEMENTS

The publication of this guide to national and provincial park campgrounds fulfilled my long ambition to write and publish a book on camping in British Columbia. A number of individuals and organizations helped me to achieve my goal. In addition, the experience I gained writing the first four editions of this book and in researching *The Best Camping Adventures: Southwestern B.C. and Vancouver Island* and *Best Camping Adventures: Northern, Central and Southeastern B.C*, and, more recently, *Camping With Kids* proved invaluable in updating the text for this fifth edition.

The data I collected from site visits was greatly supplemented by the valuable information and assistance I received from BC Parks—both from the headquarters in Victoria and the regional offices.

The enthusiasm, professional approach, advice, and expertise of the editorial staff at Heritage House improved the quality and appearance of the text. I am also grateful to the sales and marketing staff for promoting the books.

The largest debt is owed to my camping partner, Andrew Dewberry, who encourages my dreams and ambitions and who taught me to camp. Without him, the initial book and the subsequent editions would not have been possible.

**Visit the Heritage House web site at
www.heritagehouse.ca**

Camping and reading fit together. Find out which books you would like to take with you on your holiday. Learn about the history of the location you plan to visit. Take some of the children's books with you to entertain your children as they travel between campsites.

CONTENTS

CAMPGROUNDS IN
BRITISH COLUMBIA

Listed by page number.

Facilities vary between parks. Some provide playgrounds, solar showers, and amphitheatres.

Introduction

This fifth edition of *Camping British Columbia* builds upon and updates the information contained in my previous books. It was written out of a love of camping and a deep respect for British Columbia. As Canada's third largest province, B.C. covers 950,000 square kilometres, including 18,000 square kilometres of inland water. B.C. has more land designated to provincial parks than does any state in the U.S. except for Alaska and Hawaii, and it boasts over 400 different locations for day use and camping. In addition, six national parks are found in the province, four of these with developed camping facilities. With all this space for exploration and over 12,000 camping spots, it is little wonder that the "camping experience" has become an integral part of recreational life for B.C. residents and visitors alike.

The following chapters provide details of B.C.'s national and provincial park campgrounds and have been divided into six regions: The Islands, Vancouver Coast and Mountains, Thompson Okanagan, B.C. Rockies, Cariboo Chilcotin Coast, and Northern British Columbia.

The introductory chapter of this guide details important background information on camping in British Columbia, including how to select a camping spot, what to take camping, the reservation process, and potential hazards. It offers guidance to the novice and acts as a reminder to the seasoned camper.

Ensuing chapters give details of the provincial and national campgrounds in each of the six regions, their location, the facilities offered, the recreational activities available, and additional information of interest. Currently a number of changes are taking place in British Columbia's provincial parks. Services that many of us are used to, such as free firewood, campground hosts, information leaflets, free parking, and interpretive programs, have been cut or are dependent on a private service provider rather than the provincial government. This made writing this guide somewhat challenging.

For those who seek guidance on campgrounds, I have offered 7-, 14-, and 21-day camping itineraries; these are at the end of the book. The selections are based on my personal experiences and amenity evaluations and are designed to cover pragmatic travel distances on any given day.

This book has been written both for those who camp in tents and those who use recreational vehicles (RVs). It contains information only on provincial and national parks that are accessible by vehicle (with the exception of Sidney Spit and Newcastle Island) and have at least the basic amenities of water, picnic table, fire pit, and toilets. No private campgrounds are included, although many of these offer wonderful camping facilities.

Camping is a personal experience; what appeals to one person may not appeal to another. However, British Columbia is blessed with some of the most breathtaking scenery in the world. Many of the provincial and national parks nestle in the heart of this beauty and are yours to experience at relatively little cost. Over the course of the last 15 years I have travelled and camped in every region of B.C. and have been amazed at the stunning beauty the province offers. It still surprises me that many residents of B.C. do not camp. I hope this book encourages more individuals to take the plunge and use the excellent facilities provided in B.C.'s parks. A wealth of adventures and experiences can be enjoyed by those of every age. So, what are you waiting for?

Experience the old way—use a water pump at a B.C. park.

THE CAMPING EXPERIENCE

The aim of this chapter is to provide some of the basic ground rules on camping in B.C.'s national and provincial parks. While the information in this chapter is intended primarily for the uninitiated, to show them what to expect, those who regularly camp will find the data on making reservations, what to take, and how to deal with bears and other hazards a useful reminder.

Arriving at a Provincial or National Park Campground

All national and provincial park campgrounds are well signposted from major highways. A sign (blue for provincial parks, brown for national parks) 2 kilometres before the campground turnoff is the first warning you will receive, followed by another one 400 metres from the campground to direct you to the access road. The park operator will post notices on these roadside signs to state when a campground is full or closed. You will come to appreciate what a real advantage this is if the campground is located 60 kilometres from the highway on a rough gravel road.

Selecting your spot

Presuming you do not have a reservation excitement upon arrival is selecting *your* spot. Depending on the season, time of day, and location of the park, this decision may already be out of your hands. The park may be full or there may be only one place left. Some parks have areas specifically designated for tents, while most have spots suitable for both RVs and tents. A number of parks offer "double spots," ideal for two families camping together, and pull-through spots for the larger RVs. A map of the campground at the park entrance shows where these are to be found. If the park offers a reservation service, the reserved sites will be listed at the park's entrance. Once you have established which campsites are available, you should "cruise" the campground to select your spot. Campsites by a beach, lake, river, or creek are the most desirable locations, so head for these first, making a mental note of where the water tap is located. Try to avoid areas of stagnant water (mosquito breeding grounds) or spots close to the "thunderboxes" (pit toilets), which, during the park's warm summer months, may exude unpleasant odours, attract flies, and cause a disturbance from banging doors. At first glance, spots near the flush toilets and showers may seem convenient, but remember that between 5:00 p.m. and 11:00 p.m. and 7:00 a.m. and 11:00 a.m., most people at the campground will be visiting these facilities at least twice and walking past your site in order to do it. On the other hand, if you have children in your party or want to meet people, you may deem these spots ideal.

Once you have driven around and made a mental note of your preferences, return to and claim your first choice. Should you not want to pitch camp immediately, leave a plastic tablecloth or water jug on the picnic table to state to the world that this is *your* spot. If the campground requires self-registration, you need to complete a self-registration form and pin the receipt to your spot (see "Fees").

If you delay pitching your tent or going to collect water, just don't forget what time it gets dark. This is particularly relevant if you are camping in the shoulder seasons of early spring and late summer, when darkness falls as early as 7:00 p.m. Arriving at a campground late, pitching your tent in the dark, and cooking dinner by flashlight is challenging to say the least. In contrast, relaxing by the fire while the sun goes down and the stars come out is a highly pleasurable experience when you know your bed is made, dinner is over, and the dishes done. Once established in your new home, you are ready to explore the campground. The first port of call should be a return visit to the information board at the park's entrance, where you will find a map of the campground and details about any hazards in the area.

Fees

During the early-evening hours in most parks, an attendant will come and collect payment (cash only). Camping fees vary depending on the facilities provided; campgrounds with showers tend to be the most expensive, whereas less developed campgrounds have lower fees. Fees include GST and in 2004 ranged from $9.50 to $22.00 for provincial parks and up to $25.00 in national parks. Parks also request payment for firewood ($5.00 to $7.00 per bundle—and the bundles do vary considerably in size). An additional entrance fee is

Notice boards near park entrances provide useful information for campers.

charged in all national parks whether you intend to camp or not, and some of the more popular provincial parks now also charge for parking in the day-use areas ($3.00-$5.00 per day). If camping in the park, you do not have to pay the vehicle fee for parking in the day-use area as long as you display your camping receipt in your vehicle.

When registering you will be asked to provide your name, the number of people in your party, car registration number, and where you are from. You can pay for as many nights as you want, up to a maximum of 14 nights in both provincial and national parks (some parks may limit your stay to seven nights). A receipt displaying the date on which you intend to leave will be posted on your spot. Some parks operate an honour self-registration system whereby you deposit the campground fee in an envelope, place it in a box at the entrance to the park, and secure a receipt. For such instances, it is good to ensure that you have small bills and change, although fellow campers are usually willing to help you out. Instructions on self-registering are printed on a sign at the park's entrance and on the deposit envelope. Park attendants are good sources of information on weather conditions, local activities, the best fishing locations, and so on.

Before June 14 and after Labour Day, residents of B.C. who are 65 or older may camp for half price in provincial parks. From June 15 to Labour Day, full rates apply.

Facilities

With a few exceptions, all campgrounds included in this text have the basic facilities of water, wood for sale, pit toilets, picnic tables, and fire pits. (A few provincial parks offer primitive camping without the basic facilities; these have not been included in this book.) Larger campgrounds can include sani-stations, flush toilets, showers, wheelchair access, interpretive programs, visitor centres, and group camping. Washroom facilities are generally well maintained, clean, and, unlike many campgrounds I have stayed in abroad, they never run out of toilet tissue. (I was preconditioned in Europe, so it took me years to realize this and stop carrying a spare roll.) Gravel camping spots are tidied and raked after each visitor departs, garbage is regularly collected, and recycling is encouraged. Overall, the facilities provided in B.C.'s national and provincial parks are excellent.

Although some campgrounds are open throughout the year, fees for individual camping spots are collected only from April to October. I have found that even in September, despite remaining open, many of the smaller campgrounds do not collect fees.

In 2004 BC Parks started to charge $6.00 for a bundle of firewood. Hot, dry conditions sometimes result in a ban on fires. A few campgrounds (e.g. Porpoise Bay) have gone so far as to ban individual campfires at all times while others, such as Juan de Fuca, actively discourage fires for environmental reasons. When conditions are excessively hot and dry, as they were in the summer of 2003, most campgrounds ban fires. If you need a campfire to make your camping experience complete, contact the regional office for the campground you want to stay in to determine if fires are allowed, or check the campground notice board when you arrive.

Reservations

In 1996 BC Parks offered a new service that enabled advance reservations to be made in 42 of the more popular provincial parks and in two national parks. By 2001 the number of campgrounds accepting reservations was 66, reflecting the popularity of the initiative. If you do not have a reservation, campsites are available on a first-come, first-served basis. Only a certain number of campsites in each campground are available to be reserved, although this number can be as high as 80 percent. To make a reservation, phone *Discover Camping Campground Reservation Service* (1-800-689-9025 if calling from outside the Lower Mainland, 604-689-9025 from Vancouver and surrounding area) or visit its web site at www.discovercamping.ca and book your reservation on-line. In 2004 the fee to reserve was $6.42 per night to a maximum of $19.26 for 3 to 14 nights. Campers pay the reservation and campsite fees when making a reservation. Payment is taken by MasterCard or VISA and includes GST. Reservations are taken from March 1 to September 15, and sites can be reserved up to three months in advance and as late as two days prior to arrival.

For those who have found a full house at a popular campground on the times they have tried to visit, the reservation system provides a way to avoid uncertainty. While reservations offer the advantage of assuring accommodation for the night, the downside is that you have no choice over your spot and could end up next to a particularly well-used

Campgrounds that Accept Reservations

Alice Lake	Liard River Hotsprings
Bamberton	Little Qualicum Falls
Barkerville	Loveland Bay
Bear Creek	Manning
Beatton	Miracle Beach
Beaumont	Moberly Lake
Birkenhead	Monck
Blanket Creek	Montague Harbour
Champion Lakes	Mount Fernie
Charlie Lake	Mount Robson
Cowichan River	Moyie Lake
Crooked River	Nairn Falls
Cultus Lake	Okanagan Lake
Elk Falls	Otter Lake
Ellison	Paarens Beach
Englishman River Falls	Pacific Rim (National)
Fillongley	Porpoise Bay
Fintry	Porteau Cove
French Beach	Premier Lake
Gladstone	Prior Centennial
Golden Ears	Rathtrevor
Goldstream	Rolley Lake
Gordon Bay	Saltery Bay
Green Lake	Sasquatch
Haynes Point	Shuswap Lake
Herald	Smelt Bay
Juan de Fuca	Sproat Lake
Kekuli Bay	Stamp River
Kettle River	Strathcona
Kikomun Creek	Syringa
Kokanee Creek	Ten Mile Lake
Kootenay (National)	Tyhee
Lac la Hache	Wasa Lake
Lac Le Jeune	Wells Gray
Lakelse Lake	

The Rules of Park Camping

Although few formal rules exist, there is a definite camping etiquette that should be observed for the benefit of all. Most of the items in the following list are common sense and serve only as a gentle reminder.

1. Quiet time starts at 11:00 p.m. when the park gates are closed. Campsite visitor restrictions apply, and park gates are closed between 11:00 p.m. and 7:00 a.m.

2. In season, the threat of forest fires is immense, so extreme caution should be taken. At all times, light fires only in metal fire pits.

3. Store food in your vehicle, in airtight containers. If you do not have a vehicle and are in an area frequented by bears, hang food in bags suspended on a tree branch, four metres above the ground. With 100,000 black bears in B.C., this is not a rule to ignore.

4. To protect the vegetation, camp only in the designated areas.

5. Recycle as much as possible using BC Parks dispensers.

6. Burn only as much wood as you need—help preserve the environment.

7. Checkout time is 11:00 a.m., and the maximum length of stay is 14 days per year in any one park (a few parks restrict your stay to seven nights). A camping party is regarded as a family from the same address, or if not a family, a maximum of eight people, up to four of whom may be 16 years or older.

8. Cutting branches, flowers, berries, or mushrooms is prohibited in all parks. Enjoy the flora and fauna by looking, smelling, and photographing, but leave it for others to have the same pleasure.

9. Clean your campsite on departure. Remove all garbage.

10. Keep pets on a leash in campgrounds and all other restricted areas.

11. Do not use your fire pit for garbage disposal. Partly burnt food tempts wildlife, and blackened beer cans are an annoyance.

12. BC Parks allows one vehicle and trailer per site. Either one (but not both) may be an RV. A second vehicle (not an RV) may be allowed on the site for the additional nightly charge of half of the camping fee.

13. Do not take powerboats near swimmers; try not to disturb the tranquility of those enjoying the beach.

14. Alcohol is allowed at your campsite. I had camped for years before I learned it was okay to consume a glass of wine with our dinner. I guiltily hid my drink from the park attendant I thought would expel me for my transgression. On one occasion, discovered and expecting to meet the full wrath of the BC Parks employee, I cowered and apologized. All he said was, "You can drink here. This is your home away from home. It is only in the public sections of the park that alcohol is prohibited." From that point on, I've always thought of provincial park camping spots as "home away from home."

thunderbox (pit toilet) or at the busy entrance to the campground. In this book, the "Facilities" section describing each campground notes whether or not reservations are accepted. Reservations are now accepted at Kootenay and Pacific Rim national parks, in addition to the provincial park campgrounds listed in "Campgrounds that Accept Reservations."

Potential Hazards

The hazards of a vicinity are posted at the campground entrance. Here are the more common problems and how to avoid them.

Swimmer's Itch

Parasites living in freshwater snails and waterfowl can cause swimmer's itch, or *cercarial dermatitis*, a temporary skin irritation caused by the parasites' larvae entering the skin. The larvae thrive close to the shore in warm waters of lakes and ponds where Canada geese and other waterfowl are found. Because children go in and out of the water frequently and have tender skin, they are particularly vulnerable. Swimmer's itch can be avoided by applying a skin oil such as baby oil before swimming, towelling off briskly, and showering after swimming. The presence of swimmer's itch is indicated by small red spots that can develop into small blisters. Although unpleasant, the condition can be treated with calamine lotion and the condition usually clears up by itself within a week. The information board at the campground entrance will indicate whether swimmer's itch is a problem at the lake you plan to visit.

Poison Ivy

This low, glossy plant with three green leaves and white berries can produce severe skin rashes. It is prevalent in sunny areas on Vancouver Island and in the Okanagan. Calamine lotion is an effective treatment.

Sunburn

You are living largely outdoors when camping, and it is easy to forget how long you have been exposed to the sun. Always remember to apply and reapply sunscreen, wear a hat, and be especially careful when you're around water or snow, which reflect the sun and can compound burns.

Water

Lifeguards are not employed in B.C. parks, so a watchful eye must be kept on those who cannot swim. Some parks have designated swimming areas; others do not. Climatic conditions may change rapidly in some locations, with winds suddenly developing and causing a hazard for boating enthusiasts. Again, information on the park's notice board will state whether this is a problem.

Bears

B.C. is home to almost one-quarter of all the black bears in Canada and about half of the grizzlies. Although encounters between people and bears are rare, campers should remember they are always in bear country in B.C. Respect bears as strong, fast, wild animals, and act responsibly at all times.

Generally, bears go out of their way to avoid people, but all bears are dangerous. They can rip apart tents and vehicles in their search for food, run as fast as a racehorse, and they have excellent sight, hearing, and sense of smell. They are strong swimmers, and black bears and young grizzlies are agile tree-climbers. Upon leaving the city, you are in bear country and should use caution.

Anyone planning to camp or spend time in the outdoors should learn how to recognize a black or grizzly bear and how to respond accordingly. Black bears can be black, brown, cinnamon, or blond with a straight face profile, short curved claws, and a small shoulder hump. Grizzly bears can also be black, brown, or blond, but are bigger than black bears and have long curved claws and a prominent shoulder hump. When walking in bear country, watch for warning signs such as tracks, overturned rocks, clawed trees, chewed roots, and droppings. Talk loudly, wear bear bells, or sing to make your presence known. If you see a bear in the distance, leave the area immediately. If you encounter one at close range, avoid eye contact, move away slowly, and stay calm. If the bear stands up as it approaches you, it is trying to identify what you are. Talk quietly so it knows you are human. If it is lowering its head, flattening its ears, snapping its jaws, and snorting, the bear is displaying aggression. This is serious. Do not run, but continue to back away. If a grizzly shows aggression, consider climbing a tree. Generally, the key is to do nothing to threaten or arouse the animal. If a grizzly attacks,

> ➤ Avoid cooking fish, as the smell strongly attracts bears.

> ➤ Cook and eat away from your tent.

> ➤ Clean up immediately and do not leave cooking utensils, coolers, or dishwater around.

> ➤ Never bury garbage. Bears normally dig for food, and they may remember the location as a food source, thus endangering those visitors that follow.

> ➤ Avoid getting scents or food smells on clothing or sleeping bags.

> ➤ Women should consider using tampons if menstruating.

> ➤ Always use a flashlight if walking at night.

play dead and adopt a tight, curled-up position with your head on your knees and your hands behind your neck. Do not move until the bear leaves the area. If a black bear attacks, try to retreat to a safe place and use weapons such as rocks and branches to deter the animal.

Never approach or feed bears. Food-conditioned bears—those that scavenge food from garbage cans and picnic tables—begin to associate food with people, lose their natural fear of humans, and become a threat to campers and to themselves. With caution and sensible behaviour, you can safely camp in and enjoy bear country.

What to Take Camping

To the uninitiated, it would appear that some people take everything camping. On one occasion, I camped next to a couple who had a large RV with two mountain bikes tied to the front, a boat on the roof, and a small four-wheel-drive vehicle towed behind. Their picnic table displayed several coolers of assorted sizes, wine glasses, a breadbasket, and a red checked tablecloth; overhead was an ornate striped awning. Artificial grass, potted plants, lanterns, and numerous plastic lounge chairs with cushions were strategically positioned around a huge barbecue. This campsite had more accoutrements than my home (and certainly was worth more). It is impossible to provide the definitive list of necessities, but there are a number of items that will make your camping experience more enjoyable, whether you are a tenter or an RVer.

I started my B.C. camping career in 1992 with a two-person tent (designed for two *very* small people) and toured the province in a 1974 Ford Pinto. On this first excursion I was totally unprepared. My partner and I had no axe, so to make a fire we had to arrive at a campground early enough to collect the unused wood that had been cut by our predecessors. On one occasion this option was not available, so we approached a neighbouring site and asked a camper if we could borrow his axe. He came over from his well-equipped RV to supply the tool and chat. After surveying our meagre tent and picnic table (displaying two plastic plates, two plastic mugs, and one plastic grocery bag of food), he started to explain how he started as we were doing, with barely the basics, but assured us that as each year progressed our commitment to camping would grow and more "comforts" would be acquired. He was right. We now arrive at our campsite in a 1990s seven-seater van, sleep on self-inflating thermarests in a six-person tent we can stand up in, have tarps, a red checked tablecloth, clotheslines, coolers, a hibachi, and yes, even an axe. On three separate occasions we have been lucky enough to camp in a 28-foot recreational vehicle—real luxury. On occasion we see novice campers starting out as we and many others have done, and we look knowingly at each other, content in the thought that it will not be long before they too start to collect the camping necessities. One of the tremendous joys of camping is *learning* how to do it.

Camping Essentials

- aluminum foil
- axe
- barbecue, hibachi, gas stove and gas
- biodegradable dish soap, scrubbing pads
- bungee cords
- camera and film
- candles/lantern
- first-aid kit, including calamine lotion
- flashlight
- food
- garbage bags
- insect repellent
- matches and newspaper for the campfire
- paper towels
- pocket knife
- pots, dishes, cutlery
- rainy-day activities (books, portable radio, travel games)
- rope
- sleeping bag, foam or air mattress
- toilet paper
- sunglasses, hat, and sunscreen
- tarp
- tent and fly, tent trailer, camper, recreational vehicle
- toilet paper
- towels
- water container and funnel (to collect water from water pump)

British Columbia Regions

1. The Islands
2. Vancouver Coast and Mountains
3. Thompson Okanagan
4. B.C. Rockies
5. Cariboo Chilcotin Coast
6. Northern B.C.

THE REGIONS
AND THEIR PARKS

This section is divided into six chapters that reflect the main geographical regions of the province.

Maps at the beginning of each chapter show the location of each campground and the main highways and centres of population. They serve only as a guide. More accurate information can be obtained by referencing a good map of the province, such as the *British Columbia Road & Recreational Atlas* or the *Road Map and Parks Guide*. Additional information on provincial parks in the various regions can be found on the Internet; a list of useful web sites is at the back of this book.

Camper Rentals

At least 26 RV rental companies detail their equipment offerings and locations at the Super Natural Camping British Columbia web site:
http://www.travel.bc.ca

Another web site to check out is:
http://www.camping.bc.ca

To reach campgrounds on the islands, you will have to take one of the BC Ferries vessels, such as these seen at Pender Island.

Ferry Schedules

Current BC Ferries schedules are always available at Tourism BC centres, in some daily newspapers, and on the BC Ferries web site at http://www.bcferries.bc.ca, or call 1-888-223-3779.

THE ISLANDS

This chapter includes campgrounds located on Vancouver Island and the Gulf Islands. Vancouver Island is the largest North American island in the Pacific and stretches 450 kilometres. Named after Captain Vancouver, one of the first European visitors in 1778, this varied region includes mountains, farmlands, miles of breathtaking coastline (lots of it inaccessible by road), and unique wildlife. The Gulf Islands are situated between Vancouver Island and the mainland and for many residents offer a serene and alternative lifestyle away from the populations of the Lower Mainland and southern Vancouver Island. Tourists, too, find the islands a delight. Despite the number of campgrounds available, the popularity of the region and its convenient location to large centres of population mean that many idyllic spots have been reserved, especially during July and August.

Sunsets at Montague Harbour are astoundingly beautiful.

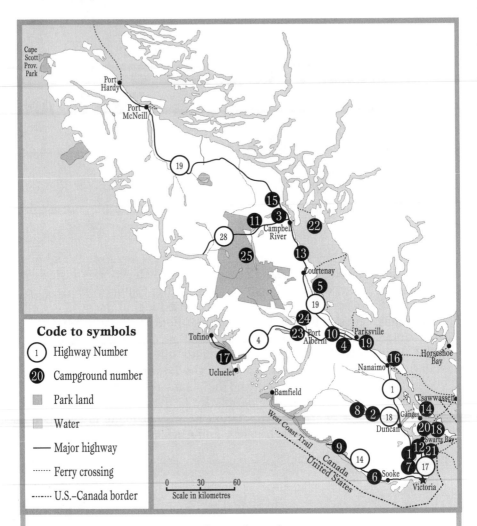

The Islands

1. Bamberton, p. 27
2. Cowichan River, p. 28
3. Elk Falls, p. 29
4. Englishman River Falls, p. 30
5. Fillongley, p. 31
6. French Beach, p. 32
7. Goldstream, p. 33
8. Gordon Bay, p. 34
9. Juan de Fuca, p. 35
10. Little Qualicum Falls, p. 36
11. Loveland Bay, p. 37
12. McDonald, p. 38
13. Miracle Beach, p. 39
14. Montague Harbour, p. 40
15. Morton Lake, p. 41
16. Newcastle Island, p. 42
17. Pacific Rim National, p. 43
18. Prior Centennial, p. 45
19. Rathtrevor Beach, p. 46
20. Ruckle, p. 47
21. Sidney Spit Marine, p. 48
22. Smelt Bay, p. 49
23. Sproat Lake, p. 50
24. Stamp River, p. 51
25. Strathcona, p. 52

BAMBERTON

Location

A true family-friendly campground
and a really picturesque location,
Bamberton looks onto Finlayson
Arm of the Saanich Inlet, across the
Gulf Islands to Mount Baker and beyond. Bamberton is situated about
half an hour's drive from Victoria, 1
kilometre east of Highway 1 at Malahat Drive. Services are available on
the highway, in Victoria to the south,
and in Duncan to the north.

Facilities

Nestled in a lightly forested area, which includes arbutus trees (only found
on Vancouver Island, the lower Gulf Islands and the Lower Mainland), are 50
well-appointed, private camping spots. There are flush and pit toilets but no
sani-station or showers. The park is wheelchair accessible, and reservations
are accepted.

Recreational activities

This is a popular family recreational area, as the warm waters of the
Saanich Inlet together with over 225 metres of beach make it a pleasant
place for families to congregate, play, and rest. Creeks that run through
the park have little fishing potential, but it is possible to catch salmon
in the inlet. Small trails lead from the campground to the beach area. As
this provincial park is so close to Victoria, 30 minutes to the south, and
Duncan, 20 minutes north, there are many additional things to see and do
outside the immediate area. For example, just north of Duncan is a forest
museum displaying logging artifacts and giving the history of an industry
that is very much a part of Vancouver Island's heritage.

Additional information

Bamberton was given to the people of B.C. by the British Columbia Cement
Company, and the name was chosen to commemorate H.K. Bamber, a
former managing director of the company. Its proximity to Victoria and the
population of southern Vancouver Island means Bamberton is a popular
place for locals to spend weekends and therefore can become very busy. It is
far more desirable than a nearby competitor, McDonald.

COWICHAN RIVER

Location

This is one of BC Parks' newer provincial parks; Cowichan River was recently designated a Provincial Heritage River because it is internationally renowned for its wild salmon and steelhead. Although less than four years old, this park has become very popular, especially amongst the angling community. Located between Cowichan Lake and Duncan, the 742-hectare park can be reached from Highway 18 on a good gravel road or from Highway 1 south of Duncan, again by a 17-kilometre paved and gravel road. Services are available in both Cowichan Lake and Duncan.

Facilities

There are two campgrounds in this park. Thirty-three vehicle and four walk-in camping spots are located at Skutz Falls (*skutz* means "waterfall" and comes from the Cowichan word *skewts*). Most of these are open and quite close together, offering little privacy. An additional 39 are located at Stolz Pool on the Cowichan River. Water, pit toilets, picnic tables, and fire pits are all provided. Reservations are available at the Stolz Pool campground.

Recreational activities

The Cowichan River is one of Vancouver Island's most popular fishing environments. It flows 47 kilometres from its headwaters at Cowichan Lake to the sea and is known as an angler's paradise with rainbow and steelhead trout and excellent salmon runs. A section of the Cowichan River footpath, a 19-kilometre trail leading to some of the best fishing holes, is within the park boundaries. As well as the excellent fishing potential, the park has swimming, canoeing, kayaking, hiking, and tubing possibilities and therefore is attractive to all ages. A section of the Trans-Canada Trail runs through the park's boundaries.

Additional information

In addition to being the delight of many fishers, this location is ideal for exploring the communities of Cowichan Lake and Duncan. Duncan calls itself the "city of totems" and is home to over 40 totem poles, which have been erected primarily in the downtown area. Some depict traditional design while others are less traditional. Duncan also houses the Native Heritage Centre, a fascinating place found on the banks of the Cowichan River that has a longhouse, theatre, and arts and craft centre. When we stayed, there seemed to be hundreds of teenagers sunbathing on the large slab rocks, with huge tubes lying by their sides. Every vehicle in the car park had a tube tied to it. In this respect, at the height of summer it is a place that attracts a younger crowd. However, these youths were not loud and seemed aware of the "rules of camping." I imagine that during the shoulder season this is a wonderful (and quieter) place for people of every age to visit.

ELK FALLS

Location

This is a beautiful provincial park that features a cascading 25-metre waterfall created by the Campbell River falling into a walled canyon. In spring, the waters tumble (and in late summer trickle) over a deep gorge and provide a beautiful vista. Elk Falls is located on Highway 28 just 2 kilometres north of Campbell River, where all services are available.

Facilities

Elk Falls boasts 122 large, private camping spots surrounded by trees. Approximately 25 of the more desirable spots are situated along the banks of the Quinsam River; the rest are among an area of second-growth forest. There is a sani-station and a couple of flush toilets, but no wheelchair accessibility. Reservations are accepted. The day-use area is separate from the campground, making for quite a peaceful provincial park.

Recreational activities

The primary attraction of the area is fishing, which is excellent in both Campbell River and Quinsam River. Depending on the time of year, steelhead, rainbow and cutthroat trout and Dolly Varden can be caught. Another feature of this provincial park is the extensive trail system. The Quinsam River Trail leads to the Quinsam Salmon Hatchery, and the Canyon View Trail takes explorers to the John Hart power-generating facility and an impressive bridge over the river. Other trails lead through woodland to wonderful waterfalls and wildlife-viewing opportunities. For children there is an adventure playground and sports field, and swimming and paddling are possible in the river at the day-use area. The nearby community of Campbell River is an attractive town to explore and if you are here in bad weather provides a number of attractions. Keep an eye out for the logger up the pole by the shopping centre, and watch for seals in the Strait of Georgia.

Additional information

In 1997 a magazine produced by BC Parks stated: "The undisputedly cheapest overnight rate in the salmon capital of the world is located in Elk Falls Provincial Park. Just $9.50/night buys a quiet river setting, a campsite, a convenient location and a fishing extravaganza … " In 2003 the price had increased to $15.00, but it is still a real bargain for those who love fishing and those who just want an idyllic place to camp.

ENGLISHMAN RIVER FALLS

Location

Established in 1940, this 97-hectare provincial park is a delight to visit at any time of the year. Englishman River Falls is found 13 kilometres south of Parksville off Highway 4 on a paved road. Qualicum and Parksville are nearby.

Facilities

The campground has 103 spacious campsites set in a forest of Douglas fir interspersed with Rocky Mountain maple trees and ferns. There are no showers, flush toilets, or sani-station and only the basic camping facilities exist (pit toilets, water, picnic tables, fire pit). The park is not wheelchair accessible. Reservations are accepted.

Recreational activities

In this park you can walk to the beautiful waterfalls amidst a mixed forest of cedar, fir, and hemlock; swim in the scenic river's swimming holes; and fish (check local fishing regulations first). A deep pool at the bottom of the canyon is a good place to seasonally view spawning salmon, steelhead, and trout. The park's proximity to Nanaimo, Courtenay, and Port Alberni means the activities and facilities of these communities are easily accessible, as indeed is the beach at Parksville, where at low tide the sea recedes nearly 100 metres and leaves a vast expanse of sand and pools to explore and beachcomb.

Additional information

Originally named *Rio De Grullas*—"River of Cranes"—by the Spanish explorers of the 18th century, this river was renamed a century later in memory of an English immigrant who died here. The campground is frequently utilized when the one at Rathtrevor Beach is full. It is well worth visiting in the fall when the trees are turning beautiful shades of golden and red, or in the spring when the wildflowers are at their best.

FILLONGLEY

Location

There is something for everyone in this 23-hectare provincial park that includes a beach, a marshy estuary, a forest rich in old-growth firs, and the remnants of what was once a large estate. Found on Denman Island and featuring views of Lambert Channel, Fillongley is reached by taking a ferry from Buckley Bay, south of Courtenay, to Denman and then driving the 4-kilometre paved road to the east coast of the island where the campground is situated. Denman Island has food, gas, and basic supplies.

Facilities

The biggest drawback of Denman Island's one provincial park is that there are only 10 camping spots available here, and they are lined up side by side at the parking area. For more privacy, it is possible to pitch tents under nearby trees. All basic amenities are provided (water, pit toilets, picnic tables, fire pit). The park is wheelchair accessible. Since 2000, reservations have been accepted.

Recreational activities

The campground is situated near a lovely rocky beach from which it is possible to swim, kayak, beachcomb, and look for oysters and clams. Hiking trails through old-growth forest have also been developed and offer an alternative to the shoreline recreational pursuits. The island is ideal for cycling enthusiasts as there is little traffic (except near the ferry terminals) and it is relatively flat. Denman Island is a delightful place to explore, for it has a beautifully relaxed atmosphere and many arts and crafts shops. In addition, nearby Hornby Island, which is also easy to reach, has hiking trails and lovely beaches.

Additional information

The park was bequeathed to the province by George Beadnell, who named it after his home in England. Beadnell, one of the first pioneers to come to the area, built up the estate, which at its peak had a tennis court, bowling green, clubhouse, and greenhouse as well as a large, impressive home. Following his death in 1958, these facilities fell into disrepair and were eventually destroyed. Beadnell is buried in the park. This is a fantastic, tranquil camping spot with a rocky beach and shallow waters. I spent a wonderful night here watching the sun set after having dinner on the beach. It's one of the best-kept secrets of BC Parks.

FRENCH BEACH

Location

French Beach Provincial Park, which boasts over 1,600 metres of beach and exceptional views across the Strait of Juan de Fuca toward the Olympic Mountains in Washington State, is a marvellous place to visit. The 59-hectare park is located just 20 kilometres west of Sooke on Highway 14 (34 kilometres from Victoria). Services are provided by a small store adjacent to the campground, as well as stores in Jordan River and Sooke.

Facilities

Set in a forest of Douglas fir, Sitka spruce, western hemlock, and western red cedar are 69 shaded camping spots. There is a sani-station, but the campground has only pit toilets. The park is wheelchair accessible and reservations are accepted.

Recreational activities

One of the biggest attractions here is whale watching. Magnificent grey whales migrate to their feeding grounds in the spring and return in the fall. If you're lucky, you can view them from the beach or, if you are an experienced paddler, at closer range in a kayak. Roaming pods of killer whales are also sometimes observed. In looking offshore it is not unusual to see river otters, seals, and sea lions playing, while ospreys and bald eagles frequent the skies overhead. The extensive sand-and-gravel beach, rimmed by the forest, is a beautiful place to swim from—although it is considerably wilder than the beaches on the other side of the island. Small nature trails wind through the second-growth forest and there is a playground for children. Once you have had enough of the natural beauty, go and explore Victoria's many attractions.

Additional information

A friend of mine tried to persuade me not to include French Beach in this book; she wanted to keep it all to herself and hated the thought of it becoming too well known. The biggest draw for her and for me to this provincial park is the huge beach—a beautiful place to sit and watch the sun go down or to stargaze. This is a rugged beach that is great to explore at any time of the year.

GOLDSTREAM

Location

The BC Parks information leaflet for Goldstream reads: "Massive trees, majestic waterfalls, a meandering river that meets the sea, flowers, birds and fascinating fish are but a few attractions that draw people to Goldstream Provincial Park." This description, coupled with the fact that the park is only 19 kilometres northwest of Victoria off Highway 1, makes it a *very* popular location for both locals and tourists. A small store and pub are located at the park entrance.

Facilities

The park has 163 well-appointed camping spots available for every type of recreational vehicle. There are showers, a sani-station, flush and pit toilets, and wheelchair accessibility. Reservations are accepted and strongly advised.

Recreational activities

Goldstream is blessed with a number of hiking and walking routes, some accessible to mountain bikers. Trails take hikers through Goldstream's two distinctive vegetation zones to views of 600-year-old Douglas fir trees and many other deciduous and evergreen trees and plants. The Gold Mine and Lower Falls trails lead to Niagara Falls, which is higher than its namesake (and fortunately much less commercialized—no honeymoon suites here). Swimming and fishing are possible within the park, and in the summer months, naturalists conduct interpretive programs in the outdoor theatre. An excellent visitor centre is also located here.

Additional information

Goldstream River was first named Gold Creek in 1858 by Lieutenant Peter Leech, an engineer with the Vancouver Island Exploration Committee, who discovered gold in the waters. Subsequent exploration revealed only small deposits, but there is nothing stopping the fortune seeker from further exploration. The Goldstream River is now the site of chum salmon spawning, and from mid-October to November it draws many thousands of visitors and millions of salmon. BC Parks produces a leaflet detailing the salmon spawning process. Long ago, this area, like many others on Vancouver Island, was used as a fishing ground by the Coast Salish people. Whether you are a fortune seeker, an angler, or just a holidaymaker, Goldstream is a lovely place to visit.

GORDON BAY

Location

Be sure you have the sunscreen if you plan to holiday in one of Canada's hottest spots, Gordon Bay Provincial Park. This 49-hectare park is found at the southern section of Lake Cowichan, 35 kilometres west of Duncan. It is accessed by taking Highway 18 just north of Duncan. The nearby community of Lake Cowichan has most services, and there is a small store at Honeymoon Bay, 2 kilometres from the campground.

Facilities

Positioned in an area of second-growth Douglas fir, this campground has 126 large, well-structured camping spots (those numbered 1 to 14 are closest to the bay). There are flush and pit toilets, a sani-station, showers, and full access for the disabled. Reservations are accepted and highly recommended, as this is one of the Island's most popular locations.

Recreational activities

Gordon Bay is located in one of the warmest valleys on Vancouver Island. The mountains pressing close to Cowichan Lake produce a heat trap that ensures the highest average daily temperature in Canada. The waters of Lake Cowichan supply relief from this heat (as do the shady camping spots). For the angler, the lake has reserves of Dolly Varden, rainbow and cutthroat trout, chum, coho, and spring salmon. There is a boat launch in the park and water skiing is permitted. An adventure playground has been constructed for children within the camping area. Two of the biggest attractions must be the excellent pebble beach—fantastic for children of every age—and the clear weed-free waters. Trails lead from the park over a forest floor covered with thimbleberry, salal, salmonberry, and, in the spring, wonderful wildflowers. (Remember, picking the vegetation in B.C. parks is prohibited.)

Additional information

In addition to the beauty of the park itself, the immediate surrounding area provides alternative activities. A small museum at Saywell Park offers local interest, and in Lake Cowichan you can tour the Lake Cowichan Earth Satellite station. This remote community is the hometown of Canada's premier female golfer of the past decade. Dawn Coe-Jones, a repeat winner on the PGA tour, learned her golf here at March Meadows, the attractive nine-hole course in Honeymoon Bay that is open to the public. In summary, Gordon Bay is a delightful family-oriented camping location equipped with all amenities. But be warned: as one of the most popular campgrounds on southern Vancouver Island, it is frequently full.

Juan de Fuca

Location

This is one of the province's newest campgrounds. Its quick addition to the list of reservable sites illustrates BC Parks' recognition that it would be immediately popular. Juan de Fuca Provincial Park consists of three main areas. In addition to the campground and day-use area (known as China Beach) there is the Juan de Fuca Marine Trail, a 47-kilometre stretch of wilderness that was used at the turn of the century as a life-saving trail. It is adjacent to the shoreline, known as the "graveyard of the Pacific" because a number of boats ran aground here. The third area of the park is Botanical Beach, a unique shoreline and one of the richest tidal areas on the west coast. The campground is situated on the west coast of southern Vancouver Island, 35 kilometres west of Sooke and 36 kilometres east of Port Renfrew.

Facilities

There are 78 vehicle-accessible campsites here in a lightly forested area. Although fire pits are available, the parks administration stresses the use of stoves to conserve the environment. There are only picnic tables, pit toilets, and water. Reservations are accepted.

Recreational activities

The main feature of this park is the Juan de Fuca Marine Trail, which was developed as an alternative to the increasingly popular West Coast Trail. Although 47 kilometres may be pretty tough going for some, it is easy to select a small section of beach to wander along. From the day-use area there is a 1-kilometre trail through the forest to the beach, while Second Beach Trail is a 2-kilometre return trip to the sea. To the west of the park near Port Renfrew is Botanical Beach. At low tide a wonderful array of shoreline and marine life is revealed here. Red, purple, and orange starfish can be seen, as well as sea anemones and blue mussels. Sea fishing is possible, as is canoeing, kayaking, and windsurfing if the seas are not too rough. Personally, I think it is just wonderful to sit and watch the ever-changing sea.

Additional information

The Juan de Fuca Marine Trail was the result of the Commonwealth Nature Legacy—a reminder of the 1994 Commonwealth Games that were held in Victoria. As early as 1901, when the University of Minnesota established a marine research station, the area was recognized as biologically significant. This is a stunning area, but there is a note of caution—the shoreline is prone to "rogue" waves that can occasionally hit the beach and drag you into the sea.

LITTLE QUALICUM FALLS

Location

Impressive waterfalls cascading into a rocky gorge characterize this 444-hectare provincial park, claimed by some people to be the most magnificent park on Vancouver Island. Little Qualicum River drops several hundred feet down the slopes of Mount Arrowsmith in a series of waterfalls. This remarkable vista is located on Highway 4, 19 kilometres west of Parksville on Little Qualicum River. Services are available at Port Alberni and Parksville.

Facilities

Ninety-four camping spots are here for the taking in the Upper and Lower campgrounds, set amongst a pleasant fir and pine forest setting. The park is accessible to the disabled, and there are flush and pit toilets but no showers or sani-station. The campground is quite close to the road and railway line. Reservations are accepted.

Recreational activities

Swimming in this provincial park is wonderful and can be undertaken in lovely little green pools at the Cameron Lake picnic site just a short drive away. (Be advised that at certain times of the year swimming is prohibited—check the park notice board.) There are over 6 kilometres of graded walking trails, and fishing in the river is rewarding. Just outside the park is MacMillan (Cathedral Grove) Provincial Park, where magnificent western hemlocks, Douglas firs, and western red cedars stand over 200 feet tall, like the columns of a cathedral. Some of these trees are more than 800 years old. Cathedral Grove has trails that lead into the depths of the spectacular old-growth forest.

Additional information

The area around the Beaufort and Cameron lakes contains salamanders and newts, which like the cool, damp cedar and fir forest area. This provincial park is conveniently located to explore the eastern Parksville/Qualicum area and the western town of Port Alberni. From Port Alberni it is possible to take the famous MV *Lady Rose* through the fjord scenery of the Alberni Inlet to Bamfield on the west coast, an unusual and rewarding trip that starts at 8:00 a.m. and returns around 6:00 p.m. If it is not raining, you are guaranteed to see some spectacular scenery and unusual wildlife.

LOVELAND BAY

Location

This is one of BC Parks' most recent additions. I visited in May 2002, well before the crowds arrived and when wonderful birds were singing their hearts out. It is situated 18 kilometres west of Campbell River on Lower Campbell Lake and is reached by taking the John Hart Dam gravel road from Highway 28, then Camp Road 5 (gravel). Both gravel roads are good and suitable for every type of vehicle. It is a relatively small 30-hectare site, but was immediately popular once opened (perhaps because it is so close to some of the best fishing in the province).

Facilities

There are 31 vehicle/tent campsites. All but five have direct access to the lake via a small pebbly beach and boast fantastic views of Lower Campbell Lake. There are 10 pit toilets, and pump water is provided. A boat launch is also available. The park is wheelchair accessible and—surprisingly—reservations are accepted.

Recreational activities

There are few organized activities here—indeed, this campground is not geared for children. But is an ideal place for reading and relaxing, and there is a small wharf to sunbathe on. Recreational activities include boating, swimming, fishing, and canoeing on picturesque Campbell Lake. Be careful of the many submerged stumps and also the wind, which can be quite strong on the lake. In the town of Campbell River, only 20 kilometres away, it is possible to rent or buy all the fishing equipment you could ever require. With the recent decline of the fishing industry, Campbell River has promoted itself as a tourist destination and is now a lovely place to wander around and people-watch. The 180-metre-long, 6.6-metre-wide pier regularly draws crowds; you can watch seals swimming below while you eat ice cream sold on the pier. Other attractions outside the park include mountain-bike trails, hiking, and the Snowden Demonstration Forest.

Additional information

As mentioned previously, a number of provincial park campgrounds on Vancouver Island fill up during the peak summer season. For those who cannot find accommodation at Elk Falls, Miracle Beach, or Strathcona, Loveland Bay provides an ideal alternative. Only 3 percent of the population of Vancouver Island lives north of Campbell River, so for those who want to explore the less commercialized, quieter side of Vancouver Island, Loveland Bay is an ideal choice.

McDonald

Location

If you have missed the last ferry to the mainland, you will be thankful for this provincial park at the end of the Saanich Peninsula. McDonald Provincial Park has good views of the nearby islands and is geared to overnight stays. Located 2 kilometres from the Swartz Bay ferry terminal, the park primarily provides accommodation for travellers waiting to take the ferry from Swartz Bay.

Facilities

Forty-four functional treed camping spots are available here for vehicles, along with an additional six walk-in spots. Despite being near considerable development, McDonald Provincial Park has only the basic facilities (fire pit, picnic tables, pit toilets, water), but it does have access for the disabled.

Recreational activities

As already mentioned, McDonald Provincial Park is used primarily by people waiting to catch a ferry, or by those who have just taken a ferry and are only staying one night. The park therefore offers little in the way of recreational pursuits. The town of Sidney, which has a pleasant harbour, craft shops, and cafés, is within easy access and can be explored. In the summer, a small passenger ferry can be taken to Sidney Island, which has delightful scenery and a provincial park.

Additional information

Victoria, only a 30-minute drive from Swartz Bay, offers a host of cultural and recreational activities for those who have time to explore. Victoria is the capital of British Columbia and houses the Legislature. Along streets lined with trees and flowers, the fascinating Royal British Columbia Museum, Empress Hotel, Parliament Buildings, Inner Harbour, and Chinatown are all within easy walking distance of one another. Shopping here is also a real treat. For those who have a choice and a vehicle, Bamberton Provincial Park is preferable to McDonald, but if you're tired after a long day's travelling and just want a place for the night, McDonald delivers the goods.

Miracle Beach

Location

Blessed with a wide sand-and-pebble beach and excellent views across the Strait of Georgia to the Coast Mountains, this campground is attractive to both adults and children and is an ideal spot for a family vacation. Miracle Beach is located on the protected shores of Vancouver Island's east coast, midway between Courtenay (22 kilometres south) and Campbell  River (22 kilometres north), 1.5 kilometres from Highway 19 on a paved access road. The campground has all required services conveniently located on the highway and in nearby communities. A small store is located in the nature house.

Facilities

Miracle Beach boasts 197 large private camping spots in a second-growth forest of Douglas fir, hemlock, and western red cedar. All amenities are here, including showers, flush and pit toilets, a sani-station, and access for the disabled. Reservations are accepted and advisable.

Recreational activities

One of the main attractions is the lovely, long, sand-and-pebble beach, perfect for swimming, sunbathing, and exploring tide pools when they are accessible. To supplement personal investigations, the excellent visitor centre has saltwater aquariums and nature displays, and interpretive programs remain here, including the Jerry's Rangers program for kids. This is one of the best visitor centres I've visited. Black Creek, which runs through the park, has a coho salmon run, and there are two small walking trails. For those who choose to travel farther afield, the salmon fishing in the area is good, and short boat trips can be taken to the nearby islands of Denman, Hornby, Quadra, and Cortes. At night, clear skies make for excellent stargazing from the beach or your camping spot.

Additional information

Miracle Beach is said to have received its name because it was miraculously missed by two severe forest fires that devastated much of the surrounding forest area in the recent past. Whenever I stay here, children seem to outnumber adults 10 to 1. This provincial park is an extremely popular camping location, especially during the summer months. If you have young children, it is the perfect place to spend a vacation.

Montague Harbour

Location

When Montague Harbour Provincial Marine Park on Galiano Island opened in 1959, it was the first provincial park to serve both visitors who arrived in their own boats and those who came by car or on foot. The park encompasses an 89-hectare area that starts five metres below sea level and rises to 180 metres above. Galiano Island can be reached via B.C. Ferries, either from Swartz Bay on Vancouver Island or Tsawwassen on the mainland. From the ferry dock at Sturdies Bay on Galiano, you must drive 10 kilometres to the park. Full services are at Sturdies Bay, and the marina has a small store and coffee bar with basic supplies.

Facilities

There are 40 beautifully positioned camping spots here, 25 of them suitable for vehicles and set in a forested area. Many of the 15 walk-in sites overlook the harbour and therefore have better views than the drive-in spots. Facilities are restricted to the basic ones found in BC Parks (pit toilets, water, picnic tables, fire pit); there is no sani-station or access for the disabled. Reservations are accepted and strongly advised.

Recreational activities

This gorgeous park has scenic hiking trails that lead through a forested area of arbutus, Douglas fir, hemlock, and Garry oak to beautiful beaches of white sand and shell, ideal for sunbathing or swimming. The abundant salmon and shellfish in the area attract a wide array of birds, including bald eagles, which can easily be seen fishing for their dinner. Canoes and kayaks can be hired from the adjacent marina, and there is a boat launch within the park. Galiano Island has quite a unique feel about it. Many artists and craftspeople have chosen to live here, and the area around Sturdies Bay has a small number of restaurants, craft shops, and an excellent bakery.

Additional information

On weekends in the summer months, the island's only neighbourhood pub offers a free hourly bus service between it and the marina (adjacent to the campground). The pub has live music and good food, and the marina serves excellent cinnamon buns and coffee in the morning. The island is named after the Spanish explorer Captain Galiano, who discovered the Gulf Islands in 1792. Smaller and less commercialized than Saltspring Island but with more amenities than Pender, Galiano is a fantastic place to spend some time. It's also a wonderful place to cycle around, and bikes can be rented at Sturdies Bay. The sunsets from the campground are astoundingly beautiful. It's one of my favourite camping spots.

MORTON LAKE

Location
A really serene camping experience can be had at this exquisite little park nestled in the Sayward Forest northwest of Campbell River on the Mohun and Morton lakes. The park is reached by travelling on Highway 19 for 27 kilometres north of Campbell River and then taking the Menzies Bay logging road (gravel) for 20 kilometres. Services are at Campbell River, 47 kilometres to the south.

Facilities
There are only 24 camping spots here, but many of them have access directly onto Morton Lake and are quite charming. Only the basic amenities are available (pit toilets, water, fire pit, picnic tables).

Recreational activities
Visitors to this area can enjoy fishing for Dolly Varden and rainbow and cutthroat trout, boating, swimming, and canoeing in either Mohun or Morton Lake. Mohun Lake provides access to the Sayward canoe circuit, a 47-kilometre trip. Alternatively, a trail leads to Andrew Lake and provides a different venue for water-based recreational pursuits, 30 minutes away. There is a good sandy beach by the campground, and as this location is away from the nearest centre of population, sunbathing and swimming can be a tranquil experience—you may even consider skinny-dipping.

Additional information
The forest around the lake was destroyed in the Great Campbell River Fire of 1938 and has subsequently been replanted with Douglas fir, while pine, cedar, and hemlock have all grown back naturally. The scars of the fire are still clearly evident in the area. Unfortunately, this is the most northerly provincial park on Vancouver Island that has the basic camping amenities. Although there are two others, Marble River and Schoen Lake, neither has fresh water, and when I tried to stay at Schoen Lake in September 1995, it was closed. In contrast to the roads south of Campbell River, Highway 19 north is a very quiet and beautiful drive; it is a great pity that there are not provincial parks located along this stretch of highway. In all my years of camping, it is only in the northern part of Vancouver Island that I have out of necessity stayed in a private campground. Although B.C. may have a large number of provincial parks in comparison to other provinces, states, and countries, there is still a need for more, especially on northern Vancouver Island.

Newcastle Island

Location

A small island barely a kilometre from Nanaimo, with spectacular views across to the mountains on the mainland, Newcastle can only be reached by water. Newcastle Island Provincial Marine Park is a popular cruising destination for recreational boaters. From Nanaimo, a charming little paddlewheeler operates from Maffeo Sutton Park, behind the civic arena, to ferry foot passengers to the island. Services are available in Nanaimo, although food can be purchased in the tearooms located in the pavilion on the island.

Facilities

There are only 18 designated camping spots, beautifully positioned at the edge of the forest, but a vast grassland meadow accommodates all additional campers. Many prefer this open space, as it is closer to the water. There are flush and pit toilets, two coin-operated showers, and the park is wheelchair accessible. The pavilion offers food from 10:00 a.m. to 7:00 p.m. during the peak summer season.

Recreational activities

The island is rich in history; the Coast Salish people inhabited the area for centuries prior to the Spanish exploration in 1791. With the help of the indigenous people, the Hudson's Bay Company opened a coal mine on the island and named it Newcastle after the famous British mining town. Coal was extracted until 1887. From 1869 until 1955 a sandstone quarry was in operation. Evidence of the past can be seen when you take the hiking trails that zigzag their way around and across the park. Bikes are permitted on two of these trails. There are a number of beaches, caves, and bays to explore and a calm sea to swim in. Canoeing around the shoreline is a favourite pastime, and there is a children's play area. Deer can be seen grazing in the early evening, and the area is also noted for its shoreline bird life.

Additional information

In July 1995, 1996, and 1997 the Cappa Big Band played in Newcastle Island Pavilion. On each of these occasions we left Vancouver with rucksacks on our backs, caught two buses to the ferry at Horseshoe Bay ($1.50), took the ferry from Horseshoe Bay to Nanaimo ($6.50), and walked the 30-minute route from the ferry terminal to the paddlewheeler to go and camp on the island, hike the trails during the day, eat on the veranda of the licensed tearooms during the evening, then dance the night away to the sound of brilliant jazz music. On these occasions I think we were the only couple wearing shorts, but we had great fun, and for only $17.00 (price includes the steamer ride from Nanaimo, normally $4.00 return). It is delightful to round off a perfect day with a glass of whiskey, good music still ringing in your ears, and to know that your bed is just a short walk away across starlit fields. Six years later, with two children under the age of five, I realize just how precious this memory is.

PACIFIC RIM NATIONAL

Location

Pacific Rim National Park boasts an 11-kilometre-long stretch of pristine surf-swept shoreline. Three distinctively different locations make up this 51,300-hectare (including 22,300 hectares of ocean) national park, and in order to see all aspects of it, you need at least two weeks. The park's features include the famous West Coast Trail, a 77-kilometre rugged excursion into west coast rain forest scenery (reservations are required if you intend to take this hike); the Broken Islands, a group of over 100 islands in Barkley Sound; and Long Beach, with its fantastic sands. Pacific Rim is on the west coast of Vancouver Island on Highway 4. Services are available at Ucluelet, Tofino, and along the highway between these two centres.

Facilities

Developed, vehicle-accessible camping facilities are available at the Long Beach area of the park (wilderness camping is possible in other areas). The main vehicle/tent campground is Green Point, with 94 blissful spots located high above the beach. Here campers are lulled to sleep by the sound of the ocean, and facilities include a sani-station, flush and pit toilets, a visitor centre, and limited access for the disabled. During the summer months this campground is almost always full, so reservations are recommended.

Long Beach.

Recreational activities

Long Beach provides a superb expanse of shoreline for surfers, windsurfers, swimmers, and kayakers to demonstrate their skills. As the wild waves of the Pacific Ocean pound along the sands, beachcombing and hiking are invigorating activities here in any season, as long as you have the correct attire. Hikers should be very cautious on rocky points and headlands, as three people were swept to their deaths in 1997 by large waves. Remember, the next wave can be higher than the one before! The ocean temperature varies from 6 to 12 degrees Celsius, bald eagles frequent the area, and there are eight small (1- to 2-kilometre) trails that can be walked to explore the rain forest or coastal flora and fauna. The community of Tofino is rapidly developing into a tourist facility and offers many commercial services, including excursions in the area.

Additional information

The Canadian Park Service has produced a number of leaflets about Pacific Rim, including one that lists the hiking trails. These can be obtained from the information centre. Long Beach is extremely popular in the peak summer months, but offers just as many delights for those who choose to avoid the crowds and visit at cooler times. Be warned that precipitation is common; the region receives 300 centimetres of rain a year, so if you are visiting out of season, dress accordingly. If you do manage to camp in the campground, you may well wake to find the previous evening's ocean view obscured by a heavy morning mist. During the course of the day the mist usually disappears, allowing you to again enjoy the sight as well as the sound of the ocean.

Contemplating the surf.

PRIOR CENTENNIAL

Location

For a get-away-from-it-all camping experience, you cannot go far wrong in selecting Prior Centennial, North Pender Island's only provincial park. Ferries to the island can be taken from Tsawwassen on the mainland or Swartz Bay on Vancouver Island. The campground is located 6 kilometres from the ferry terminal on Canal Road. There are stores in Port Washington, Hope Bay, and Port Browning.

Facilities

This is a relatively small, 16-hectare provincial park nestled in a pleasant forested area. Seventeen well-spaced vehicle/tent sites are available; unfortunately, they are close to the road. All basic services can be found here (water, fire pit, pit toilet, picnic tables). Reservations are accepted.

Recreational activities

The campground's location a few hundred metres from Medicine Beach on Bedwell Harbour is ideal for beachcombing and shoreline explorations. Hiking trails exist, and Pender Island is great to explore by bike. Watch for the historical markers that give details of the island's past. The small settlement of Hope Bay is a pleasant place to relax and watch the world go by.

Additional information

This park was donated to BC Parks in 1958 by Mr. and Mrs. F.L. Prior, hence its name. Pender Island is one of the Gulf Islands and is only a short ferry ride from Galiano Island and Saltspring Island, which both have provincial parks. Many tourists vacation by "island hopping" between these relaxed locations, while residents of the Lower Mainland and Vancouver Island visit to enjoy the altogether different ambience created by the island lifestyle. Access to South Pender Island is via a wooden bridge a kilometre from the campground, and while there is more to explore on North Pender Island, it is also interesting to travel south, as the ambience of the island changes.

RATHTREVOR BEACH

Location

Cool ocean water lapping a long white beach is just one of the many attractions of Rathtrevor Beach Provincial Park. Situated on Highway 19, just 2 kilometres south of Parksville, with views over the Strait of Georgia to the Coast Mountains beyond, Rathtrevor Beach is the most popular park on Vancouver Island for camping. Services are available in Parksville, while a small concession selling pop, coffee, candy, and other sundries recently opened in the visitor centre.

Facilities

The 175 camping spots are located in the Douglas fir-forested area of the park and accommodate every type of recreational vehicle. The campground is fully equipped with a sani-station, showers, and flush and pit toilets, and it is wheelchair accessible. Reservations are accepted, and you won't get a space without one in June, July, or August.

Recreational activities

Famed for its beautiful sandy shingle on 2,000 metres of beach leading to warm, clear waters, Rathtrevor Beach is described in BC Parks literature as "unbeatable for swimming." Windsurfing and canoeing are possible (there is no boat launch), and there are a number of walks and self-guided nature trails. Birdwatching is reputed to be good in the springtime and during the annual herring spawn. There are two children's play areas, and in the summer months the amphitheatre is used to deliver visitors' programs. The old farmhouse is now the park visitor centre. In 2004, you could rent tandem bikes there, and the bike-rental program was to be expanded to include mountain and kids' bikes.

Additional information

Rathtrevor received its name from pioneer William Rath, who settled here in 1886. In 1903 he died, leaving his wife with the farm and five children. She eventually developed the land into a campground and added the suffix "trevor" for effect. Rathtrevor was acquired by BC Parks in 1967. Today this campground is extremely popular. Visitors who arrive to find it full do not, however, have to travel far to find alternative camping, as Englishman River Falls Provincial Park is only 13 kilometres away.

RUCKLE

Location

In 1974, when the Ruckle family sold a 486-hectare parcel of land to the provincial government for a nominal fee, they gave the people of B.C. and visitors to the province a superb camping location. The largest park in the Gulf Islands, it is situated 12 kilometres from Fulford Harbour on Beaver Point at the southeastern corner of Saltspring Island. The nearest services can be found at Fulford Harbour.

Facilities

The park contains 78 walk-in camping spots in a grassy area beside Swanson Channel, as well as eight vehicle-accessible spaces. There is parking for RVs, but no campsites immediately adjacent. The walk from the parking area to the campground is flat, and in less than five minutes you can pitch your tent on a site looking directly over the water. All the basic amenities are found here (pit toilets, water, picnic tables, fire pit). There is no sani-station or access for the disabled.

Recreational activities

Campers can observe otters, harbour seals, porpoises, sea lions, and—if they're very fortunate—killer whales as they swim in the adjacent waters. Ruckle Park has more than 7 kilometres of shoreline, characterized by pocket beaches, rocky coves, and headlands waiting to be explored. There are over 15 kilometres of walking trails, leading around the headlands and through the forested areas. Swimming, beachcombing, and scuba diving are all possible here, while a maze of paved roads makes cycling a delight.

Additional information

The park area was originally settled in 1872 by the Ruckle family, which still resides and works in the area. The continuous use of the land for farming purposes from the late 1800s until today makes it one of B.C.'s oldest family farms. The Ruckle family retains its right to life tenancy within the park. Visitors can tour the historical farm buildings and learn about farming practices of a bygone age. Descriptive markers and photographs attached to the well-maintained historical buildings give details of a past life. Ruckle is another superb location to stay in to enjoy British Columbia.

SIDNEY SPIT MARINE

Location

Although effectively a marine park, Sidney Spit Provincial Marine Park on Sidney Island is a lovely camping facility that deserves mention. There is no vehicle access; it is reached by taking a foot-passenger ferry that departs from Government Wharf at the end of Beacon Avenue in Sidney on Vancouver Island. Services are found in Sidney.

Facilities

The park has 20 formal walk-in camping spots in addition to group camping facilities and plenty of space for spillover camping. All the basic amenities are provided (pit toilets, water, fire pit, picnic tables), as well as wheelbarrows for hauling gear, as the walk from the wharf to the campground is somewhat hilly and takes about 20 minutes.

Recreational activities

BC Parks literature describes Sidney Spit as "... one of the most beautiful marine parks in the Pacific Northwest," as it features thousands of metres of white sandy beach backed by towering bluffs. Beyond these, the uplands contain a second-growth forest of fir, maple, western red cedar, and arbutus. One of its main features is a lagoon affording one of the best opportunities to explore intertidal life. These salt marshes and tidal flats attract both human and animal forms: ornithologists, naturalists, seals, orcas, and dolphins are all occasionally seen. Trails lead around the park, and the stunning beach provides opportunities to swim, sunbathe, fish, and boat.

Additional information

Some of the bricks used to build the famous Empress Hotel in Victoria and the Hotel Vancouver in Vancouver were taken from a brick factory that operated at the turn of the century near the southern wharf of Sidney Island. At its peak, this factory employed 70 workers. In 1924 the Todd family began purchasing land on Sidney and by 1968 owned all but one-tenth of the island, which had been acquired by the government in 1924. This is the tenth (400 hectares) that we thankfully all have access to today. The community of Sidney is an enjoyable place for an afternoon stroll; in addition to shops that sell arts, crafts, and antiques, there are inviting delis and cafés that offer an assortment of refreshments to revitalize a tired camper.

SMELT BAY

Location

Located on the southern peninsula of Cortes Island, with stunning views to the south and west across a long pebble beach, Smelt Bay is the only provincial park on the island that permits camping. Cortes Island is not easy to reach but is well worth the effort. You must take two ferries, the first from Campbell River to Quadra Island, and the second from Quadra to Cortes. A 25-kilometre paved road leads from the ferry to the campground. Services are available on the island at Whitecove, Mansons Landing, and Squirrel Cove.

Facilities

Twenty-two camping spots are available in the woods, set back from the beach. As one would expect, only the basic facilities are supplied (water, pit toilets, picnic tables, fire pit).

Recreational activities

Leisure pursuits in the area include beachcombing, swimming, fishing, and generally relaxing. At low tide the pebble beach that leads to Sutil Point reveals a fascinating array of rock pools waiting to be explored. (Sutil Point is named after the Spanish ship *Sutil* in which Captain Galiano explored these waters in 1792.) The immediate area of the park is rich in history. For example, the mounds behind the gravel beach were built centuries ago by the Salish people to defend themselves against the Yacultas. Cycling around the island is a pleasant, easy activity as the traffic is minimal and the roads are paved. Cortes is a quiet, remote island very different from Quadra; Cortes has few settlements and a unique charm. Most of the development is concentrated in the south.

Additional information

Smelt Bay was created in 1973 to offer camping facilities and to protect an indigenous cultural site. At certain times of the year, tens of thousands of smelt spawn in this vicinity, hence the park's name. These small fish in turn attract an array of other sea life to the area, including salmon, otters, seals, herons, and sea lions. A lovely, quiet getaway spot, Cortes Island is one of the more scenic islands and has an intricate coastline ideal for canoeing and kayaking.

SPROAT LAKE

Location
Situated on the northern shore of Sproat Lake, 13 kilometres from Port Alberni off Highway 4, is the popular family campground of Sproat Lake. There is something for everyone here.

Facilities
Excellent camping can be had at Sproat Lake. The campground is situated in a forested area near the river and has showers, flush and pit toilets, and a sani-station available for tenants of the 59 spots. There are two campgrounds straddling the highway, the more desirable being the 15 sites nearer the lake. The park is wheelchair accessible. Reservations are accepted in both campgrounds.

Recreational activities
Sproat Lake is noted for its warm waters, fantastic for swimming. There is a large boat launch and good fishing. Trails lead through the forested area of second-growth Douglas fir, where at certain times of the year the ground is littered with an attractive assortment of wildflowers. The prehistoric pictographs found along trails at the southern end of the park are testimony to human presence in the area over the centuries and are considered some of the finest in B.C. In addition, the nearby town of Port Alberni is a pleasant community to explore.

Additional information
During the summer, visitors can see huge Martin Mars bombing planes take off from their lakeside base to extinguish fires. The world's largest water bombers, the planes are operated by a collective of five B.C. forest companies. Each plane can load 32 tons of water within 22 seconds by skimming across the lake at a speed of more than 110 kilometres per hour. The economy of Vancouver Island is dependent on the logging industry, and the threat of fires here and in the rest of B.C. peaks during the summer camping season. It is therefore imperative that all campfires be extinguished properly before a campsite is vacated. If the threat of fire becomes too great, fires are forbidden in provincial parks, and, as was the case in 2003, parks can be closed.

Stamp River

Location

Formerly known as Stamp Falls, this park was renamed Stamp River when it was amalgamated with Stamp River Money's Pool, increasing its area by 100 hectares. An angler's delight, this park is extremely popular with fishers, who visit the area for the excellent steelhead, coho, and cutthroat trout that can be caught. Located 14 kilometres north of Port Alberni off Highway 4, on a paved road, Stamp River has a lovely rural setting and yet is close to all amenities at Port Alberni. It is also one of the provincial parks closest to Pacific Rim National Park, approximately 100 kilometres to the west.

Facilities

There are 22 camping spots available here, some pleasantly located in a forested area near the river. Only the basic facilities exist (water, pit toilets, picnic tables, fire pit). Reservations are accepted.

Recreational activities

If you enjoy fishing, you'll love Stamp River, as the main attraction here is the fish. The campground is often used as a base camp for anglers who wish to explore the lakes and rivers in the vicinity. The park's unique feature is the fascinating display of salmon ascending the fish ladders in the summer and early fall. In July and August, 30,000 sockeye salmon use this route; lesser numbers of chinook and coho follow in September and October. Trails lead visitors from the campground to the fish ladders and to the views of the waterfalls on Stamp River.

Additional information

This 327-hectare park was created in 1940 and is named after an early pioneer who built Alberni's first sawmill. It's a pleasant and interesting picnic spot for travellers heading along Route 4. The highway between Port Alberni and Tofino is quite beautiful and follows the clear, tumbling waters of the Kennedy River for half of its route. Upon reaching Pacific Rim National Park near Tofino, the traveller is rewarded with dramatic views of the Pacific.

STRATHCONA

Location

Established in 1911, Strathcona is B.C.'s oldest provincial park. Located in a majestic wilderness of old-growth forest, mountain peaks, clear rivers, waterfalls, and lakes, it encompasses more than 210,000 hectares. The main route to the park is from Campbell River on Highway 28, which runs through the park and connects to Gold River on the west side of the Island. All services are available in Campbell River, and there is a private lodge in the park that has food, accommodation, and canoe/kayak rentals. Fuel is not available in the park.

Facilities

In addition to wilderness camping, the primary camping spots are in two locations on Buttle Lake. Buttle Lake campground has 85 units and the better beach; Ralph River has 76. Facilities at both locations include pit toilets, wood for sale, water, fire pit, and picnic tables. There is no sani-station (the nearest one is at Elk Falls) or access for the disabled. Reservations are accepted.

Recreational activities

As would be expected, there is a great deal to see and do in Strathcona Park, and it is easy to spend a week here. From Buttle Lake there are 12 hiking and walking trails that take explorers on a variety of hikes, and there are shorter nature trails as well. Other areas of the park have developed trail systems—details may be obtained from a leaflet produced by BC Parks. Swimming in Buttle Lake is good from both of the campgrounds, and there are two boat launches. Water-skiing is permitted on the lake, and the nearby lodge rents canoes and kayaks. A wealth of streams, rivers, and lakes provides angling opportunities. There are excellent wildlife viewing opportunities as well. The southern section of the park contains Della Falls, one of Canada's highest waterfalls at 440 metres, and the tenth highest in the world. With the spring runoff in May and June, the falls are particularly spectacular. Westmin Mines is located in the park, and on weekdays during the summer guided tours of the operation are offered.

Additional information

Strathcona is named after Donald Alexander Smith, Lord Strathcona, who was a Canadian pioneer and one of the principals involved with the construction of the Canadian Pacific Railway. Strathcona is an excellent location for those who enjoy hiking and the outdoor life and is definitely worth more than a one-night stay. It is not particularly kid-friendly, especially if you have young children. Interestingly, the wildlife in the park (and on Vancouver Island) differs from that on the mainland: chipmunks, rabbits, coyotes, foxes, grizzly bear, skunks, and moose are not found here. The road from Campbell River to Gold River traverses much of the park and is a pleasant, quiet drive.

VANCOUVER COAST AND MOUNTAINS

With the highest population density in the province, southwestern B.C. is undoubtedly the most popular region for provincial-park camping. Twenty-one provincial parks, all within a four-hour drive from downtown Vancouver, meet the demand for weekend getaways, and the spectacular scenery en route makes the commute enjoyable. Whether you head north on the meandering Sea to Sky Highway, east on Highway 7 to follow the mighty Fraser River, or to the Sunshine Coast via BC Ferries, your journey will include breathtaking views of mountains, clear rivers and streams, forests, and fields, as well as the comforting knowledge that services are never far away.

Birkenhead Lake is surrounded by breathtaking snow-capped mountains.

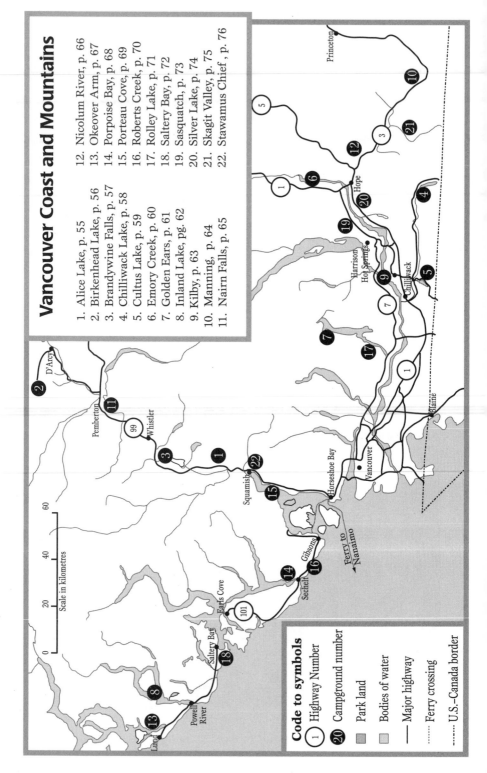

Vancouver Coast and Mountains

1. Alice Lake, p. 55
2. Birkenhead Lake, p. 56
3. Brandywine Falls, p. 57
4. Chilliwack Lake, p. 58
5. Cultus Lake, p. 59
6. Emory Creek, p. 60
7. Golden Ears, p. 61
8. Inland Lake, pg. 62
9. Kilby, p. 63
10. Manning, p. 64
11. Nairn Falls, p. 65
12. Nicolum River, p. 66
13. Okeover Arm, p. 67
14. Porpoise Bay, p. 68
15. Porteau Cove, p. 69
16. Roberts Creek, p. 70
17. Rolley Lake, p. 71
18. Saltery Bay, p. 72
19. Sasquatch, p. 73
20. Silver Lake, p. 74
21. Skagit Valley, p. 75
22. Stawamus Chief , p. 76

Code to symbols

(1) Highway Number
20 Campground number
Park land
Bodies of water
Major highway
Ferry crossing
U.S.–Canada border

Scale in kilometres

0   20   40   60

ALICE LAKE

Location

Alice Lake is situated not far from the community of Brackendale, home to the largest population of bald eagles in North America. Visitors to this campground have a good chance of seeing these splendid birds, but eagles are not the only attraction of this extremely popular park. Alice Lake, easily accessible from Vancouver, is positioned in breathtaking mountain terrain and has every amenity campers require. It is found on Highway 99—the Sea to Sky Highway—13 kilometres north of Squamish, which has all services.

Facilities

Situated in a forest of western hemlock are 108 large, private, shady camping spots suitable for all camping vehicles. The campground is equipped with showers, flush and pit toilets, and a sani-station; it has access for the disabled, and reservations during the summer months are a must.

Recreational activities

There is never a dull moment here, as the 397-hectare park has an abundance of activities to keep campers busy. One of the biggest attractions is a series of walking and hiking trails, ranging in length from half a kilometre to a day's hard walking. One of the most popular is the Four Lakes Trail, which takes hikers around the four warm-water lakes that dominate the area. Swimming, canoeing, and fishing for rainbow trout and Dolly Varden are popular pursuits, and large grassy areas provide venues for ball games. An excellent lakeside beach and a safe swimming area for children are perfect for children.

Additional information

Alice Lake is an ideal base from which to explore Garibaldi Provincial Park, which offers only primitive camping facilities. Garibaldi covers almost 200,000 hectares and during the summer months provides excellent hikes to alpine meadows, glaciers, mountains, and striking views. Alice Lake is a very popular campground even during the week, and it is frequently full during the peak summer months of July and August, so if you arrive without a reservation during these times, be sure you have other options available.

BIRKENHEAD LAKE

Location

Six kilometres long, Birkenhead Lake is surrounded by breathtaking snow-capped Coast Mountains, blessed with clear beautiful waters, and located only a 3½-hour drive (210 kilometres) from Vancouver. It is reached by taking Highway 99 to Pemberton, then turning off this road at Mount Currie toward D'Arcy. Just before D'Arcy, a 17-kilometre gravel road leads to the park. Gas and restaurants are in Mount Currie and Pemberton.

Facilities

Ninety-four camping spaces are available here, and all but a few are located in a beautiful wooded area with streams running adjacent to them (ideal for keeping your drinks cool on a hot summer day). There is a sani-station, but no flush toilets. The park has no wheelchair accessibility. The only other disadvantage is that some spots are near stagnant water pools, so mosquitoes can be a problem at certain times of year. Reservations are accepted.

Recreational activities

Birkenhead Lake has a lovely beach and protected swimming area, although the waters themselves, which come directly from the surrounding mountain snow, can be cold. There is a boat launch. Fishing for kokanee, whitefish, rainbow trout, and Dolly Varden is reputed to be good, as is wildlife watching for moose, black bear, mountain goats, and deer. Ospreys and bald eagles are often seen circling over the waters of the lake. A good trail leads along one side of the lake and is used by mountain bikers and walkers.

Additional information

The tranquil location, spectacular scenery, and pleasant drive from the Lower Mainland make this my favourite provincial park for a weekend getaway from Vancouver. I have stayed here five times in different seasons. In June the waters were so high I could not see the beach, but the hiking was excellent. In July there were millions of flies and mosquitoes, and in late August it was hot and perfect. When I stayed in July 2003, an enterprising couple had set up a really quaint "camper's store" in the back of their van near the campground. Camping provides opportunities for a variety of entrepreneurs but challenges the travel writer—you never know if the same people will be in business in subsequent years. Hopefully, this couple will be.

BRANDYWINE FALLS

Location
Stop here and learn from the interpretive signs how this stunning waterfall was formed and how it acquired its unusual name. The falls themselves are spectacular and easily justify an excursion from the highway. This small, functional roadside campground is primarily designed for overnight camping. It is located 47 kilometres north of Squamish (11 kilometres south of Whistler) on the beautiful Sea to Sky Highway. Services are available in Whistler and Squamish.

Facilities
The 148-hectare park has just 15 camping spots, each quite small and close to the others, with low vegetation that offers limited privacy. Only the basic facilities are available here (pit toilets, picnic tables, fire pit, water). The camping spots are quite close to the road, so the noise of passing traffic is easily audible. A railway line is also nearby.

Recreational activities
From this provincial park it is possible to take a short 10-minute hike to a rocky viewpoint to see the impressive 70-metre waterfall and take photographs of Daisy Lake against the backdrop of the Garibaldi Mountains. Longer trails also exist within the park's boundary. The recreational pursuits here are somewhat limited, but the nearby skiing resort of Whistler offers a host of adventurous pastimes, including heli-skiing, golfing, tennis, horseback riding, and mountain biking.

Additional information
This is very much a roadside campground, best used out of necessity, although it is an enjoyable picnic spot. My advice to anyone travelling north is to go on to Nairn Falls (40 kilometres north). If you're travelling south, you could try either of the popular parks Alice Lake and Porteau Cove. There are three interesting and distinctive waterfalls on the Sea to Sky Highway: Brandywine is the middle one; to the south is the 335-metre Shannon Falls, the third highest in B.C.; to the north is Nairn Falls, where a broad torrent of green water tumbles more than 60 metres.

Chilliwack Lake

Location

Today it is rare to find areas of old-growth forest in B.C. However, by undertaking a short walk from Chilliwack Lake, visitors can view majestic red cedar trees that are hundreds of years old. Southeast of Vancouver and situated in the magnificent Coast Mountains, this popular campground was created in 1973 to protect an area of spectacular beauty. The campground is 64 kilometres southeast of Chilliwack and can be reached by taking exit 104 from Highway 1 and following the signs for Cultus Lake until Cultus Lake Road. Rather than turning here, take Vedder Road across the bridge and turn right onto Chilliwack Lake Road, a paved/gravel access road leading to the lake—a distance of 40 kilometres. The nearest concentration of services is in Chilliwack; more limited provisions can be found at the Pointa Vista Store, 32 kilometres west of the park.

Facilities

One hundred and forty-six camping spots are available in the 162-hectare park. The majority of sites are large, private, and well positioned; about 10 of them are near the lake. The remainder are close, confined, and offer little privacy. Only the basic camping facilities are provided here (pit toilets, water, fire pit, picnic tables).

Recreational activities

The park is a delightful place to visit if you enjoy hiking, as there is a variety of trails starting at the campground. Walkers can choose whether to take an easy 6-kilometres-return route to the Ecological Reserve with no elevation gain, or the 14 kilometres to Flora Lake with a climb of over 1,000 metres. The lake has swimming, boating, and fishing for Dolly Varden, kokanee, rainbow and cutthroat trout, and is equipped with a boat launch. The water can, however, be very cold. A playground for children ensures the little ones are well entertained.

Additional information

Almost 3 kilometres along a logging road that leads from the campground and follows the edge of Chilliwack Lake is Chilliwack River Ecological Reserve. It was created in 1981 to protect a unique area of old-growth forest featuring large western red cedars. A number of ecological reserves exist in B.C., which is geographically and biologically the most diverse province in the country. The reserves are areas chosen to preserve representative and special natural ecosystems, the fauna, and flora. Ecological reserves are used primarily for scientific and educational purposes. For those who prefer the less commercialized camping experience, Chilliwack Lake is the place to stay.

CULTUS LAKE

Location

On average, almost 30,000 family groups stay at Cultus Lake per year, making it the fourth most popular campground in the province. The 656-hectare park includes both the east and west side of the 5-kilometre-long Cultus Lake, from which a spectacular vista of mountains can be seen. *Cultus* means "worthless" in the Chinook language, but the lake's immense popularity suggests that many have found it anything but worthless. Cultus Lake is located 11 kilometres southwest of Chilliwack off Highway 1 on a paved access road. While Chilliwack provides all services, a number of small commercial facilities can be found adjacent to the lake.

Facilities

This campground is the third largest in the province (after Manning and Golden Ears) with 297 spaces in four locations: Maple Bay (104), Delta Grove (57), Clear Creek (82), and Entrance Bay (52). All spaces are large and positioned well in wooded areas. There are a number of double camping spots, and 18 at Delta Grove are close to the water's edge with their own section of beach. All amenities are found here, including flush toilets, sani-station, showers, and access for the disabled. Reservations are accepted.

Recreational activities

Numerous recreational pursuits can be enjoyed. You can catch coho, chinook, chum, pink, and sockeye salmon, rainbow and cutthroat trout, and Dolly Varden if the powerboaters and water skiers do not decide to disturb the tranquility of the lake. Windsurfing is possible (if the jet skiers are not out in force), as is swimming from lovely sandy beaches. There are also several hiking trails. The most popular trek is to Teapot Hill, 5 kilometres return, where a good viewpoint rewards your efforts. Some trails permit mountain bikes and horses and have recently been extended and upgraded. For children, a play area has been constructed in Entrance Bay campground. In the immediate vicinity, commercial outlets have golf, go-carting, canoe rentals, trail rides, waterslides, jet skis, laundry, restaurants, and stores.

Additional information

Although the setting and facilities here are perfect, the park can become very busy during the summer months, especially on weekends, and somewhat loud if too many powerboats congregate on the lake. Cultus Lake attracts a youthful summer crowd and, in my mind, represents the most commercial side of provincial-park camping. The best time to stay here is in the spring, when the trees are budding, wildflowers are blooming, and the woodlands are alive with birds attracted to the deciduous forest.

EMORY CREEK

Location

I love this provincial park for, amongst other things, the unique washroom facilities (see below). This beautiful campground on the banks of the majestic Fraser River is located on the site of Emory City, which in its 1880 heyday boasted 13 streets and a population of over 500 pioneers. Two decades earlier, the same number of people worked here after coming in search of gold. If you visit today, all you'll see is a lovely, serene, wooded campground. Emory Creek is located beside Highway 1, 18 kilometres north of Hope and 6 kilometres south of Yale. A convenience store and restaurant are located opposite the campground.

Facilities

Nestled in a mixed forest area are 34 large, private camping spots suitable for every type of recreational vehicle. Some spots have views of the water. One of the most distinctive features of this campground is the "flushing thunderboxes"—from the outside, these toilets look like pit toilets, but they actually flush. During my first two stays in this park, the toilets not only flushed, but the washroom also contained small containers of dried flowers and air fresheners. Unfortunately, I didn't find this nice touch on my last stay in 2003. There is no sani-station, showers, or wheelchair access. The transcontinental railway is adjacent to the park, and the sound of trains, while audible, can be quite soothing in the night.

Recreational activities

Although there is not a lot to do at Emory Creek, the park seems to attract the retired folks looking for a tranquil spot in which to spend a few days. There is a small trail, and visitors can fish for salmon in the Fraser, which is easily accessible from a pebbled beach. When I last visited, two grey-haired gentlemen were busy panning for gold, an activity that struck me as an extremely pleasant way to spend an afternoon.

Additional information

This campground has a wonderful feeling about it. Its lack of defined or structured activities makes it particularly appealing to older campers, while the well-cared-for and unique washroom facilities are a welcome surprise to seasoned campers who often approach pit toilets with a deep dread, especially in the height of summer. The area was the site of one of the richest finds during the 1858 gold rush, before prospectors moved farther north. When Simon Fraser first travelled here in 1808, this attractive valley was inhabited by the Coast Salish people, who hunted and fished in the region. A short drive north on the Coquihalla Highway is Coquihalla Canyon Provincial Park, where visitors can walk through a series of disused railway tunnels, which were blasted through the rock in the early years of this century.

GOLDEN EARS

Location

Almost 40,000 camping parties regularly visit Golden Ears, making this large, well-appointed provincial park one of the most popular campgrounds in B.C. Like Cultus Lake and Manning Park, Golden Ears is close to Greater Vancouver. Although this proximity may dissuade some campers from visiting, let me add that whenever I have stayed here—even at the height of summer—the park has never felt crowded or busy, although the campground itself can get a little noisy. Named either for the twin peaks that shine golden in the sunlight or, as some locals claim, a nesting place for eagles, "Golden Eyries" is located 11 kilometres north of Haney off Highway 7, on a paved access road, and is an easy 45- to 60-minute drive from Vancouver. All services are available at Haney, and there are a few additional stores close to the campground itself.

Facilities

Alouette, Gold Creek, and the newer North Beach campground provide the camping options in Golden Ears, offering a total of 409 spaces. All have large, private spots within a forested area. There are showers, flush toilets, a sani-station, and wheelchair access. Reservations are accepted in all three campgrounds.

Recreational activities

The park is blessed with a number of trails suitable for both hikers and horses (horseback riding can be arranged from local facilities). Outings vary from 20-minute interpretive trips to overnight excursions up to the Golden Ears. Fishing for rainbow trout, coastal cutthroat, kokanee, Dolly Varden, and lake trout is popular in Alouette Lake and Alouette River, Pitt Lake, Mike Lake, and Gold Creek. Good swimming beaches are available at Alouette Lake in both the day-use and camping areas. Boating and water-skiing are permitted on the lake away from the swimming area, and canoes can be rented in the park. An adventure playground keeps young ones entertained, and more than 20 kilometres of horse trails are available to those who love riding.

Additional information

The area around Alouette Lake was originally the hunting and fishing ground of the Interior Salish and Coast Salish peoples. During the early 1900s, the area was the primary site for B.C.'s railroad logging operations, and there are stories of loggers in the 1920s felling trees up to four metres in diameter. A huge fire that ripped through the area in 1931 stopped the logging operations. Today, Golden Ears is characterized by a second growth of western hemlock, western red cedar, and Douglas fir, but evidence of the earlier logging is everywhere.

Inland Lake

Location

Inland Lake is 12 kilometres north of Powell River, next to 1,065-metre-high Mount Mahony. Turn right off Highway 101 onto Alberni Street. Go up the hill to Manson Avenue, turn left, and follow Manson to Cassiar Street. Turn right onto Cassiar (which becomes Yukon Street), and continue to Haslam Street. Turn right onto Haslam and stay on it until the first junction, where you take the left fork to the campsite.

Facilities

Camping provisions at Inland Lake make this one of the choicest parks for disabled campers. It has ramps and larger toilets, and 13 kilometres of flat, wheelchair-accessible trail, six piers jutting out onto the lake for easy fishing, a concrete ramp sloping into the water, and cabins specially designed for the handicapped. The main campground is next to the day-parking area and accommodates 24 parties, with spaces for large RVs. Pit toilets, fire pits, garbage bins, and picnic tables overlooking the lake are in a lightly wooded area. Pumps are used to collect lake water, which should be boiled before using. Four overnight camping spots are located around the lake. There are some cabins for the disabled, and services are available in Cranberry and Powell River.

Recreational activities

The biggest draw at Inland Lake is the 13-kilometre trail circling the lake. Convenient for people in wheelchairs or those with strollers, it has kilometre markers placed along it and wooden carvings of local pioneers, animals, and other subjects. The most impressive is a totem pole created by Sliammon carver Jackie Timothy. You can take two paths from the trail: one to Lost Lake, then on to Haywire Bay on Powell Lake, the other directly to Powell Lake. Or you can hike along the shoreline, then on a small bridge to Anthony Island. Inland Lake is great for canoeing and kayaking; although powerboats are permitted, they are limited to 10-horsepower engines. For fishers, the 349-hectare lake contains cutthroat and kokanee, but fishing is not permitted between November 1 and March 31. Loons, eagles, ducks, ravens, grouse, blue jays, and hummingbirds can be seen and sometimes, beavers, otters, and bears. The lake water is calm, clear, and warm—ideal for swimming.

Additional Information

This campground and lake are wonderful. During our last visit, on a day that started with rainy skies, we set off on our hike in waterproof gear. Halfway around the trail the skies cleared, and by the time we returned to the car, we were hot and sweaty. Three families were playing in the lake, proving it was not cold, so we got changed and revelled in the warm water. We were there on a Labour Day weekend, when there was no shortage of space and few people on the trail.

KILBY

Location

If you want a taste of the life experienced by early settlers in the province, visit Kilby Provincial Park and pay a visit to the marvellous museum nearby. This delectable three-hectare provincial park is situated 1 kilometre off Highway 7 at Harrison Falls on the Fraser River. Services can be found on the highway or at Harrison Mills, Agassiz, and Harrison Hot Springs.

Facilities

Twenty-two large campsites on the river provide excellent spots from which to watch the Fraser meander on its course—unless the river level is very high, as it was in June 1996 when the campground had to be closed because it was under water. There are flush and pit toilets and water, but no sani-station, showers, or access for the disabled.

Recreational activities

This campground is ideally located for those who want to explore the surrounding communities of Mission, Agassiz, Chilliwack, and Harrison Hot Springs. It also provides its own attractions in the form of a wide sandy beach and river for boating and swimming. As the campground is positioned near both the Fraser and Harrison rivers, a variety of fishing spots in the immediate vicinity are available, where anglers can try their luck for cutthroat and Dolly Varden.

Additional information

One of the biggest attractions here is the Kilby General Store Museum, which is the two-hectare historical site of a general store dating back to the early 1900s. The two-storey general store was built in 1904 and operated by the same family up until 1976. The museum contains a small working farm (with pigs, goats, and hens—a delight for children) and orchard, in addition to a number of buildings that have been faithfully restored. Guides dressed in period costume provide fascinating details of the development of the area at the turn of the century. Kilby General Store Museum also boasts a gift shop and an excellent tea room that serves traditional tea and scones. Both children and adults will find it is easy to pass the hours in the museum, reading and learning about the Fraser River's colourful past. Specifically, the photographs of huge sturgeon caught in the Fraser River should not be missed. I must admit, though, that whenever I have visited this campground it's populated with the younger and louder crowd, and it doesn't foster the get-away-from-it-all camping experience that I tend to seek.

Manning

Location

Manning is the second most popular provincial campground (after Golden Ears). Within three hours of Vancouver (224 kilometres away) and covering over 65,000 hectares of the Cascade Mountains, this is a fantastic area for recreational use. The Highway 3 park entrance is 30 kilometres east of Hope. Accommodation, gas, food, and other commercial facilities are located in the park.

Facilities

In addition to wilderness camping, there are four campgrounds with 355 spots: Hampton (99), Mule Deer (49), Coldspring (64), and Lightning Lake (143). Lightning Lake has showers and flush toilets, and its 143 campsites are included in the reservation system of BC Parks. The other three campgrounds operate on a first-come, first-served basis. All spaces are large and set among trees offering privacy, although some campsites are close to the road and Coldspring is a little sparse on vegetation, thanks to a recent attack of pine beetle. There is a sani-station near the visitor centre and reservations are accepted.

Recreational activities

Manning Park offers an abundance of things to do and see. Upon arriving, visitors should go to the visitor centre located a kilometre east of Manning Park Resort to pick up a detailed map of the area. The centre also has human and natural history displays of the park and area. Manning is a hiker's paradise; extensive trail systems meander through the mountains to alpine meadows, waterfalls, and rivers. Some trails are mountain-bike accessible, and there are also riding trails and self-guided interpretive trails. Anglers can fish in the Similkameen and Sumallo rivers for Dolly Varden, rainbow and cutthroat trout, and also in Lightning and Strike lakes. Lightning Lake has a beach, a swimming area, and good canoeing (rowboats and canoes can be rented). Powerboats are not permitted anywhere in the park, a rule that ensures a peaceful stay.

Additional information

Manning Park is named after E.C. Manning, chief forester of British Columbia from 1936 to1941. It is at the north end of the Pacific Crest Trail, a six-month trek. Almost 4,000 kilometres in length, the trail runs all the way to Mexico, crossing 24 national forests and seven national parks in the United States. Manning provides a number of delightful hiking options. For an easy 45-minute trail, try the Canyon Trail (2 kilometres); for a slightly longer walk, the Lightning Lake Loop (9 kilometres) is appealing. The Lightning Lake Chain Trail is 24 kilometres, but there's no elevation gain.

NAIRN FALLS

Location

One year I stayed here in July, when the temperature was in the high 20s, and I really appreciated the shady canopy this wooded campground offers. Just 3 kilometres south of Pemberton on Highway 99 and considerably less popular than Alice Lake, its nearest big neighbour to the south, this is an exquisite, laid-back provincial park. Services are conveniently located at Pemberton or at Whistler, 29 kilometres to the south.

Facilities

Ninety-four spacious, forested camping spots are available (the 40 reservable are the best ones, as they overlook the canyon, but the others are not bad). All accommodate the largest recreational vehicle. Facilities include water, fire pit, picnic tables, pit toilets, and a sani-station. Since 2000, Nairn Falls has accepted reservations.

Recreational activities

Nairn Falls is regularly used by travellers as a picnic spot. An easy 20-minute trail (1.5 kilometres) leads to the falls, which tumble down 60 metres into a beautiful canyon of Douglas fir, cedar, and hemlock. The park contains other trails, but when I visited, signage left a lot to be desired and some trails were washed out. Fishing is possible in Green River, while a short drive/walk from the park on Highway 99 toward Pemberton there is a lake for swimming, a real luxury on a hot summer's day. The shady, peaceful campground is perfect for reading and relaxing, and Nairn Falls gives the impression of offering an almost sophisticated camping experience for those who want to escape from life's pressures.

Additional information

When I stayed here, my calm camping environment was occasionally disturbed by the noise of powerboats ascending the rapids to take groups of visitors whitewater rafting. Excursions of this nature can be organized in Pemberton and Whistler. Nairn Falls is an ideal location from which to explore Whistler (and is also considerably cheaper than staying right at the year-round resort). It also offers a far more enjoyable environment in which to camp than does its southern neighbour, Brandywine Falls. The lack of recreational pursuits may put some people off; there is little to do in the park itself for those with young families, although just to the north of Nairn Falls before you reach Pemberton is a small beach on a lakefront that is pretty, despite there being a lot of reeds in the water. For the majority of people, Nairn Falls is a haven.

Nicolum River

Location

This park may not be open for camping. Information from BC Parks in 2003 said it was, but when I drove past in June and July of that year it was closed. In any case, for those who want to camp for more than one night, other provincial park campgrounds in the vicinity (namely Manning and Emory Creek) offer superior camping to Nicolum River. Nonetheless, this is not a bad roadside campground and quite a nice place to stop for a picnic or for one night. Located on the banks of the river for which it is named, this small campground is often overlooked by those heading to or from its nearest neighbour, Manning. It is located just 8 kilometres east of Hope on Highway 3. Services are available at Hope.

Facilities

Claustrophobia will not be a problem here, as the campground has only nine spots in a pleasantly wooded area. The basic facilities are provided (pit toilets, water, picnic tables, fire pit). The park is quite close to the main road, but the slight noise of traffic is offset to some extent by the rush of the river.

Recreational activities

There is little to do here other than relax and fish for cutthroat, coho, and squawfish on the banks of the river. The town of Hope is less than 10 kilometres away and is a pleasant community to wander around. Hope has acquired a number of large, carved wooden statues that can be seen in the downtown core. A short drive up the Coquihalla Highway and well worth a visit is Coquihalla Canyon Provincial Recreational Area. It houses a chain of tunnels built for the construction of the Kettle Valley Railway in 1914 at a cost of $300,000. Go marvel at this engineering feat, walk through the tunnels, and stand in awe as the water crushes down over the rock formations.

Additional information

This is very much a one-night camping spot. Those who seek activity are better advised to stay at Manning, where there are a multitude of things to do. Be aware that two mountains overshadow Nicolum River Provincial Park: Tulameen (2,286 metres) and Outram (2,438 metres). They create an early barrier to afternoon sun and promote cold late afternoons and evenings. I have found that this little campground has an erratic opening schedule; for some reason, it is not always open during the summer months.

OKEOVER ARM

Location

Over the recent past the waters and islands of this area have become known as a kayaker's dream. Consequently, Okeover Arm Provincial Park is a kayaker's campground. At the end of the Sunshine Coast road (Highway 101), overlooking Okeover Arm on the eastern side of the Malaspina Peninsula, this small campground is ideal for campers who plan to kayak in Desolation Sound Marine Park. The park is located 19 kilometres north of Powell River, 5 kilometres on a paved road from Lund. The small community of Lund has a store and accommodation, and Powell River provides all services.

Facilities

Okeover Arm was upgraded in 1997 to ensure more camping spots were available for both vehicles and tents. Nineteen vehicle camping spaces, some with tent pads, are available, and a few have views of the water. Only the basic amenities are available here (pit toilets, water, fire pit, picnic tables).

Recreational activities

The main recreational activities here are canoeing, kayaking, swimming, boating (there is an undeveloped boat launch), and walking in a lightly forested area. As mentioned, the campground is an ideal base for those who wish to explore Desolation Sound Marine Park, B.C.'s largest marine park, with more than 60 kilometres of shoreline, several islands, and a multitude of bays and coves.

Additional information

There is little to do here if you don't plan to canoe or kayak. Lund seems to be geared to providing a base for these recreational pursuits. When I arrived at Lund, I had planned to spend a few hours exploring the community; it could be done in a few minutes, although there are a couple of coffee bars and restaurants where you can people-watch. Lund was originally settled in 1895 by two brothers from Sweden and is named after the Swedish city. The renovated hotel, which dates back to the turn of the century, is the hub of the community.

Porpoise Bay

Location
Reaching this campground from the Lower Mainland requires a lovely excursion on BC Ferries to the Sunshine Coast. Take the ferry from Horseshoe Bay to Langdale, then Highway 101 to just north of Sechelt, where a 5-kilometre paved road leads to the campground. Services can be found in Sechelt, where the wide selection of restaurants, bakeries, and coffee bars offers a great alternative to campground food.

Facilities
Campers here want for nothing. Porpoise Bay has flush and pit toilets, showers, a sani-station, wheelchair access, and it accepts reservations. There are 84 large camping spots, including a few double units in a second-growth forest of Douglas fir, western red cedar, western hemlock, and alder. Campfires at individual campsites are prohibited here, but group campfires are encouraged, so this integral part of the camping experience is not altogether lost.

Recreational activities
This popular park and campground offers a wide sandy beach and a protected swimming area, making it ideal for family camping. A large number of grassy areas great for ball games are a feature here, and there are small trails, one of which leads to Angus Creek, a salmon-spawning waterway for chum and coho. The park is a base for kayakers who wish to explore the many coves and inlets of the surrounding area. At low tide it is really pleasant to beachcomb, wander through the rock pools, and turn over the rocks looking for the marine life. My children adored fishing with nets for "toe biters" and small crabs.

Additional information
Porpoise Bay is near Sechelt Inlet's Provincial Marine Recreational Area, which includes eight wilderness campsites located in the sheltered waters of Sechelt Inlet—a paddler's delight. The area is also rich in marine life. I last stayed here in June, when only half the camping spots were taken. The waters were somewhat cold, but the tranquility was wonderful. I had reserved a space but need not have bothered, as the park does not get busy— except on weekends— until July and August.

PORTEAU COVE

Location

The views from this campground off the fantastic Sea to Sky Highway (Route 99) are stunning if the weather is good, and for this reason alone every attempt should be made to stop here. Although almost impossible to see from the road, Porteau Cove is an enchanting roadside campground with an astounding vista of Howe Sound, the most southerly fjord in North America. Thirty-eight kilometres north of Vancouver, just over 8 kilometres south of Britannia Beach, Porteau Cove is a haven for campers and day trippers. Britannia Beach has food; gas and other provisions are available in Squamish.

Facilities

The campground has 44 vehicle camping spots and 16 walk-in sites and all amenities (showers, flush toilets, sani-station, wheelchair access, and reservations). Some spots look directly onto the water's edge over to the mountains on Vancouver Island, and while the sites are not as large as those in other provincial parks, they are private thanks to the surrounding Sitka spruce trees. The campground is set away from the road, so traffic noise is not a problem, but the railway runs close by and a number of trains pass during the day and night (if you're in a tent, it feels like the train is passing right over your head).

Recreational activities

One of the biggest attractions of this location is scuba diving. Three ships have been sunk in the nearby waters to attract marine life and create a destination for diving enthusiasts. They also provide entertainment for those of us who just want to watch funny rubber-clad individuals plunge into the cool waters. Away from the diving area it is possible to swim in the waters of Howe Sound and to fish. The public boat launch at Porteau Cove is the only one between Squamish and Horseshoe Bay. The park is an extremely popular camping and picnic spot for people travelling along the highway. When I last camped here I used Porteau Cove as my base, but swam and sunbathed at Alice Lake, less than a 20-minute drive north.

Additional information

The mining museum at Britannia Beach is well worth a visit if you have time. Visitors are given hard hats and taken on a tour that includes a rail trip underground and a demonstration of past mining machinery. Britannia Beach also has a large number of arts and craft shops and cafés to visit. Porteau Cove is a *very* popular location, so don't plan to camp here without a reservation during the peak months of July and August.

ROBERTS CREEK

Location

If you want to spend your time relaxing, beachcombing, and staring out to sea to look for whales, stop at Roberts Creek. With fantastic views of the Strait of Georgia and beyond to the mountains of Vancouver Island, this campground is found 12 kilometres north of Gibsons on Highway 101. From the Lower Mainland, visitors take a beautiful ferry ride from Horseshoe Bay to Langdale. Services are available at Gibsons or Sechelt, 15 kilometres to the north.

Facilities

Camping facilities at this 40-hectare park are situated in a lightly forested area of second-growth Douglas fir and western red cedar. There are 21 spaces and a sani-station, but no flush toilets or showers. The park is wheelchair accessible. It is quite near the main road, and traffic noise may be a problem for some people. The day-use area is a short drive from the campground.

Recreational activities

Beachcombing is a favourite activity here. At low tide a cobblestone beach reveals sea stars, mussels, oysters, and an array of marine life. From the beach it is also possible to see whales, seals, and sea lions, but don't count on it—they were somewhat elusive when I visited. Although the waters tend to be cold, swimming and fishing are also enjoyed by some.

Additional information

The area of coastline from Langdale to Lund is called the Sunshine Coast because of its warm summers and mild winters. Precipitation here is almost 170 millimetres less than in Vancouver, making the Sunshine Coast a desirable place to live. Roberts Creek campground is located on one of the busiest sections of the area. The community of Gibsons to the south is famous because the TV series *The Beachcombers* was filmed here. It also has a small maritime museum. To the north, Sechelt has a number of great bakeries and cafes—don't stop here if you are on a diet, but if you're not, it's a nice little community to wander through.

ROLLEY LAKE

Location

Some parks are criticized for being too big, some for being too small. In my opinion, Rolley Lake is the perfect size. It is also easily accessible from Vancouver, has a delightful setting, boasts a number of recreational activities, and is well equipped. It is located 23 kilometres northwest of Mission (70 kilometres east of Vancouver). Although well signposted from Highway 7, the location is a little hard to find. In Maple Ridge, turn off Highway 7 north at 287th onto the Dewdney Trunk Road, turn right onto Bell Road, then make a left turn toward the park. The road is paved all the way. Maple Ridge and Mission both have comprehensive services.

Facilities

This popular campground has 64 spacious units set in a woodland area of western hemlock and mature vine maple, offering privacy and shade. The facilities are among the best provided by BC Parks and include showers, sani-station, flush and pit toilets, and wheelchair access. Reservations are accepted.

Recreational activities

The 115 hectares of Rolley Lake Provincial Park provide a relaxing environment for campers. The lake is surrounded by forest, and because powerboats are prohibited, it is a peaceful place to relax, canoe, swim, and fish (the lake is stocked with cutthroat and rainbow trout). There are a couple of short walks: one leads to a waterfall, while another leads around the lake, includes a section of boardwalk, and takes about 90 minutes to complete. Children can have fun in the play area. Rolley Lake is also a good place for observing bird life, and there is a wildlife-viewing site for B.C. Wildlife Watch.

Additional information

Rolley Lake, which takes its name from Fanny and James Rolley, who settled here in 1888, has played an active part in the logging industry of B.C. In the early part of the century the lake stored shingle bolts destined for a mill located at Ruskin, 5 kilometres away. In the 1930s, when all the old-growth forest had gone, it became home to a small Japanese-Canadian logging operation harvesting Douglas fir. BC Parks acquired it in 1961, and today it provides a tranquil environment for those who wish to escape the main centres of population. The park has the advantage of being relatively small and yet supplying all amenities. These characteristics, together with its serene location and proximity to the Lower Mainland, ensure a pleasant camping experience. The only problems with this idyllic setting are the mosquitoes, which can be troublesome at times, and sometimes the sandy beach is littered with Canada geese droppings—so watch your step.

SALTERY BAY

Location

Come and see Canada's first underwater statue at Saltery Bay, but remember to bring all the correct diving gear! Saltery Bay Provincial Park is located about 27 kilometres south of Powell River on the north shore of Jervis Inlet. Visitors must take two delightful short ferry rides, one from Horseshoe Bay to Langdale, the other from Earls Cove to Saltery Bay. The land and sea route from the Lower Mainland and the ocean-view scenery at Saltery Bay make this camping excursion a real delight. Thirty kilometres north, Powell River has all services.

Facilities

There are 42 large, private camping units in an evergreen forest. The campground has a sani-station, but only pit toilets and no showers. It is wheelchair accessible and accepts reservations.

Recreational activities

In addition to the superb ocean-view scenery, the shallow offshore waters of the park are the biggest attraction here. Scuba divers are enticed to the area by the variety of marine life, underwater cover, and shipwrecks (there is also access for divers with disabilities). To the delight of many divers, a three-metre bronze mermaid has been sunk at Mermaid Cove. It has the distinction of being Canada's first underwater statue. For those who do not dive, the park offers beaches for swimming and sunbathing (in the day-use area), a 2-kilometre hiking trail to Little Saltery Falls, the chance to see killer whales, seals, and sea lions who occasionally bask in the area, and salmon fishing from April to October. What more could you ask?

Additional information

Saltery Bay is named after the fish saltery that was located here at the turn of the century; prior to that time, First Nations inhabited the area. This popular diving area has been featured by *National Geographic* and is an excellent spot from which to explore the Sunshine Coast.

SASQUATCH

Location

This really is a great place to take the kids, but even for those without little ones, a lot of fun can be had at Sasquatch. With four pristine lakes, including the freshwater fjord of massive Harrison Lake, and over 1,220 hectares of land, it is easy to see why this park is popular. The park offers a vast expanse of beautiful mountain scenery to explore. Sasquatch is located 6 kilometres north of Harrison Hot Springs off Highway 7. All services are found at Harrison.

Facilities

The 176 camping units are set in an area of second-growth deciduous forest and are divided into two areas. Hicks Lake campground has 71 spots, some close to the lake, while the Lakeside (my favourite, with 42 spaces) and Bench (63 spaces) campgrounds are nearer to Deer Lake. Lakeside has some wonderful spots with access directly onto the lake, whereas the spaces at Bench are heavily shaded. There are flush and pit toilets and a sani-station, but no showers. The park accepts reservations but is not wheelchair accessible.

Recreational activities

The four lakes at this location (Harrison, Hicks, Deer, and Trout) vary in size and in the recreational pursuits they offer. Harrison and Hicks lakes permit powerboats, and at Deer Lake only boats powered with electric motors are allowed. Trout Lake prohibits powerboats and thus is ideal for canoeing and kayaking. Trout fishing here is reputed to be excellent. A number of trails lead around the park, and some of these are suitable for mountain bikes. Two beach locations ensure sun-worshipping opportunities—one is at the southern end of Hicks Lake and the other is by the group-camping area. From this second location it is possible to swim to two small forested islands ideal for exploring. A play area for children is located at the Lakeside campground, and the day-use area on Harrison Lake has tons of picnic tables, and sunbathing and swimming opportunities. Canoe rentals are also offered (the cost was $15.00 per hour in 2003, from Hicks Lake). The nearby town of Harrison Hot Springs, famous for its mineral pools, holds a sandcastle-building contest in September.

Additional information

The name "sasquatch" is an English corruption of the Coast Salish word *sasqac*. The sasquatch is a mythical creature believed to possess a certain type of spirit that should be avoided—a sort of Bigfoot. Local Native people still report sightings of the sasquatch around Harrison River, so be warned! This area is spectacular in the fall when the colours are at their height; fall is also a good time to visit Harrison Hot Springs, which can become very busy during the peak summer months.

SILVER LAKE

Location

Confession time: I do not much care for this campground. When I visited (on my way to Skagit Valley—a far superior campground), groups of teenagers from Hope were loud and boisterous and consequently shaped my impression. The relatively small lakeside campground is located 12 kilometres from Hope off Highway 1. The last 6 kilometres are on a good gravel road. All services are available at Hope.

Facilities

There are 25 sites at this 77-hectare park; some are little more than pull-ins at the side of the road. However, the surrounding Fraser Valley scenery is great. Only the basic facilities exist (water, pit toilets, picnic tables, and fire pits).

Recreational activities

One of the other problems I have with Silver Lake is that there is little to do here, in stark contrast to its neighbour, Skagit Valley. It is possible to swim in the lake and fish for trout. A small 1-kilometre trail follows the water's edge, and there is a boat launch that is accessible only with a four-wheel-drive vehicle. The town of Hope is an interesting place for a wander, as there are a number of carved wooden sculptures in the downtown and a number of restaurants and eateries.

Additional information

I cannot tell a lie—I would not want to camp here. Although the scenery is stunning and the campground's proximity to Hope attractive, my advice to other campers is to journey to Skagit Valley or, if you cannot face the gravel road, to Emory Creek, or even to the Alaska Highway! Anywhere is better than here—unless, of course, you are 18 years old, have a four-wheel-drive truck with monster wheels, love loud music, and want to hang out with like-minded people.

Skagit Valley

Location

For me, the words "Skagit Valley" and "mosquitoes" are synonymous. Had I visited when these insects were not biting, Skagit Valley would probably rank as one of my top 10 campgrounds. Encompassing over 32,500 hectares, this park is in the Northern Cascades. West of Hope, a gravel road leads 32 kilometres to Skagit Valley, but the main camping area is an additional 26 kilometres on bumpy gravel. Once at Ross Lake (the main campground), the scenery is awesome. The nearest services are back at Hope, so stock up before making the journey.

Facilities

Two campgrounds offer 142 sites; 44 are at Silvertip, adjacent to the Skagit River near the park's entrance, and the rest are at Ross Lake. Silvertip is set among trees; Ross Lake tends to be more open, with sites near the water's edge. There is no sani-station or wheelchair access, and facilities are basic (water, fire pit, picnic tables, pit toilets).

Recreational activities

At Silvertip, trails lead along the Skagit River. Ross Lake has hiking trails in the immediate vicinity, and there are more than 50 kilometres of hiking trails in the park itself. There is also a boat launch, an adventure playground for children, and a large grassy field. The lake is surrounded by fantastic snow-covered mountains. The Skagit River is one of the best fly-fishing streams in North America and the most productive stream in the Lower Mainland. Fishing for Dolly Varden, char, eastern brook trout, and cutthroat trout is good. Wildlife here includes deer, black bear, cougar, coyote, mink, and raccoons. There is also a wide array of birds. Swimming is possible from Ross Lake's sandy beach.

Additional information

Over 20 years ago, a public protest saved the valley from being flooded by a Seattle hydro company. Today, the water level at Ross Lake is controlled by a hydro dam in Washington State and is subject to fluctuations. As I bounced along the 58 kilometres of gravel road, I cursed the fact that the park entrance is so far from the campground and that this information is not conveyed to the uninitiated. Then I beheld the mountain scenery that surrounds the lake and suddenly the journey was worth it. I did not stay the night due to the mosquitoes, out in force on that July day. It appears others have had the same experience, so be forewarned.

STAWAMUS CHIEF

Location

This campground takes its name from the majestic piece of rock under which it is situated. Less than 10 years old, the campground has been developed primarily for climbers and hikers; when I visited, it was dominated by skinny Lycra-clad individuals setting out to climb "the Chief." If you're a climber it's the place to be; however, others may not find it so appealing. It is located on Highway 99, 5 kilometres south of Squamish, where all services are available.

Facilities

There are 15 vehicle sites that are not suitable for larger RVs, as they are very close together, and 45 walk-in sites. Because the campground is relatively new, the ground vegetation is sparse, making the camping spots under the trees look quite dark and sad. Pit toilets and water are available, but not fire pits.

Recreational activities

The primary reason for camping here is to scale the tremendous Stawamus Chief rock. The second-largest granite monolith on Earth, it is a world-class climbing destination. Generally, the 700-metre-high rock is closed to climbers from March 15 to July 31 to protect the nesting peregrine falcons. For those who do not wish to climb, it is also possible to hike up the rock, but be warned: This excursion is not for the faint of heart. I attempted it a few years ago. A sign at the outset read "unsuitable for dogs." Upon reaching the top, another small rock climb was required, after which it was necessary to walk a narrow pathway with dramatic crevices on either side. I turned back, believing this hike was not just unsuitable for dogs, but also for many two-legged individuals. You can also hike the adjacent Stawamus Squaw. Shannon Falls Park is less than 2 kilometres away and is a great place for a picnic and a stroll to a platform for viewing the 335-metre falls—B.C.'s third-highest waterfall. The restaurant across the road also provides good views of the falls. The railway museum at Squamish and the mining museum at Britannia Beach are also well worth a visit.

Additional information

This is not a picturesque campground; the views are minimal and the spaces small. There is also the distant sound of traffic. But if your passion is climbing, it is the place to be, as you will inevitably meet like-minded people. For all others, my advice is to stay at Porteau Cove, Alice Lake, or Nairn Falls.

THOMPSON OKANAGAN

The Thompson Okanagan region includes a huge central region of land from the U.S. border in the south to the Canadian Rockies in the north. Pack the sunscreen if your plans include a trip to the southern portion, as temperatures here are often the hottest in the province. This region features miles of orchards and vineyards, crystal-clear lakes, warm-hearted communities, and undulating countryside giving way to beautiful mountains in the north. The southern Okanagan region incorporates Highway 3 from Kettle Valley to Princeton, Highway 33, Highway 97, Highway 5A south of Aspen Grove to Princeton, and Highway 6. Further north, three of the province's most spectacular provincial parks can be found: Mount Robson is named after its majestic mountain, the highest in the Canadian Rockies; Wells Gray is B.C.'s fourth-largest park and is known as "the waterfall park"; Shuswap Lake has over 1,000 kilometres of waterways and many sandy beaches. The northern region encompasses campgrounds accessible from Highway 16 from the border of Alberta to Route 5, Highway 5, Highway 5A, Route 1 as far as Lytton, and the northern section of Highway 23. With such diversity, there is something for every camper in this area of B.C.

Fish and swim in the Similkameen river at Bromley Rock Provincial Park.

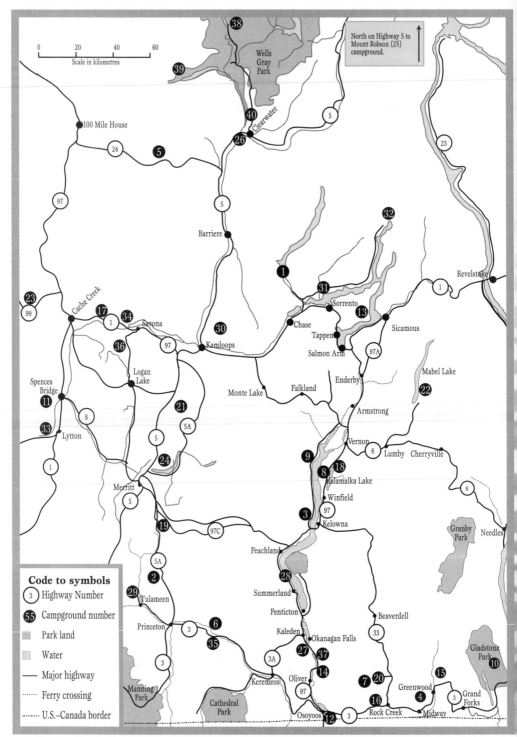

Adams Lake

Location
Visitors to Adams Lake discover a paradise of pristine beaches covering over 2,500 metres of shoreline. The campground is beautifully situated near the warm southern end of the 60-kilometre-long lake. Turn off Highway 1 at Squilax and take a paved road that turns into a gravel road for 15 kilometres. The park is 30 kilometres from Chase, which houses the nearest services.

Facilities
The small, lightly forested campground has 28 spots, which are really only suitable for smaller RVs, tent trailers, and tents. Facilities are restricted to the basic ones found in B.C. parks (pit toilets, water, picnic tables, fire pit).

Recreational activities
Caves nestle along the shore, and all types of water sports can be enjoyed, including swimming, boating, sunbathing, fishing, windsurfing, and paddling. Many visitors simply enjoy relaxing in this remote location. The campground is located 15 kilometres north of Roderick Haig-Brown Provincial Park, dedicated to preserving one of B.C.'s primary natural resources and also the site of the largest sockeye salmon run on the continent. Every four years, millions of sockeye return here. In the intervening years, the runs are smaller but still significant. Trails allow riverside access to this amazing phenomenon. A number of archaeological sites exist in the park.

Additional information
Adams Lake Provincial Park was established in 1988 and is a relatively recent addition to BC Parks. The park, which incorporates an area of 56 hectares, is an idyllic spot for those who seek a tranquil location that is easily accessible from Route 1. Although the park is scheduled to open on May 15 each year, the snow load could mean that this date is a little optimistic in certain years.

Thompson Okanagan

ALLISON LAKE

Location
On the relatively quiet Highway 5A at the southern end of Allison Lake there is an enchanting little 23-hectare campground, perfect for those with time on their hands. Services can be found at Princeton, 28 kilometres south.

Facilities
Twenty-four large, well-positioned camping spaces are found in a lovely forested area of mature Douglas fir. The sites are suitable for every type of vehicle, and although some are quite close to the road, there is not a lot of traffic. All the basic amenities exist (fire pit, water access, picnic tables, pit toilets).

Recreational activities
The primary recreational activities here centre on beautiful Allison Lake and include swimming (although there are quite a few reeds), fishing (the lake is stocked with blackwater rainbow trout), canoeing, and kayaking. The lake is bordered by aspen trees, and the area is particularly attractive during the fall when the trees turn golden and red and present fantastic photographic opportunities. A single-width gravel boat launch is located in the day-use area.

Additional information
This is one of the better roadside campgrounds used primarily for overnight camping. Highway 5A between Kamloops and Princeton is a lovely quiet route on which to appreciate the scenery of the Okanagan. And for those who have the time, it is far more pleasant to travel than the busy Coquihalla Highway. The route is 118 kilometres longer than the main highway, but avoids the long, steep hills of the Coquihalla as well as the $10.00 toll. Be prepared for little development and a scenic drive if heading south from the campground, as the road follows Allison Creek to Princeton. The area is rich in mining history; information is available from the visitor centres in Princeton and Merritt.

BEAR CREEK

Location

Go to sleep to the sound of tree frogs at this popular 167-hectare campground. Bear Creek exhibits a variety of geological features, including sandy beaches and spectacular canyons and waterfalls. These features are supplemented with a diversity of vegetation, which encourages wildlife populations. Bear Creek is situated to the north of the Okanagan, 9 kilometres west of Kelowna (where services are found) on the western side of Okanagan Lake, off Highway 97 on a paved access road.

Facilities

Bear Creek provides 122 camping spots and every type of camping service, including flush and pit toilets, a sani-station, showers, and access for the disabled. Sites accommodate all recreational vehicles, and there are a number of double spots. Some of the more desirable spots overlook Lambly (Bear) Creek, where campers can be lulled to sleep by the sound of the trickling waters (not recommended for those with weak bladders). The park administrators operate a small concession selling ice cream, juice, pop, etc. Reservations are accepted.

Recreational activities

This stunning location facilitates a variety of recreational pursuits. The beach is over 400 metres in length, ideal for swimming and sunbathing. The lake has rainbow trout, whitefish, and kokanee, as well as boating potential. In addition to a number of smaller interpretive trails, over 15 kilometres of well-maintained hiking trails exist, some of which lead to views of the lake and canyon. Remember to pack your camera, as there are excellent photographic opportunities. Children can enjoy an adventure playground, and there is also a horseshoe pit. Bear Creek is home to an array of wildlife, including swallows, hawks, and owls. Tree frogs can be heard in the spring, and rattlesnakes live in the vicinity but are rarely seen.

Additional information

In the early fall, kokanee can be seen spawning in the lower reaches of the creek. The quality of the creek's water was recognized by the Kelowna Brewing Company, which many years ago established a brewery nearby. This park is extremely popular in the summer months, and is particularly appealing for those with children. I strongly advise making a reservation if you hope to camp in July or August.

BOUNDARY CREEK

Location
If you are debating whether to spend the night at Boundary Creek or at another location, my advice would be to choose the alternative. Conveniently situated on the banks of Boundary Creek 3 kilometres west of Greenwood, where all services are found, this two-hectare roadside campground has little to recommend it.

Facilities
The 18 camping spots are quite large, but the lack of dense vegetation makes them open and without privacy. The campsites adjacent to the creek are somewhat more private, as cottonwood trees line the banks of the creek itself. All the basic facilities offered by BC Parks are available (picnic tables, flush and pit toilets, water, fire pit). As the campground is close to the main road, it can be quite noisy.

Recreational activities
This is very much an overnight campground and therefore offers little recreational activity. It is possible to catch rainbow and brook trout in the creek. The mining industry developed the area adjacent to the campground. A nearby slag heap and crumbling stack are evidence of the B.C. Copper Company's smelter, which employed over 400 men during its years of operation in the first part of the 20th century. The historic town of Greenwood contains some beautiful turn-of-the-century buildings, including a courthouse and post office, and is a pleasant place to stroll around.

Additional information
Out of necessity, I stayed at Boundary Creek in late September one year. The proximity to the road coupled with the openness of the sites themselves marks this as one of BC Parks' less desirable spots; however, it does have the advantage of being the only campground in the immediate area. I had visited Greenwood during the late afternoon and enjoyed it, so I went back in the evening, only to find it extremely quiet. Despite its claim to be Canada's smallest city, in Greenwood little occurs after 6:00 p.m.

Bridge Lake

Location
This area, known as the "Interlakes District," is an angler's paradise. Hundreds of lakes offer fishing for eastern brook and lake trout, burbot, and kokanee. Bridge Lake Provincial Park was established by BC Parks in 1957 and covers a modest six hectares. There are two main ways to reach Bridge Lake. The first entails turning off Highway 97 east of 93 Mile House on Highway 24. The campground is 50 kilometres east of Highway 97. The second is to turn off Highway 5 at Little Fort and travel west on Highway 24. Full services are available at 100 Mile House.

Facilities
Thirteen vehicle/tent sites and three walk-in campsites are available. The sites are large, set amongst trees, and have views of the lake. Facilities are basic and consist of picnic tables, fire pit, water, and pit toilets. There is no sani-station.

Recreational activities
Activities at this location include fishing for burbot, lake and rainbow trout, boating (there is a boat launch), and swimming. The lake is also ideal for canoeing and kayaking. A small hiking trail skirts the lakeside, and there is an archaeological site in the park itself.

Additional information
Recently a number of resorts have developed in the area, and these now offer holiday excursions. The easy access from two main highways means that this campground is a convenient stop-off for the traveller during the busy peak months of July and August. The location seems to be particularly popular with anglers.

BROMLEY ROCK

Location
Set astride a rock bluff on the Similkameen River, 21 kilometres east of Princeton on Highway 3, is the riverside campground of Bromley Rock Provincial Park. In staying here, campers trace the footsteps of the early pioneers who came in search of gold and other minerals. Services are located at Princeton, 21 kilometres west, or Hedley, 15 kilometres east.

Facilities
The campground has 17 spots set in a forested area near the Similkameen River. All the basics are here (fire pit, water, picnic tables, pit toilets), and the park is wheelchair accessible.

Recreational activities
The river offers swimming in delightful cool swimming holes, and there is fishing potential. When I visited, local young male adventurers could be observed "tubing" downstream to Stemwinder Provincial Park, an activity not recommended for the uninitiated. Just outside the park, hiking trails lead to fantastic views of the Similkameen Valley. The nearby town of Princeton was named in 1860 to commemorate the visit of the Prince of Wales that year. Princeton has a pioneer museum with displays of clothing, mining items, and furnishings. Artifacts from the Salish people and Chinese immigrants who played a major role in the early development of mining and the railway are also on display.

Additional information
This campground is only 14 kilometres from Stemwinder Provincial Park, which is slightly larger in capacity and may provide an alternative should Bromley Rock be full. Bromley Rock is a great place to stop for a picnic even if you do not want to camp. The area was originally inhabited by the Salish and Shuswap people, who have left traces of their existence. More recently, the area was explored by miners and trappers. Anyone travelling west along Highway 3 should make time to visit the Grist Mill and Gardens (see Stemwinder Provincial Park). Even if you do not have time to tour this BC Heritage site, just call in for coffee and the wonderful home cooking.

CONKLE LAKE

Location

If you are looking for a backcountry retreat to get away from the crowds and you can endure a bumpy road and navigate around herds of cows, this is the place for you. The campground is in a beautiful location amidst the Okanagan Highlands, but BC Parks warns that the access route along twisting gravel roads is not suitable for large motorhomes or towed trailers. Consequently, those travelling in these types of vehicles may wish to choose another spot. The park can be reached by gravel access roads from three points: From Highway 33 at Westbridge, it is found after driving for 16 kilometres on a gravel road; from Highway 3, 6 kilometres east of Bridesville a 26-kilometre gravel road leads to the site; and from Highway 97 at Okanagan Falls, a 35-kilometre gravel road can be taken. Services are available at Westbridge and at the junction of Highways 3 and 33.

Facilities

There are 34 private camping spots located in a lightly forested area of western larch, lodgepole pine, alder, and willow on the northwest corner of the 3-kilometre-long lake. Some spots overlook the lake. Only the basic facilities are provided by BC Parks (pit toilets, picnic tables, pump water, cooking pit). There is no sani-station.

Recreational activities

Conkle Lake has a beautiful beach, where you can sunbathe, swim, or fish for rainbow trout. A steep dropoff, however, means non-swimmers and children should be cautious. There is a boat launch and a number of hiking trails that lead from the campground. The 1.7-kilometre Falls Trail includes a beautiful multi-tiered waterfall. For rainy days, a covered picnic shelter is available.

Additional information

The park is named after an early settler to the Kettle Valley, W.H. Conkle. The fact that this park is relatively difficult to access by the RV population may suggest it is a campground only for four-wheel-drivers and their passengers to enjoy. When I visited, there were quite a few large recreational vehicles that had obviously managed the routes and whose owners were enjoying the beautiful Okanagan scenery. However, the roads should not be attempted by those with low-loaders or long vehicles, as there are a number of tight switchbacks.

ELLISON

Location

If diving is your game, then Ellison Park should be your aim. In addition to the diving opportunities it provides, Ellison is an excellent spot for a family vacation, perfect if you have children to entertain. Set on the northeastern shore of Okanagan Lake and encompassing 200 hectares between the Thompson Plateau and the Monashee Mountains, the park is reached by travelling 16 kilometres southwest of Vernon. All services are available in Vernon.

Facilities

The park has 71 spacious, well-appointed sites set in a natural forest of Douglas fir and ponderosa pine and is suitable for every size of recreational vehicle. There are flush and pit toilets, but no sani-station or showers. The park is wheelchair accessible and reservations are accepted at 49 sites.

Recreational activities

Ellison Provincial Park is home to Canada's only freshwater dive park. A number of objects and artifacts have been sunk here to attract fish and create a diving haven for the rubber-clad enthusiasts who explore the dark, cold waters. If diving is not your passion, there is a wide array of other activities to enjoy, including 6 kilometres of hiking trails that take visitors to many of the park's natural features and viewpoints. (Watch out for porcupines, often seen on the popular Ellison Trail.) Two protected beach areas ideal for swimming and sunbathing are equipped with changing facilities and an outdoor shower. A little farther away is a third beach, which allows dogs. Fishers can try their luck for large carp, burbot, kokanee, and trout, and while there is no boat launch in the park, one is located 6 kilometres to the north. A number of the camping spaces overlook the playground and are ideal if you have young children. There is also an almost manicured green field that many golf courses would be envious of for ball games.

Additional information

Ellison is in the heart of the fruit-growing region of the province, and orchards, ranches, and farms dominate the area, as they have since the 1800s. This park provides an excellent base from which to explore the North Okanagan and savour the produce of the region. When we stayed in 2004, yurts were available for rent.

FINTRY

Location

This is a wonderful provincial park to explore, as it has so many facets. It is quite distinctive and one of my favourites in the area. Ideally situated for exploring the Okanagan and found in one of the region's few remaining natural areas, Fintry started to register campers in 1996. The park is on the northwest side of Okanagan Lake, 32 kilometres north of Kelowna and 37 kilometres south of Vernon. It is clearly signposted from Highway 97 and accessed by 8 kilometres of paved road. Services are available at Kelowna and Vernon.

Facilities

Camping facilities here include flush toilets and showers. Camping spots are in a large open area. Some are shaded by pine trees, and others have views of the lake. A hundred camping spots are available, and reservations are accepted for 70 sites.

Recreational activities

In close proximity to the campground is a beautiful 2-kilometre sandy beach, ideal for swimming, sunbathing, and family activities. Although no boat launch is provided in the park itself, the regional district public boat launch is found a kilometre from the park's boundary. Fishing in the warm waters of Okanagan Lake can be rewarding, and hiking the Shorts Creek Canyon Trail provides opportunities to view white-tailed deer, bighorn sheep, and a variety of birds. BC Parks warns that caution should be exercised on sections of the trails; in places it is quite narrow and near steep cliffs.

Additional information

The park is a heritage site occupying the former Fintry Estate. Its history dates to the last century, when fur dealers traded with the Native inhabitants of the area. In 1909 James Cameron, originally from Scotland, purchased the land and called it Fintry. He built many of the buildings that exist today, including the manor house and farm buildings. Fintry has the advantage of being located in a popular area, but being a relatively new camping haven, it has yet to be fully exploited by the camping public. It will not be long before this situation changes. I first visited this park in 1999 and adored wandering around the undeveloped trails and shady lanes that had once been part of the farm. BC Parks is currently in the process of restoring many of the old buildings on the site.

GLADSTONE (TEXAS CREEK)

Location

Gladstone (formerly Texas Creek) Provincial Park is located just east of the community of Christina Lake, off Highway 3—turn onto East Lake Drive and drive for 6 kilometres on a paved road. Residents of Christina Lake boast that the waters here are the warmest in B.C.; however, Wasa Lake and Osoyoos Lake make the same claim. Whatever the truth, Christina Lake is an immensely popular recreational place where all services can be found.

Facilities

Sixty-three large camping spots are set in an open pine forest in this 112-hectare provincial park. Facilities include the basics: fire pit, water, picnic table, pit toilets. Gladstone is wheelchair accessible, and reservations are accepted.

Recreational activities

Nineteen kilometres long and only 55 metres deep, Christina Lake supplies a wealth of leisure pursuits, including swimming from delightful secluded pocket beaches, and boating and fishing in the clear waters. There is a hiking trail that leads north along the lakeshore, and another leads to Deer Point Lookout—26 kilometres return. The nearby popular holiday centre also has golf courses and country clubs to enjoy.

Additional information

For years I avoided staying here, as I found the community of Christina Lake very busy and commercialized and envisaged the campground having similar traits. How wrong could I be! This is a wonderful, quiet camping spot where very lucky campers gain sites overlooking the water. I spent a gorgeous summer night here in 1998 and cursed my previous preconceptions about the place, which were grounded in the knowledge that the population of Christina Lake swells from 1,000 to 6,000 in the summer months.

GOLDPAN

Location
Watch out for river rafters and gold prospectors if you plan to sojourn here. Goldpan is a five-hectare roadside provincial park conveniently located on Highway 1, 10 kilometres south of Spences Bridge, where services are located. There is also a restaurant just down the road.

Facilities
There are just 14 camping spots available here beside the mighty Thompson River. Facilities are basic (water, fire pit, picnic tables, pit toilets). Railway trucks and the noise of road traffic can be heard from the campground.

Recreational activities
Goldpan's main draw is fishing, and the park attracts steelhead anglers, especially in October, November, and December. In addition, the area is known for whitewater rafting, and often adventurers can be seen navigating the currents of the Thompson River in their rubber rafts. Consequently, the area is heavily used during the peak summer months by commercial river-rafting companies looking for a resting place for their downriver trips. As one would surmise, gold panning is also a pursuit that can be undertaken here. Osprey frequents the area—so keep looking up.

Additional information
Spences Bridge, named after Thomas Spence, who built the original bridge in 1865, is where the Thompson and Nicola rivers meet. This area has been fished for hundreds of years by the Thompson Nation, whose people continue to fish here today, as indeed do many others. For those who want a taste of adventure by whitewater rafting, this location is ideal. Be warned—in summertime the area is prone to very high temperatures, often the highest in the country, so remember the sunscreen. The campground was established in 1956 and is primarily a one-night stop for travellers on Highway 1. Having visited again in 2004, my feeling is confirmed that this park serves well as a picnic spot for breaking the journey on Route 1, rather than an ideal place to camp. Skihist, a short drive south, is far superior and not as noisy.

HAYNES POINT

Location
It is a great shame that this popular campground is not larger. For the longest time, whenever I attempted to stay in this idyllic setting, it was full. I finally succeeded in September 2002 and got the last remaining space, even at this supposedly quiet time of the year. Haynes Point is located at the southern end of the Okanagan River Valley, in the rain shadow of the Cascade Mountains on Osoyoos Lake, just 2 kilometres from Osoyoos on Highway 97.

Facilities
It is little wonder that Haynes Point is a popular retreat, as all of the 41 camping spots are located on a narrow sandspit with over half of them having direct access to the beach. There are both flush and pit toilets, but no sani-station or showers. The park is accessible by wheelchair. Reservations are accepted.

Recreational activities
The deep Okanagan River Valley, formed by glacial erosion, receives less than 35 centimetres of rain per annum and is Canada's only true desert. The lake is reputed to be the warmest in the country, making it a magnet for swimming, boating (there is a boat launch), and for rainbow trout and bass fishing. The fish are huge here and can easily be seen from a trail in the park. The park trails have recently been upgraded and extended. The warm climate and lack of precipitation promote desert-loving plants such as ponderosa pine, bear cacti, sagebrush, and greasewood, which in turn provide a habitat for a wide array of bird, animal, and reptile life, including species unique to this area, such as the spadefoot toad, burrowing owl, and desert night snake.

Additional information
The park is named after Judge John Carmichael Haynes, who came to Osoyoos in 1866 and became a renowned legal authority and landowner. Native people lived, hunted, and fished in the area; two archaeological sites in the park provide proof of this long history. Haynes Point is an extremely popular location during the peak summer months, and the climate ensures a pleasant stay for those who visit in the spring and fall. Some of the Okanagan's finest vineyards and fruit farms are found in this region. From May to November, fresh fruit and vegetable stands at the side of the highway provide produce for campers to enjoy around an open fire. The only disadvantage to this campground is that at certain times it can be a little noisy, as the sound of traffic and music is easily audible from the town of Osoyoos across the water.

HERALD

Location

A variety of flora and fauna and easy access to the calm waters of Shuswap Lake are just two of the many attributes of Herald Provincial Park. The vegetation is attributable to the park's distinctive position amid steep uplands and flat deltas. It includes Douglas fir, juniper, dryland shrubs, red cedar, hemlock, cottonwood, aspen, and paper birch. A naturalist's delight, Herald is found on the Salmon Arm of Shuswap Lake, 12 kilometres east of Tappen off Route 1. Services are available at Tappen.

Facilities

On the calm lakeside are 119 beautiful, wooded camping spaces with all the services required for a comfortable camping experience, including showers, flush and pit toilets, a sani-station, and wheelchair access. The campsites are at three locations: Reineker, Bastion, and Homestead. Reineker's sites are closer to the water, and Bastion's are larger and more secluded. The sites at Homestead don't have much shade. Reservations are accepted.

Recreational activities

Shuswap Lake is a relatively warm lake and therefore a delightful place to swim. The park has sand and fine-gravel beaches ideal for sunbathing. Fishing and boating are pursuits enjoyed by many, and there are a number of trails, including a 20-minute one that leads through an area of cedar growth to the beautiful Margaret Falls. Reineker Creek runs through the park near the campground, and evidence of Shuswap Nation pit houses is visible west of the creek. The boat launch is 1 kilometre from the campground in the day-use area. Birding is reputed to be fantastic, as more than 70 species frequent the park.

Additional information

The lake is named after the Shuswap First Nation, who recognized it as bountiful for hunting and fishing. Cliff faces around the lake display pictographs (rock paintings) that provide evidence of humankind's long inhabitation of the region. Although the lake is named after the Aboriginal people, the park takes its name from the Herald family, who were early settlers of the area. The remains of the family's farm buildings can still be seen today. Herald Provincial Park is very popular with both locals and tourists, as it offers every facility yet is not tremendously large. It's a delightful place to camp. This park has a sani-station with the best view of any sani-station in the province, so even the mundane chores of camping become a delight.

INKANEEP

Location

Inkaneep is an ideal spot from which to experience the excellent local fruit and wine; however, little else is offered by this campground. It's primarily geared to overnight camping. On the shores of the Okanagan River, this 21-hectare campground is 6 kilometres north of Oliver on Highway 97. Services are found in Oliver. It was established in 1956 and plays a role in protecting old cottonwood trees.

Facilities

Inkaneep offers seven camping spots, more suitable for tents than RVs, set in a shady oasis of cottonwood trees on the edge of the Okanagan River. Only the basic facilities are available here (pit toilets, picnic tables, water, and cooking pit). The campground is very close to a group of houses, and in this respect it is quite suburban.

Recreational activities

From this campground it is possible to fish in the Okanagan River and to canoe (although it is quite a trek from the campground to the water). The arid desert habitat around the park is home to many species of wildlife; consequently, one of the main activities here is birdwatching. The area is home to blackheaded grosbeak, American redstart, northern oriole, yellow warbler, Lewis's woodpecker, and warbling vireo. An ecological reserve is located nearby. A small path amidst old-growth cottonwood trees leads from the campground to a small dike on the Okanagan River, where there are birdwatching opportunities.

Additional information

Just south of Oliver is a "pocket desert." When I visited, it was somewhat difficult to find, as there were no signposts. However, in 2001 it was designated as a provincial park, and it will be developed in the future. The area supports subtropical flora and fauna such as cactus, horned lizards, rattlesnakes, and burrowing owls. The town of Oliver was established in 1921 under a land grant by then-B.C. premier John Oliver as a settlement for veterans from the First World War. Now it is known for housing some of the best wineries in the country, which can be toured by visitors. Be sure to make time to explore the local caves and perhaps purchase a bottle of wine for savouring around the campfire.

JEWEL LAKE

Location

Somewhat off the beaten track, Jewel Lake provides the camper with a get-away-from-it-all camping experience, and if that camper is keen on fishing, then this place must be heaven. Found 12 kilometres north of Greenwood off Highway 3, it is accessed by travelling toward Jewel Lake Resort. All services are available at Greenwood, but the resort also has some provisions and boat rentals.

Facilities

There are 26 vehicle-accessible sites here, and the basic facilities (water, picnic tables, fire pit and pit toilets). All sites are in a heavily forested area of Douglas fir, hemlock, birch, and larch and are not suitable for larger RVs.

Recreational activities

Like so many out-of-the-way places in the province, Jewel Lake is primarily a location for fishing. Stocked with brook and rainbow trout from the Summerland Trout Hatchery, the 3-kilometre-long lake attracts anglers by the score. Fly-fishing is also popular. There is a car-top boat launch, and boats can be rented at Jewel Lake Resort. Boats are restricted to 10 horsepower, making canoeing a delightful alternative. Swimming is also possible. The historical town of Greenwood has a number of interesting buildings, but be warned that it closes early, even at the height of summer.

Additional information

Now for my confession: I have not personally visited this campground in my 15 years of camping in B.C. But when undertaking the research on this location and speaking to people who have, the words "fish" and "mosquito" always punctuate their sentences. Sometimes there are good reasons why even the most dedicated travel writers should gain their information second-hand.

Johnstone Creek

Location
Established in 1956 for day use only, this small 38-hectare roadside provincial park recently started offering camping. It is located near Bridesville and Rock Creek on Highway 3 about 45 kilometres from the town of Osoyoos, where all services are available.

Facilities
Situated in an area of Douglas fir, pine, and aspen are 16 campsites a little distance away from the road. The trees make a good sound barrier, so noise from traffic is not a huge issue. The spots seem to be evenly split between those that are quite open with only a few shrubs dividing them to those with more privacy, thanks to the trees. There are four pit toilets, picnic tables, fire pits, and water. I stayed in the springtime, so the smell of blooming spring vegetation was an added bonus.

Recreational activities
A pleasant waterfall where the waters of Johnstone Creek and Rock Creek converge is the main attraction here. There are also good photographic opportunities at Rock Creek Canyon. According to BC Parks information, white-tailed deer and woodpeckers are often seen in the park. There is very limited hiking and fishing potential in the immediate vicinity, as the campground is geared to the overnight camper.

Additional information
For those interested in prospecting for gold, a visit to the ghost town Camp McKinney is a must. Situated 11.5 kilometres northwest of Highway 3 on Mount Baldy Road are the ruins of a mining town, which between 1887 and 1903 yielded more than 80,000 ounces of gold. A stop at the Osoyoos visitor centre provides more details. For those who plan to camp in the area longer than one night (and have a vehicle that can take the terrain), Conkle Lake is the preferred option; for others, Johnstone Creek is a superior roadside campground.

JUNIPER BEACH

Location

Juniper Beach is distinct from many other provincial parks you may stay in because of its dry desert setting. Established in 1989, it is one of B.C.'s newer parks. Juniper Beach is located 19 kilometres east of Cache Creek on Highway 1. Services are available at Cache Creek or at Kamloops, 53 kilometres to the west.

Facilities

On the banks of the Thompson River, 30 camping spots are yours for the taking. The vegetation consists of sagebush, prickly pear cactus, juniper, and cottonwoods. Although the camping spots accommodate every type of recreational vehicle, they are somewhat open. A special area has been designated just for tents, and some of the vehicle sites have the advantage of being close to the water. The campground is wheelchair accessible and has pit toilets, a sani-station, electrical hookups, and a shower. Located a fair distance from the road, the campsites are not affected by the noise of road traffic, but two railway lines are close by, and when I stayed here, there were quite a few trains to lull me to sleep.

Recreational activities

This provincial park provides one of the few access points to the Thompson River between Savona and Spences Bridge and is excellent for steelhead and rainbow trout fishing. A large natural pool separated from the river is perfect for swimming, and canoeing and kayaking are also possible.

Additional information

This campground is located in the desert area of the Thompson–Nicola region and so looks quite barren compared to B.C. parks in more fertile regions. Do not expect to find much shade here on a hot summer day! The easy access down to the Thompson River makes Juniper Beach a pleasant place to stay, and picnics on the shoreline are a delight. BC Parks says this is a good place to view sockeye salmon and to witness the summer migration of chinook and coho, although when I stayed here, there was no evidence of fish, either in the river or being caught by the patient anglers. I came here from the waterlogged Alice Lake campground and really appreciated the fantastic hot, dry climate. This is not the place to be if you hate trains, as there is considerable rail traffic.

KEKULI BAY

Location

This is one of BC Parks' newest additions, and unlike many other recent arrivals, it is not small in capacity. Although only 57 hectares in size, it has space for 69 camping parties, and all sites have fantastic views of the lake. It is located on a gorgeous bay on the west side of Kalamalka Lake, 11 kilometres south of Vernon, where services are available.

Facilities

Kekuli has flush and pit toilets, water, showers, and all other basic amenities. Reservations are accepted and advisable, especially on the weekends. The noise of traffic may be an issue for some, and a railway line, though not much used, is also close to the campground. The lack of shade in the campsites also makes for very hot camping from mid-June to September.

Recreational activities

The boat launch at this location is reported to be the best on Kalamalka Lake. Kayaking and canoeing are also pleasant here. With a sandy beach close by, those who don't want to ride on the waters can certainly have fun splashing in them. A small trail circles the campground, and there is a great kids' play area. If the weather isn't accommodating, a host of activities awaits in the town of Vernon. Kalamalka Lake Provincial Park, just north of Kekuli Provincial Park, provides a habitat for a variety of birds and wildlife (including rattlesnakes), while the high rodent population at Kekuli Bay ensures a healthy population of birds of prey, including ospreys and vultures. Yellow-bellied marmots run around the campground and are great fun for preschoolers to chase. The campground is the closest to Predator Ridge golf course, which reputably has some of the best greens in the Okanagan.

Additional information

Kekuli Bay Provincial Park takes its name from semi-subterranean homes built by the Interior Salish people. I visited for the first time in June 2002 and loved the views but hated the intense heat and lack of shade. It is also quite noisy. I cannot imagine staying here in the height of the summer without an air-conditioned RV. Trees have been planted, though, so in a few years' time there will be shade. Until then, my advice is to travel to Okanagan Lake instead.

The recreated Gitskan village near Seeley Lake in the Hazelton Mountains includes six longhouses with painted fronts, totem poles, and a carving school.

Two fishermen wait for a bite.

Strathcona is B.C.'s oldest provincial park.

Pumping water is a good workout.

A deer inspects a campsite at Buttle Lake.

Campers, hikers, and picnickers enjoy the ambience and great trails on Newcastle Island.

Newcastle Island is a little bit of paradise, and easy to reach by ferry from Nanaimo.

The view from the summit of Mount Norman on Pender Island is awesome.

Porteau Cove is an enchanting roadside campground with an amazing view of Howe Sound.

The amphitheatre at Porteau Cove is good place to meet other campers.

Nairn Falls tumble down 60 metres into a beautiful canyon.

Chilliwack Lake is great for fishing and swimming, but the water can be a little cold.

Saltery Bay Park is on the north shore of Jervis Inlet, just south of Powell River.

Campers take in the scenery at Saltery Bay.

If you enjoy fishing, you'll love Stamp River—it's an angler's delight.

Skihist Provincial Park includes part of the old Cariboo
Wagon Road.

Kokanee Creek's beautiful setting in the Slocan Range of the Selkirk
Mountains is just one of the features that make it one of the best
campgrounds in the province.

Windsurfing and sailing are popular activities on Okanagan Lake.

Campsites at Okanagan Lake Park fill up fast.

Okanagan Lake is great for water babies of all ages.

Kentucky-Alleyne

Location
Campers from the Lower Mainland looking for a weekend getaway cannot go wrong in choosing Kentucky–Alleyne, a real gem of a campground. Situated 38 kilometres south of Merritt, it is found by turning off Highway 5A (south of the Okanagan Connector) and taking a 6-kilometre paved road. Services are available in Merritt.

Facilities
The park has 63 camping spots. Although the units do not have the advantage of vegetation to afford privacy, they are well spaced and suitable for every type of recreational vehicle. Four camping spaces are set a kilometre away from the rest, at the other end of the lake, and some spots are on the lakeside. Facilities are basic (pit toilets, fire pit, picnic tables, water).

Recreational activities
This is a stunningly beautiful area consisting of glacial undulating hills and grasslands surrounded by forests of pine and fir in the heart of cattle country. The many lakes offer fishing potential for rainbow trout (I love the way that one of the smaller lakes is restricted for "children only" fishing) and are annually stocked. Swimming is a delight here, as is canoeing. A number of trails take visitors around the lakes to different areas of the park where it is possible to see beaver lodges. As the campground is spread out, cycling on the many gravel roads and trails is an enjoyable activity for all ages; however, there are a number of private roads displaying NO TRESPASSING signs.

Additional information
I love this park. Although the camping spots themselves are not stunning, the size of the camping area, the many dirt trails and roads around the park, and the glacial topography make Kentucky–Alleyne a pleasant place to explore. The sunsets are gorgeous—it is magical to cook dinner on an open fire while watching the beautiful red sunset over the water, as ospreys circle above. For those who want to avoid other people and do not mind a bumpy road, the four detached camping spots at the far end of the lake make a good retreat. We stayed here in 2003, when my husband and I escaped without our children for a few days. We camped with just our tent, alcohol, and a plastic bag of sandwiches. The BC Parks attendant, on collecting our fee and seeing our meagre provisions, asked if this was my first camping trip ever … In 2004 we camped with the children. Our four-year-old went running to the children's lake, straight through mud that resembled sand, and sank in it almost up to his waist. So, be warned of sand that is actually mud, especially if you have little ones.

KETTLE RIVER

Location

Between 1860 and 1864, this region was worked by more than 500 miners, who scoured the gravel for gold. Today, it provides a more tranquil setting for camping enthusiasts and is characterized by old-growth cottonwood and ponderosa pine trees. Named after the river that runs through it, Kettle River Provincial Park is located 5 kilometres north of Rock Creek on Highway 33. Some services (pub, gas, store, accommodation) are located at Rock Creek.

Facilities

At a bend on the west bank of the river are 87 well-spaced camping spots nestled in an area of ponderosa pine and birchgrass. The sites are suitable for every size of recreational vehicle. In addition to the basic facilities offered, there is a sani-station, flush toilets, and pit toilets. Reservations are accepted.

Recreational activities

The Kettle Valley Railway discontinued its service in the early 1970s, and in 1979–80 the track was removed between Midway and Penticton. The abandoned route runs through the park and is an excellent hiking and biking trail. There is fishing, swimming, and canoeing in the park; tubing is another river-based activity popular with locals and regular campers. On the eastern banks of the river, remains of gold and silver mines can be seen—evidence of the pioneers who travelled and worked in the area at the turn of the century. Excellent opportunities exist for the photographer and artist in this locale, and many people resurrect the past by panning for gold.

Additional information

For those who decide not to cook over an open fire, there is an interesting although limited collection of eateries at Rock Creek, including a pub and some good breakfast cafés. Rock Creek dates back to 1857, when a prospector called Charles Dietz started a gold rush here. There were never large quantities of gold found, only copper. During the winter the area is popular with cross-country skiers and snowshoers. This is a lovely place to stop and relax.

LAC LE JEUNE

Location
If you are looking for a base from which to explore the region, this relatively small (47 hectares) lakeside provincial park, easily accessible from Kamloops and Merritt, is an excellent bet. It is situated 37 kilometres south of Kamloops on Highway 5 and 53 kilometres north of Merritt, and a full range of services can be found at these locations, or at Logan Lake, 26 kilometres away.

Facilities
Set among a forest of pinegrass and lodgepole pines at a cooler elevation of 1,280 metres are 144 large, well-positioned campsites. A few of these spots have the added advantage of being close to the lake. A sani-station and flush toilets are in the day-use area. The park is wheelchair accessible and accepts reservations for 70 percent of the spaces.

Recreational activities
Lac Le Jeune is equipped with a boat launch (powerboats are limited to a speed of 20 kilometres per hour), and swimming is possible in a protected swimming area. All the literature on the park states that the lake is famous for "fighting rainbow trout," so go win a battle! A trail leads from the day-use area to the Stake/McConnell trail systems in the adjacent Stake/McConnell Lakes Park. This area has 160 kilometres of trails for hiking, mountain biking during the summer, and cross-country skiing in the winter. The Gus Johnson Trail rings the lake and is an easy 8-kilometre hike. There is an adventure playground and a horseshoe pit. Walloper Lake Provincial Park, a short drive from here off Highway 5, has only wilderness camping, but it does offer canoe and boat rentals and therefore access to the beautiful waters of the area.

Additional information
During the hot, dry days of summer, this campground offers a welcome respite from the heat, as it is at a higher elevation than Thompson Valley to the north and Nicola Valley in the south. Lac Le Jeune is an excellent base from which to explore the towns of Merritt, Kamloops, and Logan Lake. When I visited, we took a short 20-minute trail to a trout-spawning stream that the camp host had told us about. My only criticism of this park is the lack of information boards or maps detailing the trails in the area. Hopefully, this will have been addressed by the time you visit.

Mabel Lake

Location

Mabel Lake is perfect for those who want to appreciate the Okanagan from a cooler vantage point. Somewhat off the beaten track, it is a lovely 182-hectare provincial park between the Thompson Plateau to the west and the Monashee Mountains to the east. Temperatures here tend to be cooler than in many other areas of the Okanagan, providing a pleasant respite from the summer heat. The campground is 76 kilometres northeast of Vernon. Travel on Highway 6 to Lumby, then take a mostly paved road for 36 kilometres (only 3 kilometres is unpaved). Services are available at Lumby; there is also a small marine store by the campground, which sells candy, milk, propane, and other supplies.

Facilities

You can camp here in one of two campgrounds: the Monashee or the Trinity. Together, they provide a total of 81 well-situated spaces in a wooded setting, some with great views of the lake. There is a sani-station, but no flush toilets or showers. The park is wheelchair accessible.

Recreational activities

A 2,100-metre shoreline that includes two lovely beaches (and a pet beach) with safe swimming areas provides access to the waters of 35-kilometre-long Mabel Lake. Fishing is good both from the shore and in the deeper waters where anglers hope to catch rainbow trout, Dolly Varden, lake trout, kokanee, and chinook salmon. Water-skiing and boating are popular, and the nearby marina offers boat rentals. The area is attractive to canoeists, who paddle down the Shuswap River just south of the park. For those who like to see more unusual wildlife, painted turtles can be observed in Taylor Creek. The park also has a one-hour interpretive trail, tons of grassy areas, and a kids' playground.

Additional information

The adjacent area offers interesting alternatives to the recreational activities found in the park. The road between Lumby and Mabel Lake takes travellers through the distinctive landscape of ranches and farmland—quite beautiful and somewhat "un-Okanaganish." Wilsey Dam has a picnic spot with trails leading to the awe-inspiring Shuswap Falls. I adore this park and highly recommend it. The 36-kilometre approach road is a lovely drive, and the reward at the end is well worth the effort. Bears and deer are often seen in the vicinity. The only note of caution—there can be mosquitoes.

MARBLE CANYON

Location

Marble Canyon Provincial Park is popular with rock climbers, who are attracted to the area for its rugged terrain. It is not difficult to see why mountaineers and others choose to visit this park nestled on a lakeside below towering limestone cliffs and amid the beautiful scenery of Marble Canyon. The campground is found by travelling 40 kilometres northwest of Cache Creek on Highway 99. It is about 35 kilometres northeast of Lillooet. Services are available at Cache Creek or Lillooet or at the Butterfly Creek Store, 2 kilometres from the campground. The park was established in 1956, but in April 2001 Pavilion Lake was added to preserve unique, freshwater stromatolite features (fossilized remains of micro-organisms considered by some to be some of the oldest life forms on Earth).

Facilities

There are 26 relatively small gravel campsites with little privacy, some directly overlooking the lake, and some with tent pads. The services provided are limited to the basics (pit toilets, picnic tables, water, fire pit).

Recreational activities

Leisure activities include fishing, swimming, kayaking, and canoeing. Only electric motors are permitted on the lake. A trail along the side of the lake leads to a waterfall and is an easy 30-minute trek. There are two archaeological sites where Native pictographs have been found. People interested in fauna and flora will find the vegetation and the bird and animal life here fascinating.

Additional information

Reaching this campground is a beautiful and scenic drive. Close to Lillooet, travellers see some of the ginseng farms for which B.C. is now known, easily spotted by looking for vast expanses of black plastic. At the junction of Highway 97 and Highway 99, the historical 1861 Hat Creek Ranch, an original stopping place on the Cariboo Wagon Road, offers guided tours. The area is noted for its rock formations, scenery, and the beautiful lake. The disadvantage in camping here is the campsite's proximity to the road; although the route is not tremendously busy, campers may be kept awake by the sound of traffic. When I stayed here in 1995, noise was not a problem, and we enjoyed an evening meal cooked at the lakeside, as our campsite was on the water's edge. I found a marked difference in 2004—there seemed to be a lot more traffic from around 6:00 a.m. onward. Wasps can also be a problem here, although these annoying insects never seem to dampen visitors' enthusiasm for the location. I have not been bothered by them on the four separate occasions I have camped there. As always, black bears inhabit the vicinity.

Monck

Location

With fantastic views of the Nicola Valley south of Kamloops and within easy reach of Merritt, the nearest large settlement, this campground has a great deal to offer. Monck Provincial Park is found by taking Highway 5A to Nicola, then a paved road to the campground, situated 22 kilometres north of Merritt. All services are available in Merritt.

Facilities

With the exception of showers, this 71-space campground has all the necessary requirements for camping (including a sani-station, flush toilets, and access for the disabled). The cheery camping spots, set among a lightly forested area of ponderosa pine and fir on the north side of Nicola Lake, are suitable for every type of recreational vehicle. Most have views of the water. Reservations are accepted.

Recreational activities

Monck Provincial Park is an ideal family vacation spot. There is a safe sandy beach leading to the beautiful waters of Nicola Lake, where a cordoned-off swimming area is provided. The beach shelves quickly, so you do need to use caution. A change house is provided. Fishing for kokanee is reputed to be excellent, and a further 25 species of fish, including rainbow trout, can be caught in the waters. There is a concrete boat launch to facilitate boating and sailing pursuits. A number of trails lead from the campground through a forest to various vantage points. First Nations pit house depressions can also be found here, and a walk along an old road to Second Beach leads to a fine example of Native rock paintings (pictographs).

Additional information

The Nicola Valley is surrounded by green fields and rich marshland. Originally settled by ranchers, the area is now home to Canada's largest working cattle ranch, the Douglas Lake Ranch, which offers horseback riding and ranch tours. The land that now includes Monck was donated by Major Charles Sidney Goldman in honour of his son, Lieutenant-Commander "Pen" Monck, a British Second World War soldier who changed his name to Monck to improve his chances of survival should he be captured by the Germans. Goldman moved to the Nicola Valley in 1919, purchased 6,550 acres of land, and built up a cattle ranch with over 5,000 head.

Mount Robson

Location

Mount Robson Provincial Park provides a camping experience that should not be missed. Mount Robson, "the monarch of the Canadian Rockies," is the highest peak in the Rockies at almost 4,000 metres. In 1913 a special act was passed by the B.C. legislature to ensure that this area of exceptional beauty is preserved for all to encounter and enjoy. The park is easily accessed from the Yellowhead Highway (Highway 5). Services such as gas, food, and a store are located in the park itself at Mount Robson Motor Village.

Facilities

There are three campgrounds in the park, and two of them are located at the western end: Robson Meadow has 125 spots; Robson River has 19 spots. Both have flush toilets, showers, and are wheelchair accessible. The third campground is Lucerne, 10 kilometres west of the Alberta border, with 36 spots on Yellowhead Lake. The sani-station is located at Robson Meadow. Most sites are large, private, and situated well in the evergreen forest. (Robson River is my favourite; it's smaller than Robson Meadow, but has all amenities and is adjacent to services). Reservations are accepted at Robson Meadow.

Recreational activities

The spectacular scenery, which consists of lakes, waterfalls, rivers, glaciers, and mountains, makes this a paradise for hikers, climbers, canoeists, and anyone who loves the outdoors. There are over 200 kilometres of hiking trails within the park, one of the most popular being the Valley of the Thousand Waterfalls, which takes explorers past the fantastic azure brightness of Berg Lake and on to views of Tumbling Glacier's spectacular waterfalls. I believe this to be one of the best hikes in B.C. Boat launches are available at Moose Lake and Yellowhead Lake, but fishing tends to be poor, as the glacial waters yield low fish populations. The Mount Robson Visitor Centre at the Mount Robson Viewpoint has details of all the park's activities and staff to advise on climate and camping conditions.

Additional information

The First Nations called Mount Robson *Yuh-hai-has-hun*, meaning "Mountain of the Spiral Road." It is unclear whether the park is named after Colin Robertson, a Hudson's Bay Company factor and later member of Parliament, who sent Iroquois fur hunters to the area in 1820, or John Robson, premier of B.C. from 1889-1892. This is one of my favourite B.C. parks, as there is so much to do and the scenery is so breathtaking. When you're arranging a holiday tour of British Columbia, Mount Robson is a lovely destination to include on your itinerary, but plan to spend at least three nights in order to even begin to appreciate its true beauty.

North Thompson River

Location

The most amazing feature of this park is the meeting of two distinctly individual water systems. The 126-hectare provincial park is located where the Thompson and Clearwater rivers meet, 5 kilometres south of the town of Clearwater, just off Highway 5. Clearwater has services such as gas, propane, food, and accommodation, as well as a number of commercial tour operations.

Facilities

The campground itself is on the banks of the Thompson River in a mixed forest of Douglas fir, pine, cedar, and spruce. There are 61 camping spots, the more desirable ones being closer to the river. A word of caution: These sites are not suitable if you have young children, as the riverbank is steep. The park is wheelchair accessible, and there is a sani-station. A railway line runs close by, so expect the noise of trains.

Recreational activities

A number of short trails lead through the campground. All take less than 30 minutes to complete. A small wading and swimming area is located on a back eddy where the Clearwater River flows into the North Thompson. BC Parks cautions that during the flood season of June and July, currents can be powerful. Canoeing, kayaking, and fishing for rainbow trout and chinook salmon are also possible here. In addition to the recreational activities available in the park itself, there is the fantastic "poggy playground" for kids—one of the best playgrounds I've seen anywhere, and in the last four years I've seen more than my fair share of these. The nearby community of Clearwater offers bikes and canoes to rent, horseback trail rides, and rafting trips. Nearby Dutch Lake has swimming.

Additional information

From a viewpoint in the park you can take in the vista of the distinctive green waters of the Clearwater River meeting those of the muddy brown Thompson. This was once the site of a Shuswap Nation encampment, and there are two archaeological sites in the park. This campground is very sedate and peaceful, ideal for the older RV crowd and for family camping. This is a lovely campground from which to explore Wells Gray. The visitor centre in Clearwater is worth a visit—there is a life-sized moose outside that my kids liked, and excellent tourist information.

OKANAGAN FALLS

Location

Native legend recalls how the waters here
once fell with "a voice like thunder" and a
spray as white as cherry blossom. Today,
development has ensured that visitors
cannot experience the original natural
beauty of the falls, but instead there is a
lovely provincial park. Okanagan Falls,
known as "OK Falls" to the locals, is
found at the community that bears its
name, on Highway 97 south of Skaha
Lake. All services can be found here.

Facilities

The picturesque campground with 25 camping spots is set amongst a forest
of deciduous trees just above the Okanagan River. It has an extremely neat
and tidy feel about it, and when I last visited all the spots were taken by large
RVs whose owners seemed as if they'd been there for years. It is wheelchair
accessible and provides flush and pit toilets, but no sani-station or showers.

Recreational activities

Like the two other provincial parks in the immediate vicinity (Vaseux Lake
and Inkaneep), the area is rich in bird and animal life and therefore a good
location for nature study and photography. A species of small sonar-equipped
bats is found here, in addition to a wealth of other birds and animals.
Fishing is possible in the Okanagan River, and the park has horseshoe pits.
Christie Memorial Provincial Park, which has 200 metres of beach and
good swimming, is located just north of Okanagan Falls. The area is rich
in grapevines, and visitors can tour the local wineries. The community of
Okanagan Falls has an excellent ice cream store and chocolate shop, which
campground research has required me to evaluate in depth in 1998, 2000,
and 2002. I suggest you do the same.

Additional information

Anyone looking for spectacular waterfalls will be disappointed, as the falls
here have been reduced to rapids due to rock blasting for water control
in the area. The museum at Okanagan Falls is housed in a restored 1909
prefabricated building that was ordered from a catalogue, shipped in pieces
and assembled here. It contains artifacts and memorabilia of the pioneer
Bassett family. I really have the impression that this is a campground for the
retired RV owner who wants to put down roots for weeks and do little other
than sit in the shade, listen to the river, and pass the time of day with fellow
campers. It's a campground geared more to adults than to children.

Okanagan Lake

Location

Okanagan Lake is the most popular camping location in the Okanagan. Like other provincial parks such as Haynes Point and Bear Creek, Okanagan Lake is very busy in the peak summer months of July and August. Located 24 kilometres north of Penticton between Peachland and Summerland, where services can be found, this park has fantastic panoramic views of the Okanagan Mountains and Lake.

Facilities

The park has 168 vehicle/tent campsites, 80 in the north campground and 88 in the south, some with views of the lake. I prefer the camping spots in the north campground, which are better spaced and less confined than those in the south. Both are set in an unusual forest area. Each campground has showers and flush and pit toilets. The south campground has a sani-station and boat launch. The park is wheelchair accessible and reservations are accepted.

Recreational activities

With more than 1 kilometre of beach (some of it pebbly), Okanagan Lake Provincial Park is a paradise for swimmers, sunbathers, anglers, and water-sports enthusiasts. The lake is popular for windsurfing and sailing, and for those who prefer other activities a number of small hiking trails exist in the 98-hectare park. One of the unique features of the park is an arboretum of more than 10,000 exotic trees, including Russian olive, Chinese elm, Norway, Manitoba and silver maples, and red, blue and mountain ash. This woodland enhances the birdlife, so keep your eyes peeled for hummingbirds, larks, and woodpeckers, which can be easily seen. Fantastic photographic opportunities abound.

Additional information

Due to its popularity, you may well be disappointed if you arrive at this campground without a reservation in the peak summer months. The Kettle Valley Railway operates a quaint steam train during the summer months. Each year this attraction employs wonderful volunteers and enthusiastic employees, dressed in period costume, who provide tons of information for the tourist (train rides cost $15.00 per adult in 2003). The fires of summer 2003 did not affect this segment of the railway.

OTTER LAKE

Location

Literature from BC Parks states that Otter Lake is ideal for "old-fashioned camping," where campers can find privacy in a natural setting. This provincial park is found 47 kilometres northwest of Princeton off Highway 5A. From Princeton, drive to Coalmont and Tulameen on Coalmont Road, then to Otter Lake, which is well marked with signs. The park can also be accessed from Highway 97C. Turn at Aspen Grove (which is Highway 5A) and follow the signs. Services are available in the small towns of Coalmont and Tulameen.

Facilities

Otter Lake boasts 45 beautifully spaced, large camping spots on the northwest shore of the lake, some with views of the water. Large trees provide much-needed shade—be warned: This area of the province can become very hot. There are flush and pit toilets but no sani-station or showers. The park is wheelchair accessible and accepts reservations.

Recreational activities

The 5-kilometre Otter Lake provides the main recreational activity in the form of fishing for lake trout, swimming from a warm beach in the day-use area (5 kilometres from the campground), and boating (a boat launch is provided). There is also a horseshoe pit. The surrounding area is home to a variety of animals, including otter, beaver, red squirrel, mountain goat, cougar, and grizzly bear—but don't expect to see them all on your first visit! A few kilometres away, the now disused Kettle Valley Railway offers a fantastic mountain bike or hiking route amid some spectacular scenery. Bikes can be rented in Tulameen. Recently, this section of track became part of the Trans-Canada Trail—a trail winding across the country and covering 17,898 kilometres. This section is the link between Princeton and Merritt.

Additional information

Otter Lake is an ideal base from which to explore the mining history of the Tulameen region. The town of Tulameen (the name is a Native word that means "red earth") is located 5 kilometres south of the campground. Tulameen was first used by First Nations for hunting and fishing, and then explored by gold miners in the last century. The Hudson's Bay Company used a road that passed through Tulameen and called the settlement *encampment des femmes*, as it was populated primarily by women waiting for their men to return from trapping and hunting. The town of Coalmont, also south of the park, sprang to life during the gold rush; in 1925 it produced 100,000 tons of coal, making it the region's largest producer. By 1940 the mine was exhausted, and most residents moved away. Today, Coalmont contains a café, a general store, and a hotel dating back to 1912 that you won't be able to miss—it's painted bright pink.

Paul Lake

Location

Provincial parks near populated areas often offer the best amenities for family camping, whether it be in a tent or RV. Paul Lake is one such park. Residents of Kamloops and visitors regularly patronize this popular provincial park, conveniently located 24 kilometres northeast of Kamloops. It is found by turning off Highway 5 and following a well-maintained twisting road across a meadow landscape for 17 kilometres. Gas and food are available at the turnoff from Highway 5; all other needs can be accommodated in Kamloops.

Facilities

The campground has 90 large, well-maintained, private camping spots. They are set in a lightly forested area of Douglas fir and aspen and are suitable for every type of recreational vehicle, making the park popular with RVers. There is a sani-station, flush and pit toilets, and access for the disabled.

Recreational activities

The lake provides a host of activities, including swimming in a protected area from a 400-metre sandy beach, boating with canoes and paddleboats available for rent, and fishing. Paul Lake is stocked with rainbow trout. Over 7 kilometres of trails lead from the campground. A pleasant hike, with over 900 metres in elevation gain, leads up Gibraltar Rock—the last section is the steepest. The park is particularly appealing to people with young children; it has a playground, horseshoes, and wide grassy areas, and a maze of paved roads connecting the camping facilities ensures fun for young cyclists and rollerbladers. In 1996, 268 hectares were added to the park to protect the habitat of ospreys, falcons, bald eagles, coyote, and mule deer. The area is popular with the birdwatching community.

Additional information

At certain times of the year the park is blessed with an array of beautiful wildflowers. (Remember, visitors are forbidden to pick vegetation in the provincial parks.) For good views of the vicinity, campers with stamina are advised to climb Gibraltar Rock. The park's proximity to Kamloops means it is often filled to capacity, and reservations are not accepted. For some reason, I find this park to have little atmosphere and not as much character as most others. In some respects, it appears too ordered and regimented, almost clinical. This is purely a personal observation and clearly not one shared by everyone, for when I visited, a number of campers, especially family groups, seemed to be well established. I just find it to be one of B.C.'s more formal parks.

SHUSWAP LAKE

Location

For people who love water-based activities, Shuswap Lake, with over 1,000 kilometres of waterways, is a real magnet. The provincial park of the same name is one of the larger B.C. parks and accommodates 272 vehicles. It is conveniently located 90 kilometres east of Kamloops on Highway 1 at Squilax. A 20-kilometre paved road leads to the campground. Some supplies can be found at a store adjacent to the entrance of the park, while more comprehensive supplies are found in Sorrento, 35 kilometres away.

Facilities

Because Shuswap Lake is one of B.C.'s largest provincial parks, the facilities offered here are comprehensive and include 271 camping spots suitable for every type of recreational vehicle, flush and pit toilets, sani-station, showers, and full access for the disabled. Reservations are accepted, and BC Parks describes Shuswap Lake as operating at capacity from mid-July to Labour Day. Those who arrive without a reservation are assigned a camping spot at the entrance of the park, so there is no opportunity to "cruise" the campground to find the most desirable spot.

Recreational activities

One of the most popular recreational pursuits here is cycling, as there are over 11 kilometres of paved road in the park itself. Water sports are also actively undertaken on the 1-kilometre-long beach and in the designated swimming area. There is a boat launch, and 2 kilometres offshore is Copper Island, which has a hiking trail and lookout. Anglers can fish in the lake and share it with windsurfers and paddlers. To entertain the entire family there is an adventure play area and visitor centre. Commercial recreational activities (kayak rentals and go-carts, for example) are also easily accessible in the North Shuswap and surrounding area.

Additional information

The park was established in 1956 and named after the Native people of Shuswap, whose artifacts were found here. Although there is no overnight boat mooring at Shuswap Lake, the nearby Shuswap Lake Provincial Marine Park offers this facility, as well as six developed and eight undeveloped camping locations along all four arms of the lake. As already noted, this area is extremely popular during the summer months and may not be to everyone's taste at that time, as it presents the more commercial side of camping in B.C. parks. For those who want to experience the delights of the lake from a quieter vantage point, Herald and Silver Beach provincial parks are tranquil alternatives.

SILVER BEACH

Location
Campers who wish to enjoy the waters but not the crowds of Shuswap Lake should head for Silver Beach. This somewhat remote provincial park is located 65 kilometres from Scotch Creek. Turn off Highway 1 just east of Squilax and take the paved road to Scotch Creek. The road to the park from Scotch Creek is only partially paved. Gas and limited provisions are available near the campground.

Facilities
There are 30 vehicle/tent campsites and five walk-in campsites located in a forest of Douglas fir and aspen at the head of the Seymour Arm of the Shuswap Lake. Silver Beach contains the basic amenities (pit toilets, picnic tables, water, fire pit).

Recreational activities
As this quiet campground is at the northern end of Shuswap Lake, all activities related to the lake can be enjoyed here: swimming at a delightful sandy beach, fishing (for trout, among others), boating, canoeing, windsurfing, water-skiing, etc. In August and September it is possible to view sockeye salmon spawning in the Seymour River, which runs into the lake near the campground. Wildfowl observation is good and there is also a small trail along the top of the beach.

Additional information
The remains of Ogden, an old gold-rush town of the late 19th century, can be seen here if you are prepared to navigate a somewhat overgrown trail. An old graveyard and archaeological sites are also in the park. With its beautiful sandy beaches, this area is popular with sailors and houseboaters exploring the lake, so expect to share your tranquility with more than just your fellow dry-land campers. Houseboating is a very popular activity on the four arms of the Shuswap. At the height of the season, as many as 350 houseboats are navigating the waters of the lake. Silver Beach provides a quieter and less commercialized view of Shuswap Lake than Shuswap Lake Provincial Park, but does not have all the facilities that the larger park offers.

SKIHIST

Location

Anyone stopping here will be rewarded with brilliant views of the Thompson Canyon, but be sure to remember the sunscreen, as Skihist is situated in an area prone to very high summer temperatures. This quaint 33-hectare provincial park is found 8 kilometres east of Lytton on Highway 1. Services are available in Lytton.

Facilities

Fifty-eight well-positioned camping spots set in a lightly forested area high above the Thompson and Fraser rivers are available. The park has both pit and flush toilets; it has a sani-station and is wheelchair accessible. It is one of the few B.C. provincial parks with hook-ups. There is a large day-use area, which is a popular resting place in the summer.

Recreational activities

Recreational activities in the park including picking saskatoon berries, which are plentiful at a certain time of year, taking photographs, admiring the fantastic views, and looking for the elk that have been introduced to the area. The campground is a good base for those who wish to try whitewater rafting; trips are easily arranged through commercial businesses in Lytton and Spences Bridge. Hiking is possible from the trailhead in the campground. The trail leads to Gladwin Lookout; this one-and-a-half-hour trip rewards hikers with excellent views of the mountains. Remember to take lots of water, as this area can be very hot.

Additional information

Skihist Provincial Park includes part of the old Cariboo Wagon Road used by the early pioneers of the province. Its main attraction must be the fantastic views of the Thompson Canyon, where water gushing over thousands of years has cut into the pre-glacial valley floor. (The fact the park has flush toilets is another attraction!) Lytton, at the junction of the Fraser and Thompson rivers, claims to be the official hot spot in Canada, although this claim is disputed by Lillooet to the north. As neither community has a weather station, the debate continues. Be prepared for some hot days if visiting Skihist in the peak summer months.

Steelhead

Location

Set in an almost desert environment, Steelhead, which began operating in 1997, really is the baby of provincial parks. It is located on the site of one of the oldest homesteads in the Interior, which was also a ferry stop and a stagecoach depot. Steelhead is an excellent base for exploring the town of Kamloops, Kamloops Lake, the mighty Thompson River, and the surrounding plateau scenery. The campground itself is rather spartan and is found 45 kilometres west of Kamloops on Highway 1 just west of Savona, which has food, gas, and supplies.

Facilities

The campground is situated at the outflow of Kamloops Lake. Forty-two camping spots are available, all quite open, and there are flush toilets and showers. Twenty-two sites overlook the lake. This is one of the very few B.C. parks with hookups (10 sites). The park is wheelchair accessible. Reservations are not accepted.

Recreational activities

Campers can enjoy swimming and canoeing in Kamloops Lake. There is also fishing here and in the many plateau lakes in the region. There is no boat launch. Naturalists appreciate the wildlife in the area, which includes deer, elk, and mountain sheep in addition to migratory waterfowl, shorebirds, and songbirds. The town of Kamloops is only a short drive away and is the major centre of the region. Just south of the campground is the community of Logan Lake, where fascinating tours of the Highland Valley Copper Mine can be taken.

Additional information

BC Parks should be sincerely thanked for establishing a number of additional campgrounds in the High Country Region in 1997. Steelhead is the most developed; other recent additions are Momich, Tunkwa, and Roche Lake. All were previously forestry campsites, but in 1997 BC Parks became responsible for their administration. These other locations have only primitive camping facilities. If staying in this region, be prepared for some very high temperatures, and remember to put on the sunscreen. On a personal note, I do not find this campground very appealing, probably due to the lack of vegetation and the near-desert surroundings. I prefer Juniper Beach, just down the road, which is more spacious and offers better views.

STEMWINDER

Location

Between 1904 and 1955, $47 million in gold was taken from the mountains adjacent to Stemwinder Provincial Park, and rumour has it that there is still some left—so what are you waiting for? "There's gold in them thar hills!" This small (4-hectare) roadside campground is very much geared toward overnight stops. It is found 35 kilometres east of Princeton on Highway 3, next to Hedley. Services are available in Hedley and at a store adjacent to the campground.

Facilities

The campground provides 27 spots on the banks of the Similkameen River. Only the basic amenities are available (water, pit toilets, picnic tables, fire pit), and the camping spots are quite close to the road, so expect the noise of traffic. The park does have access for the disabled.

Recreational activities

Because this campground is geared toward overnight camping as opposed to long-term recreational camping, it provides limited recreational activities. The waters of the Similkameen River can be fished, but are fast-flowing. Caution must be taken by those who wish to swim; only strong swimmers should consider it. Alternatively, you could try your luck at panning for gold, an activity that started here at the turn of the century. Be careful to avoid the poison ivy found along the riverbank. If you are prepared to travel a little farther, the Grist Mill and Gardens at Keremeos cannot be too highly recommended. When I visited, a man on a penny farthing cycled around the wonderful gardens. My children delighted in feeding chickens and collecting eggs, and the tea room served delicious pastries and desserts. Grist Mill is a BC Heritage site illustrating the last remaining pioneer flour mill dating back to 1881. Well worth a visit.

Additional information

When visiting this area, it is worth turning off Highway 3 to explore the museum, the back roads, and the older architecture in the quaint Similkameen community of Hedley. Hedley dates to the early 1900s, when the Nickel Plate Mine, one of B.C.'s first hardrock mining operations, was established 1,200 metres above the town. The mine operated from 1904 to 1956, producing gold, silver, and copper. The remnants of the Mascot Mine's buildings can be seen perched on a cliff high above the town.

TUNKWA LAKE

Location

Tunkwa Lake Provincial Park covers a massive 5,091 hectares of land not far from Logan Lake, a town established in 1970 for the 1,000 employees of the Highland Valley Copper Mining Corporation. The park is situated 14 kilometres north of the town, off Highway 5, but can also be accessed off Highway 1 at Savona and also from the Coquihalla Highway. All access roads are good gravel routes. The nearest services are at Logan Lake. Kamloops is 40 kilometres away.

Facilities

There are three campgrounds here with a total of 265 spaces, some with excellent views of the lake. Only the basic amenities are available (pit toilets, picnic tables, fire pits, and water). Reservations are not accepted.

Recreational activities

There are two boat launches here, at Tunkwa and Leighton lakes, and fishing is popular not only at this location, but also in the multitude of lakes in the vicinity. Tunkwa and Leighton lakes are known for their excellent trout fishing. Tunkwa was voted one of the top 10 provincial rainbow-trout locations. (I have a firm mental image of the individuals involved in this research.) It is also possible to swim and kayak here. Logan Lake has a nine-hole golf course, and tours of the copper mine can be arranged. Horseback riding is available at a few of the corrals in the area and is an excellent way to experience the rugged landscape. Be advised that ATV use is also popular here, so noise can be a problem.

Additional information

Formerly the site of a forestry campground, the park was initially established to protect an area of fragile grassland and wetland. It is popular in winter for ice fishing, snowmobiling, and cross-country skiing, but in the summer it is really a venue for the fishing community. Be warned: This area of the province can become extremely hot during the peak summer months, so come prepared.

Vaseux Lake

Location

Vaseux is French for "silty." This shallow, weedy lake, 4 kilometres long and 1 kilometre wide, is one of Canada's foremost birding areas and a real magnet for ornithologists. Between the highway and the lake sits Vaseux Lake Provincial Park, a 12-hectare roadside campground. It is located 4 kilometres south of Okanagan Falls, 25 kilometres south of Penticton.

Facilities

This 12-spot campground, surrounded by cliffs, contains all the basic amenities found in BC Parks (pit toilets, picnic tables, water, fire pit) and is wheelchair accessible. There is no sani-station. As the highway is close to the campground, noise from traffic is audible and constant, but the advantage is that camping spots are right on the lake. Visitors should be aware that the regional health department has issued a year-round boil-water advisory for this park.

Recreational activities

This area attracts ornithologists and wildlife enthusiasts. A variety of grasses, weeds, and willow vegetation provides a home for birds and animals. Waterfowl and birds of the area include trumpeter swans, widgeons, Canada geese, wood ducks, blue-winged teal, chuckar partridge, wrens, swifts, woodpeckers, and dippers. California bighorn sheep inhabit the cliffs near the park, and smaller mammals in the area include beavers, muskrats, deer, mice, rattlesnakes, and turtles. The lake is excellent for fishing in both winter and summer and yields largemouth bass, rainbow trout, and carp. The park has a beach for sunbathing and swimming. There is no boat launch and powerboats are prohibited, but canoeing and kayaking are permitted on the lake.

Additional information

Near the park is the Canadian Wildlife Service wildlife sanctuary, in addition to two wildlife management units operated by the federal and provincial governments. Vaseux Lake really is the place to be if you are an ornithologist. The park is also a popular location for winter sports such as ice fishing and skating.

WELLS GRAY/CLEARWATER/MAHOOD LAKE

Location

How do I even begin to describe one of the best provincial parks in B.C.? There are hundreds of things to see and do at Wells Gray. BC Parks calls it a "vast, untamed and primitive wilderness exceeding 520,000 hectares in area and encompassing the greater part of the Clearwater River Watershed." The park contains two large river systems, five huge lakes, numerous small lakes, streams, waterways, rapids, and waterfalls. The main entrance to Wells Gray is 40 kilometres from the community of Clearwater on a paved access road. The road from Helmcken Falls to Clearwater Lake is gravel. The park can also be reached by travelling 88 kilometres on a secondary road from 100 Mile House. There is also access from Blue River. Services are located at Clearwater and 100 Mile House.

Facilities

In addition to numerous wilderness camping spots, there are five campgrounds in the park. Three of the other four campgrounds are accessed from the Clearwater approach road and include Pyramid, opened in 1998, which has 50 units; Clearwater Lake, with 32 sites; and Falls Creek, which has 41 units. A sani-station is available at Clearwater Lake. The fourth campground, on Mahood Lake, is reached from the 100 Mile House entrance off Highway 97 and has 34 splendid, huge sites. Facilities are basic (pit toilets, water, picnic tables, fire pit). Reservations are accepted at Clearwater Lake and Falls Creek campgrounds.

Recreational activities

Wells Gray is B.C.'s fourth-largest provincial park and offers a wealth of things to see and do. Numerous trails run through the park and lead to waterfalls and creeks; some of the trails are open to mountain bikes. Boat launches are provided at Mahood and Clearwater lakes, and canoeing and kayaking are very popular in the park (powerboats are prohibited on Murtle Lake). Fishing is reputed to be good in Canim River, Mahood Lake, Murtle Lake, and the Murtle River. Swimming is possible at Mahood Lake.

Additional information

The park, named after the Honourable Arthur Wellesley Gray, minister of lands for B.C. from 1933 to 1941, displays a landscape formed by volcanoes and water. It is impossible to count the number of waterfalls in the park, but two of the best known are Helmcken Falls and Dawson Falls, which are spectacular in both winter and summer. BC Parks publishes informative leaflets on the recreational activities available here, and this information is a must for anyone wanting to gain maximum benefit from a holiday. A travel information centre at the junction of Highway 5 and Clearwater Valley Road supplies these details and has a wonderful huge moose outside that makes for a good photograph.

Wells Gray/Spahats Creek

Location

Until 2000, Spahats existed as a separate campground, but in 2001 this campground was included in Wells Gray Provincial Park. I included it here as a separate campground. I have found it to be quieter yet just as accommodating as those in Wells Gray. *Spahats* is the Native name for "bear," so watch out for these beasts at this 306-hectare provincial park. Spahats is located approximately 11 kilometres north of Clearwater, off Highway 5 on a paved access road (en route to Wells Gray Provincial Park). Services can be found in Clearwater.

Facilities

The facilities provided here are the basic ones (pit toilets, water, picnic tables, fire pit). Twenty well-spaced, private camping spots are available within a forested area.

Recreational activities

Spahats Creek's main attraction is the magnificent Spahats Creek Falls. From a lookout, visitors can view the 122-metre-deep canyon carved by Spahats Creek to the 61-metre falls that cascade down the volcanic precipice to the Clearwater River below. Be sure to bring a camera to record this spectacle. I think these falls are more spectacular than the famous Dawson and Helmcken Falls, and because they're less popular, they offer great photographic opportunities. An interpretive display describes the geology of the area. The day-use area is a short walk away and has excellent views of the Clearwater Valley. A number of hiking trails lead from the campground. Fishing in the creek is also possible.

Additional information

This area of the North Thompson is becoming increasingly popular for outdoors people who come to explore the hectares upon hectares of undisturbed forest, abundance of lakes, rivers, and streams, fantastic mountain scenery, kilometres of trails, and moderate summertime temperatures.

Premier Lake.

Jimsmith Lake.

B.C. ROCKIES

Just mentioning the famous Canadian Rockies conjures images of high snow-capped mountains, icefields, glaciers, huge lakes, fertile valleys, rushing rivers, and dramatic waterfalls. When you travel in this region, you will not be disappointed—you will see all these splendid features and more. Despite its great beauty, the area is not densely populated. This chapter provides details of the national and provincial parks situated in the Rockies/Kootenay area of the province accessible from Highways 1, 93/95, 95, 3, 3A, 31, and 6. There are few large camping spots here; instead, the accommodation tends to consist of campgrounds with fewer than 100 camping spots, nestled in some of the most breathtaking scenery you'll ever see.

Spectacular alpine meadows, glaciers, and waterfalls await visitors to Yoho National Park.

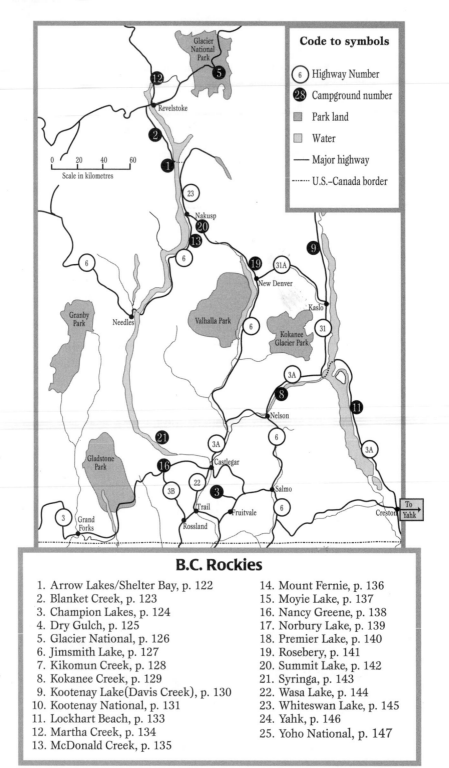

Code to symbols

- (6) Highway Number
- (28) Campground number
- ▢ Park land
- ▢ Water
- — Major highway
- ······ U.S.–Canada border

Scale in kilometres
0 20 40 60

B.C. Rockies

1. Arrow Lakes/Shelter Bay, p. 122
2. Blanket Creek, p. 123
3. Champion Lakes, p. 124
4. Dry Gulch, p. 125
5. Glacier National, p. 126
6. Jimsmith Lake, p. 127
7. Kikomun Creek, p. 128
8. Kokanee Creek, p. 129
9. Kootenay Lake(Davis Creek), p. 130
10. Kootenay National, p. 131
11. Lockhart Beach, p. 133
12. Martha Creek, p. 134
13. McDonald Creek, p. 135
14. Mount Fernie, p. 136
15. Moyie Lake, p. 137
16. Nancy Greene, p. 138
17. Norbury Lake, p. 139
18. Premier Lake, p. 140
19. Rosebery, p. 141
20. Summit Lake, p. 142
21. Syringa, p. 143
22. Wasa Lake, p. 144
23. Whiteswan Lake, p. 145
24. Yahk, p. 146
25. Yoho National, p. 147

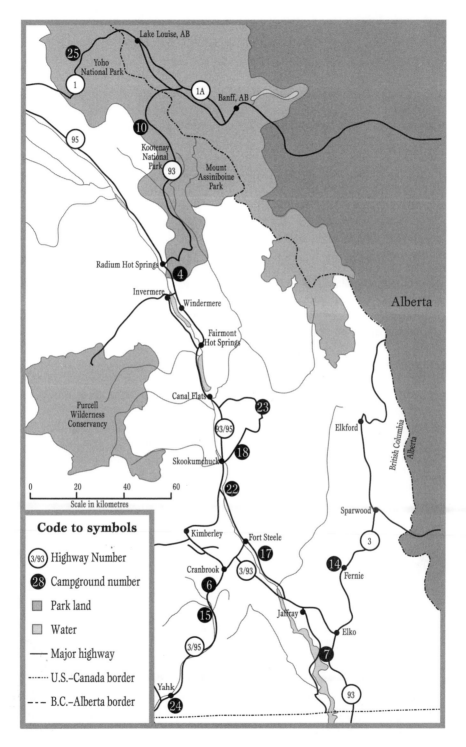

Code to symbols

(3/93) Highway Number

28 Campground number

☐ Park land

☐ Water

— Major highway

······ U.S.–Canada border

--- B.C.–Alberta border

Arrow Lakes/Shelter Bay

Location

Take the camera and marvel at the sunsets from this quaint little roadside campground. Located on the western side of Upper Arrow Lake and found by travelling 50 kilometres south of Revelstoke on Highway 23, it is near the ferry crossing for Galena Bay. The nearest services are at Revelstoke.

Facilities

Twenty-three camping spots are available. They are positioned quite close together and as there is no vegetation they afford little privacy. Some do, however, overlook the lake; these spots provide beautiful views of the water and the landscape beyond. All the basic amenities found in B.C. parks are available (pit toilets, picnic tables, water, fire pits), and those who prefer flush toilets and sinks can find them a short walk away at Shelter Bay.

Recreational activities

This campground is primarily for overnighters. The lake is excellent to swim in, and fishing for rainbow trout, Dolly Varden, and kokanee is possible. There is also a boat launch.

Additional information

This is a pleasant place to stop because of its proximity to the lake and to the views of the rugged Selkirk Mountains that reach over 3,000 metres. Although the campground is near the road, traffic ceases at 9:30 p.m. when the ferries stop, so the location is very peaceful during darkness. The ferry ride from Shelter Bay to Galena Bay is free and provides a beautiful break from driving to enjoy the scenery. I stayed here in August, and the campground was barely half full. With no traffic noise and a beautiful lake in which to bathe, this is definitely one of the better roadside camping spots.

BLANKET CREEK

Location
In its former life, Blanket Creek was a busy homestead, and today it is easy to see why the original pioneers chose to settle here. Created as a provincial park in 1982, this delightful 316-hectare park is located at the point where Blanket Creek enters the Columbia River, 25 kilometres south of Revelstoke on Highway 23. The nearest services are available at Revelstoke.

Facilities
Sixty-four well-positioned, large camping spots for every size of vehicle, set in a lightly forested area and all with spectacular views of the Monashee Mountains, are available here. Some of the better spaces are adjacent to meadow areas. There are flush and pit toilets but no sani-station or access for the disabled. Reservations accepted.

Recreational activities
In the day-use area of Blanket Creek, a large beach-rimmed lagoon ideal for swimming has been constructed. A trail leads from the campground to the pool. A five-minute walk along the Old South Road takes campers to the beautiful 12-metre-high Sutherland Falls, and there is also a route suitable for bikes. Fishing in both the creek and Upper Arrow Lake can yield Dolly Varden, rainbow trout, and kokanee, and in the fall, kokanee can be seen spawning in the mouth of the creek. The nearby town of Revelstoke is a lovely place to visit. Revelstoke offers a golf course, railway museum, piano museum, and local history museum, as well as a number of cobbled streets and turn-of-the-century buildings to explore.

Additional information

The site contains the remains of the Domke homestead, one of the few properties unaffected by the flooding of the Arrow Reservoir. The original log home dating back to the 1920s is still standing, but many of the other brick buildings were dismantled. The land was abandoned in the late 1960s when the Hugh Keenleyside Dam near Castlegar and the flooding of Arrow Reservoir were completed. Blanket Creek supplies a pleasant, quiet camping experience. I stayed here one year in early June when the place was deserted, the weather good, and the lake warm. This campground is suitable for every age group.

Champion Lakes

Location
The true Kootenay experience can be tasted at this provincial park. Situated in the Selkirk Mountains east of Trail at an elevation of 1,067 metres, this chain of three lakes is known as Champion Lakes. The park is 18 kilometres northwest of Fruitvale and is reached by turning off Highway 3 and taking a paved road. There are services at Fruitvale and at Trail, half an hour's drive away.

Facilities
The facilities at this 95-spot campsite include water, a sani-station, flush and pit toilets, and a large day-use area. The campground itself is located between Second and Third Champion lakes, with trails leading to the water. All spots are large, shady, and private, set in a forest of Douglas fir, pine, and spruce. There is no wheelchair access. Reservations are accepted.

Recreational activities
Described as a canoeist's dream, this campground supplies a ribbon of lakes and portages and offers brilliant paddling potential. Development is concentrated around Third Champion Lake, which has a boat launch, playground, picnic area, and change house. Second and First lakes remain in their natural states. Powerboats are prohibited. Swimming is a popular pastime here, and there is a buoyed swimming area for the kids. Another popular pursuit is angling for rainbow and cutthroat trout. Over 6 kilometres of hiking and walking trails lead from the campground. The Third Lake Trail is a 1.5-kilometre trek and is a popular stroll between Main and Campers Beach. In addition, Second Lake Trail is about 2.5 kilometres long and has sections of boardwalk and good views.

Additional information
These lakes are named after James W. Champion, who was an early settler and orchardist in the area. First Champion Lake is about 1,500 metres long, and Second and Third are about 800 metres each. The park's location between the Coastal and Dry Biotic zones results in a diversity of plant species, as well as more unusual animals such as beaver, porcupine, mink, and muskrat. If canoeing is your passion, you should definitely include Champion Lakes on your list of prime paddling locations. Families are also big winners here, as there is a wonderful beach and the waters are relatively warm. Another wonderful B.C. provincial park.

DRY GULCH

Location

If hot springs are your passion, you'll love Dry Gulch. This beautiful little campground is 5 kilometres south of Radium Hot Springs, at the foot of Redstreak Mountain amid steep-sided gullies eroded by glaciers. All amenities can be found at Radium Hot Springs, just a short drive away. It's 1 kilometre in from Highway 93 to the campground.

Facilities

Dry Gulch Provincial Park consists of 28 campsites set in a lightly forested area of Douglas fir and ponderosa pine. All sites are large, private, and able to handle every type of recreational vehicle; some have tent pads. There are flush and pit toilets, but no sani-station or showers. The park is wheelchair accessible and located just far enough from the main road that traffic noise is not a problem.

Recreational activities

One of the biggest attractions of staying here is the world-famous Radium Hot Springs, which are located in Kootenay National Park. Prior to their formal development in 1911, the springs had been used for centuries by the Interior and Plains First Nations. In addition to the springs, the resort has a café and shop. Additional recreational activities in the vicinity include golf courses, Kootenay National Park, and the town of Radium. Watch for bighorn sheep, which are often observed on the grassland behind the campground. There is a boat launch in Invermere.

Additional information

As this park is adjacent to Kootenay National Park, the campground is often used as an overspill location when the national park campgrounds are full. Kootenay National Park is situated on the west slope of the Continental Divide. It has more than 200 kilometres of hiking trails and features alpine meadows, snowfields, lakes, and mountains. Dry Gulch is an excellent quiet campground for enjoying the mineral waters. It's one of the better small campgrounds.

GLACIER NATIONAL

Location

A region of spectacular high-mountain scenery shaped by avalanches and snow, Glacier National Park is found in the Northern Selkirk Range of the Columbia Mountains, 49 kilometres east of Revelstoke on Highway 1. The park is aptly named. Nearly 12 percent of its total 136,500-hectare area comprises more than 400 active glaciers and icefields. Services located adjacent to the Rogers Pass Information Centre in the park include a gas station, hotel, café, and shop.

Facilities

Two camping areas are located here, and there is talk of establishing a third. Both sites are very popular. Loop Brook has 20 spots and is located 14 kilometres from the western entrance; Illecillewaet, 17 kilometres from Loop Brook, has 60 spots. Neither site is open until mid-June. There are no showers or a sani-station, but there are flush toilets.

Recreational activities

Anyone visiting the park should stop at the visitor centre, which has displays of natural and human history as well as videos illustrating various aspects of the park, its early relationship with the railroad, and subsequent development. The centre, designed in the shape of a massive snow shed, is an attraction in itself. Park staff are always willing to provide advice on Glacier's numerous attractions and can gear suggestions to your preferences and time lines. Twenty-one hiking trails zigzag across 140 kilometres of park and include the Abandoned Rails Interpretive Trail, which starts at the information centre. Renowned for climbing and mountaineering opportunities, the park also offers potential for canoeing, horseback riding, and fishing for whitefish, Dolly Varden, and trout in the Illecillewaet River. Interpretive programs are offered over the summer months.

Additional information

Even if you do not intend to stay at Glacier, stop and visit the information centre and learn about the history of Rogers Pass. The pass was first discovered by railway engineer Major A.B. Rogers in 1882, and by 1885, railway construction had been completed. In 1956 the Trans-Canada Highway was surveyed through the area, and the road linking the Illecillewaet River on the west to the Beaver River on the east was completed in 1962. Videos and displays give testimony to how hazardous and challenging this construction process was. Today, experts constantly monitor the snow conditions, and there is an avalanche control program.

JIMSMITH LAKE

Location

It's easy to see why this park is popular with both visitors and locals. Although Jimsmith Lake is relatively small (1.5 hectares), it is well situated at the western end of the Rocky Mountain Trench and surrounded by a forest of Douglas fir, spruce, western larch, aspen, and lodgepole and ponderosa pine. The campground is located 4 kilometres south of Cranbrook on Highway 3/95. All services are available in Cranbrook.

Facilities

Twenty-eight large, private, well-spaced campsites suitable for every type of vehicle are available here (as long as you can navigate a gravel road with a few potholes). A couple of sites have views of the lake. There is no sani-station. The park is wheelchair accessible and contains all basic amenities (water, fire pit, picnic tables, pit toilets).

Recreational activities

Campers can enjoy a lovely, sandy, developed swimming beach, grassy picnic area, canoeing and kayaking (powerboats are not allowed), and fishing for rainbow trout and largemouth bass. The park is frequently used for picnics and day trips by locals who relish the tranquility it offers. The nearby town of Cranbrook houses the Canadian Museum of Rail Travel, where trains from an earlier era are shown and tea can be taken. Cranbrook also boasts a self-guided heritage tour that highlights buildings dating from 1898 to 1929. Sixteen kilometres from Cranbrook is the heritage town of Fort Steele, where more than 60 buildings from the turn of the century have been restored to recreate a bygone era.

Additional information

This 12-hectare park is a popular destination in the wintertime for ice fishing, ice skating, Nordic skiing, sledding, and tobogganing. The economy of Cranbrook has been built on mining, fishing, and the railway. It is the largest town in the region (population 16,000) and has five provincial parks all within a 30-minute drive. This campground has a very "local" feel about it. When I last visited, there were several groups of teenagers in the day-use area, which made me presume this area was used well into the evening. Fortunately, the day-use area is located far enough away from the campsites that noise from adolescents is not a problem. Jimsmith Lake offers a more urban (although pleasant) camping experience.

KIKOMUN CREEK

Location

Sometimes the human influence on the geography of an area is beneficial. Such is the case at Kikomun Creek Provincial Park in the southern part of the Rocky Mountain Trench by Lake Koocanusa. This man-made lake was created by the construction of Libby Dam on the Kootenay River in Montana. The park is reached by turning off Highway 3/93 at Jaffray and travelling 11 kilometres south on a paved road. Jaffray has limited services, and there is a marina 4 kilometres from the campground with gas, propane, food, etc.

Facilities

Located in three campgrounds are 135 sites that can accommodate every type of recreational vehicle. There are flush and pit toilets, a sani-station, and showers, and wheelchair access. Reservations can be made in the Surveyors' campground, which is where the showers are found and which is by far the best location. Camping at the other sites is somewhat regimented, but the sites are closer to the boat launch and Koocanusa Reservoir.

Recreational activities

Fishing in this park is varied and good. The smaller lakes (Hidden Lake and Surveyors' Lake) offer potential for catching bass, eastern brook, rainbow trout, and Dolly Varden, while the 144-kilometre-long Koocanusa Reservoir has cutthroat trout and Rocky Mountain whitefish. Powerboats are not permitted on the smaller lakes, thus ensuring a peaceful time. There are two beaches, and picnic areas are found at Surveyors' Lake. Hiking trails around the smaller lakes (30 to 90 minutes) offer opportunities to see elk, deer, badger, and ospreys. Old roads and railway beds give hikers and bikers easy access to the 682-hectare park. For young campers, there is an adventure playground.

Additional information

Kikomun Creek Provincial Park houses one of the largest collections of western painted turtles, so-called because of the bright pattern underneath their shells. The turtles can easily be seen soaking up the sun. Kikomun Creek is a beautiful and varied place, ideal for a family vacation. It reminds me of an English country estate because of its size and the many roads that meander through the park.

KOKANEE CREEK

Location

It is difficult to imagine anyone not enjoying a visit to Kokanee Creek, situated amidst the beautiful scenery of the Slocan Range of the Selkirk Mountains. On the west arm of Kootenay Lake, 19 kilometres east of Nelson on Highway 3A, this popular provincial park has a wealth of activities for campers of all ages. Services are conveniently located in Nelson or Balfour (12 kilometres away).

Facilities

Kokanee Creek has 132 wooded camping spots in two locations, Sandspit (numbers 1-113) and Redfish (114-132), off paved lanes suitable for every size of vehicle. Redfish is closer to the road, making Sandspit my personal preference. The site is home to the West Kootenay Visitor Centre, so the facilities here are good and include flush toilets, showers, a sani-station, and access for the disabled. Reservations are accepted.

Recreational activities

You can easily spend a week at Kokanee Creek campground. There is a wealth of things to see and do, both in the park itself and in the immediate vicinity. Activities linked with the water include swimming from wide sandy beaches, boating, water-skiing, and sailboarding. The fishing is reported to be excellent for both rainbow trout and kokanee. Dolly Varden, char, burbot, and whitefish are also regularly caught. There is a large children's play area, a visitor centre that contains exhibits of natural and human history, and a number of walks. The nearby town of Nelson boasts the largest concentration of heritage buildings in B.C., and farther north on Highway 3, visitors can walk through caves at Ainsworth Hot Springs and relax in therapeutic mineral pools.

Additional information

The spawning channel and visitor centre here make this a truly educational place to visit. The word *kokanee* means "red fish" in the Kootenay Native language and is the name given to the landlocked salmon that spawn here in large numbers (the average is 2,000-4,000, but the number has been as high as 20,000). When I first stayed here, it was late August and the spawning was at its peak. At dusk, bald eagles and ospreys can be seen diving for salmon, and although it is sad that a few of these fish who have come so far with the sole thought of spawning will meet their demise so close to their destination, the spectacle is straight from a *National Geographic* television program. The salmon, together with the many other activities and the beautiful location, make this provincial park well worth a visit in August/September. In June the wild roses are in full bloom, and the colours spectacular. This campground must be considered one of the best in B.C.

Kootenay Lake (Davis Creek/Lost Ledge)

Location
These adjacent campgrounds used to be known collectively as Kootenay Lake, but in 1998 BC Parks decided to give them separate names, although their facilities and locations are very similar. Then, in 2003, BC Parks decided to revert to the original name—Kootenay Lake. These beautiful, quiet campgrounds are located on the west side of Kootenay Lake, north of Kaslo on Highway 31, in the heart of Kootenay country. There is little to distract the camper other than mountain scenery and bald eagles flying overhead. Services can be found in Kaslo, a 20-minute drive south.

Facilities
Twenty-six campsites are available at two locations: Davis Creek offers 18 sites, and Lost Ledge has 14. Some sites are very close to the lake and afford fantastic views of the Purcell Mountains. There is no sani-station, and facilities are the basic ones found in BC Parks (pit toilets, water, fire pit, and picnic tables).

Recreational activities
Leisure pursuits include swimming (but take it from one who knows—the water here is very cold), boating (there is a boat launch at Lost Ledge), and fishing for kokanee, Dolly Varden, and rainbow trout. In addition, the quaint town of Kaslo is well worth a visit. In Kaslo you can rent canoes, kayaks, and bikes to explore the lake and surrounding area. To the south, Ainsworth Hot Springs provides a relaxing afternoon's activity in mineral hot waters.

Additional information
The campgrounds are located on a very quiet section of Highway 31. When I stayed, I cycled north to Duncan Dam, then on to Howser, which has a small café. The highway follows the lake and has excellent views. There is another provincial park children and adults will adore located a short distance from Kootenay Lake. Cody Caves has no camping facilities and is located in the Selkirk Mountains just above Ainsworth Hot Springs, 11 kilometres down a good forest road off Highway 31. Visitors to this provincial park are treated to a full array of spectacular cave formations, including stalagmites, stalactites, waterfalls, draperies, rimstone dams, and soda straws, and must wear protective clothing and hard hats (the necessary equipment is provided) when taking the highly informative tours offered by BC Parks.

KOOTENAY NATIONAL

Location

Along with Banff, Yoho, and Jasper, Kootenay National Park was designated a World Heritage Site in 1985 when UNESCO officially recognized the beauty and significance of the Rocky Mountain landscape. The only national park to contain both glaciers and cactus, Kootenay National Park is found on Highway 93 only a kilometre north of Radium Hot Springs (west park entrance) and straddles over 90 kilometres of the highway as it heads north. Services are located in Radium.

Facilities

Backcountry camping is possible here, and there are three locations for vehicle/tent camping. Redstreak campground (my preference, and reservations are accepted here) is just 1 kilometre from Radium Hot Springs and is a good spot from which to gain access to the pools (a 30-minute trail leads from the campground to the water). Redstreak has 242 spots set in a lightly forested area; showers, flush toilets, and a sani-station are available. It also has RV hookups, which is unusual for a national park. Marble Canyon campground has 61 spots and is 86 kilometres north of Radium, near the park's information centre. Set in a dense subalpine forest, Marble Canyon is the quietest of the three campgrounds. Mcleod River campground, 26 kilometres north of Radium between Meadow Creek

and Kootenay River, has 98 shady spots—some close to the water's edge, some quite small. These two smaller campgrounds have only the basic facilities (pit toilets, water, picnic tables, fire pit).

Recreational activities

One of the biggest attractions here is, of course, the hot springs. Valued for centuries for their rich healing powers, they are within easy access of Redstreak campground and are open in the summer from 9:00 a.m. until 11:00 p.m. The park has a number of hiking trails, covering over 200 kilometres, in addition to self-guided trails. One of the more impressive shorter trails is Marble Canyon, a 30-minute walk that takes visitors into an ice-carved limestone and dolomite canyon; interpretive boards detail the canyon's 500-million-year development. It's an easy hike for old and young alike—my two-year-old managed it without assistance. Other recreational pursuits include horseback riding, mountaineering, canoeing and rafting down the Kootenay River, swimming, and wildlife viewing. While it is possible to fish for brook and rainbow trout, most of the streams and rivers are glacier-fed, so the waters are too cold to yield high fish populations.

Additional information

As in all national parks, visitor permits are required by all who plan to stop. These are available at the park entrance and can be used in any Canadian national park. There are hundreds of things to do here, and wildlife (moose, black bear, elk, deer, and over 179 species of birds) does appear to be readily observable. The Banff–Windermere Highway, which runs through the park, was built in 1922 and was the first road constructed through the Canadian Rockies. It is a very pleasant drive, and you can often spot animal life while travelling.

LOCKHART BEACH

Location

This quaint, lakefront provincial park, established in 1939, covers just three hectares and is therefore one of the smallest in the province. It's located on the east side of the south arm of Kootenay Lake, 19 kilometres south of Kootenay Bay/Crawford. Food and lodging are available at Crawford Bay; more comprehensive services are located at Creston, an hour's drive south (40 kilometres).

Facilities

The campground, primarily for overnight stops, was recently rebuilt. It has 18 camping spots, suitable for every type of camper, across the road from the lake. It features the basics—pit toilets, pump water, fire pit, and picnic tables—and there is no sani-station or access for the disabled. Traffic noise from the road is audible; a couple of sites are close to the creek, and there you'll hear the babble of water instead.

Recreational activities

The park has a lovely, quiet beach area where you can swim or fish for rainbow trout and Dolly Varden. A trail leads from the park and through a forest of Douglas fir, red cedar, and ponderosa pine along Lockhart Creek; rainbow trout can be caught in the creek. It takes about three hours to hike the trail, which has an elevation gain of 800 metres.

Additional information

Highway 3A from Creston to Kootenay Bay is a lovely drive that takes tourists past small stores, galleries, and an amazing circular glass house that a retired funeral director constructed out of 500,000 square embalming-fluid bottles. Definitely the only one in Canada, if not the world, the house is 7 kilometres south of the campground. At Kootenay Bay, travellers can take the Kootenay Lake ferry—the world's longest free ferry ride—across the lake to Balfour. When I took this trip, there was an excellent little café on board. Be sure you're hungry when you embark: the breakfast is very good, as is the entertainment that goes with it. This boat trip offers excellent photographic opportunities and is recommended to everyone holidaying in the area. Lockhart Beach is definitely one of the better roadside campgrounds.

MARTHA CREEK

Location

The views from this campground, which overlooks the Revelstoke Reservoir, stretch on to the Monashee Mountain Range and provide fantastic photographic opportunities. In June a blanket of colourful wildflowers covers the campground. For these reasons alone, Martha Creek is a delightful place to sojourn. Martha Creek is situated 19 kilometres north of Revelstoke on Highway 23. All services are available at Revelstoke.

Facilities

Located on an old river terrace on the western shore of Revelstoke Reservoir, Martha Creek has 25 paved campsites, many with access directly onto the beach, although some are quite close to each other. There are flush and pit toilets but no sani-station. The park is not wheelchair accessible.

Recreational activities

A swimming beach is located near the campground, and a boat launch is found at the eastern boundary of the park. You can fish in the Revelstoke Reservoir for kokanee, rainbow trout, and Dolly Varden. An enchanting 7-kilometre hiking trail leads walkers through wildflowers, cedar, and hemlock and on to flowering meadows and alpine lakes within the Sleeker Mountains. There is a children's playground and a large grassy field with volleyball net. The historic town of Revelstoke has been restored over the last few years and is an appealing place for shopping and wandering. In the summertime the bandstand (or gazebo) in the town's plaza has evening entertainment for visitors. I spent a lovely August evening dancing to a local band as the sun went down—just the sort of light exercise needed before retiring to the tent or RV.

Additional information

When staying in this vicinity, you must visit the Revelstoke Dam, one of North America's largest and most modern hydroelectric developments, located five minutes from Revelstoke on the road to Martha Creek. Mica Dam, two hours north of Revelstoke on Highway 23, is also worth a visit. Both offer fascinating tours of their facilities and interesting programs on how and why they were constructed. In 1999, as we travelled toward Revelstoke over Robson Pass with the rain pouring, I called in to the hotel to inquire about a room for the night: $125.00 plus tax! We travelled on to Martha Creek, and the skies cleared and the sun shone. We spent $9.50 to camp in a field full of wildflowers and wonderful smells! Although in 2003 the camping fee had increased to $15.00, on this trip we discovered Canyon Hot Springs, about 20 kilometres east of Revelstoke on Highway 1. Here there are two wonderful hot mineral pools where you can soak in therapeutic waters while surrounded by mountains. Recently renovated and well worth a visit.

McDonald Creek

Location
Ten kilometres south of Nakusp, where all services can be found, this 468-hectare park occupies land on both the eastern and western shores of Upper Arrow Lake. Camping facilities are situated adjacent to the highway on the eastern side of the lake. It's a perfect location for an evening's beach barbecue or lunchtime picnic.

Facilities
Thirty-eight relatively private campsites are available in a lightly forested area; some overlook the lake. Facilities are confined to the basics—water, fire pit, picnic tables, and pit toilets.

Recreational activities
Massive Arrow Lake is the central source of activity. You can fish for kokanee, Dolly Varden, and rainbow trout, swim, sunbathe, and sail. The water levels in the lake change. In June there is mud, but in July and August a sandy beach is revealed. A boat launch is available in the park. The nearby town of Nakusp is renowned for its hot springs, located north of the town, 12 kilometres down a gravel road. The pools are high in the Selkirk Mountains; one is 38 degrees Celsius, the other 41 degrees. The views from these outdoor pools to the Selkirk Mountains are quite spectacular, and if you visit at the right time you could have this facility all to yourself. A 20-minute drive farther north of Nakusp on Highway 23 is Halcyon Hot Springs Resort, which was re-established in 1999. The original world-famous hotel was destroyed by fire in 1955. Today, the timber-frame day lodge offers a licensed restaurant, two mineral hot pools, and a heated swimming pool, situated on a steep hillside next to the Upper Arrow Lake.

Additional information
Arrow Lake, like Kootenay Lake, holds Gerrard trout, the world's largest rainbow trout. When I visited, I had to stay at the overspill site, but even so I had a wonderful time cooking dinner by the lakeside on a hibachi and watching the sun go down. Although it was full, the campground did not appear crowded, and it has a good ambience. As with other communities in the Kootenays, the economy of Nakusp has depended on the logging industry since 1910 and, notwithstanding some diversification, remains so today. Evidence of the logging industry is never far away from the traveller vacationing in the Kootenays.

MOUNT FERNIE

Location

Rich in Native legends of unrequited love, broken promises, and catastrophes, this 259-hectare park in the shadow of Mount Fernie has been described as the eastern gateway to the Kootenays. It is located 3 kilometres west of Fernie on Highway 3. Services are provided at Fernie.

Facilities

The campground has 38 sites set amongst a parkland of diverse vegetation including western larch, Douglas fir, black cottonwood, trembling aspen, western red cedar, and spruce. There are flush and pit toilets, but no sani-station or showers. The park is not wheelchair accessible. Sites can accommodate all sizes of RVs. Reservations accepted.

Recreational activities

The main attraction of this park is a 3-kilometre interpretive trail that winds its way through the park and takes visitors to picturesque Lizard Creek and waterfalls. The walk from the parking lot to the falls also makes a pleasant short trip for those people not intending to spend the night here. The trail continues on past the falls, but when I was last here that trail was badly signposted and no maps were available so I couldn't explore it to the extent I would have liked to. Hopefully, BC Parks will have updated the signposting when you visit. I am told that mountain biking is becoming popular here, so perhaps the trails will improve. The park has areas of old-growth forest and there are wildlife-viewing opportunities where you may see black bears, elk, or deer, which are common here. The town of Fernie, just 3 kilometres from the park, has a historical museum, buildings dating back to 1904, a historical walking tour, and a cultural centre and restaurant on the site of the former Canadian Pacific Railway station.

Additional information

Fernie is named after William Fernie, who was instrumental in the development of coal mining in the area. Legend has it that William Fernie found out about the coal deposits from the Tobacco Plains people by promising to marry one of their young women. After gaining this information, he rejected her, thereby provoking her father to place a curse on the name "Fernie." The town has suffered calamities: a mine explosion killed 128 men in 1902; there were two fires in 1904 and 1908, the latter leaving 6,000 people homeless; and there have been floods. In 1964 Chief Red Eagle of the Tobacco Plains Nation lifted the curse. Some people still believe that on summer nights the ghost of the Native woman, led by her father, rides across Hosmer Mountain in search of William Fernie.

Moyie Lake

Location

A restful, relaxing time awaits campers at this beautiful provincial park. Adjacent to the eastern fringe of the Purcell Mountains near the northern end of Moyie Lake, this campground is a wonderful retreat, especially for folks with young children. Moyie got its name from the French word *mouillé*, meaning "wet." It was established in 1959 and is located 20 kilometres south of Cranbrook (where all services are available) and 10 kilometres north of the community of Moyie.

Facilities

There are 111 camping spots, and the park has full disabled access, a sani-station, flush toilets, and showers. The sites themselves are all large and private, but they do not have views of the water. Reservations are accepted. The only downside here is that there's a railroad near the campground, and this may cause problems for light sleepers.

Recreational activities

A wealth of activities can be enjoyed at Moyie Lake. Campers can take the 2-kilometre Meadow Interpretive Trail, which describes the forest typical to the area, or the Deep Pond Trail (a half-hour return). Swimming is easy from a protected swimming area, and there are 1,300 metres of beach. For anglers, the lake contains Dolly Varden, kokanee, burbot, rainbow trout, and eastern brook trout. A boat launch is available and windsurfing is possible, weather permitting. Children can be kept busy at the adventure playground. For those who enjoy mountain biking, a half-day excursion up a gravel road to Mineral Lake, formally a forestry recreational site, is a fun excursion.

Additional information

This park is an ideal place to spend time in if you have a young family, but it is not just for those with children. For campers who decide not to cook over an open fire, the pub situated about 10 minutes south of the campground on Highway 3 is worth a visit, and the nearby town of Cranbrook supplies all services should you have forgotten a basic camping item. Moyie Lake is a delightful place to set up camp. When I stayed, the only drawback was the three jet-skiers who shattered the calm of the afternoon and made me appreciate the lakes on which powerboats are prohibited. My advice to those who prefer a smaller, quieter experience is to try Jimsmith instead.

NANCY GREENE

Location

This lovely park is by all accounts just as popular in the wintertime as it is in the summer. Named after Canada's world-famous Olympic skier Nancy Greene, who came from the Rossland–Trail area, the park is nestled in the Rossland Range of the Monashee Mountains, 35 kilometres north of Rossland on Highway 3, at the intersection of Highway 3B. The park itself and the adjacent recreational area of the same name contain the subalpine Nancy Greene Lake. Services can be found at either Rossland or Castlegar; both communities are about a half-hour drive from the campground.

Facilities

There are 10 formal campsites here, primarily geared to tenters and smaller recreational vehicles. These sites are not great, being closely packed and adjacent to the car park. Larger RVs are allowed to camp in the parking lot. All the basic facilities exist (pit toilets, picnic tables, pump water, fire pit). There is no sani-station or access for the disabled. Noise from traffic is audible, but the road is not tremendously busy, especially at night.

Recreational activities

The park contains a subalpine lake and a lovely beach area, where you can swim, fish for rainbow trout, or sail (powerboats are not allowed). A self-guided, 5-kilometre nature trail leads around the lake, and the adjacent Nancy Greene recreational area offers more than 20 kilometres of hiking trails. The area is popular in the winter for both downhill and cross-country skiing. The park has a covered picnic shelter and an old log cabin with wood-burning stove.

Additional information

The picturesque town of Rossland dates back to the turn of the century. More recently, it has gained a reputation for mountain biking. Just outside Rossland is the Le Roi gold mine, where visitors are taken underground to become acquainted with the life and work of a hardrock miner. Between 1900 and 1916, the Le Roi mine produced 50 percent of B.C.'s gold and swelled the population of Rossland to 7,000 before its demise in the 1920s. Although the actual camping spots here are disappointing, the views of the lake are tremendous.

Norbury Lake

Location

Norbury Lake is nestled in the Hughes Range of the Rocky Mountains and supplies excellent views of the Steeples—a distinctive feature of the Hughes Range and also of the Purcell Mountains. The park is easily found 13 kilometres southwest of Fort Steele on a paved road from Highway 93/95. Services are available at Fort Steele. The campground is approximately 1 kilometre away from the day-use area at Peckhams Lake.

Facilities

This is a secluded location for 46 gravel camping spots set amongst a lightly forested area of Douglas fir, lodgepole pine, ponderosa pine, and western larch. The number of trees decreased considerably in June 1998 when a strong wind blew through the area, causing the campground to close for more than two weeks. Fortunately, the two families camping during this time were not hurt. There is no sani-station or disabled access, and facilities are restricted to the basics (pump water, fire pit, picnic tables, pit toilets).

Recreational activities

Recreational pursuits within the park include fishing for rainbow trout in Peckhams Lake, swimming, and boating (powerboats are prohibited). Two trails are available to lead explorers over a diverse area of lightly forested landscape where it is possible to see elk, deer, and Rocky Mountain bighorn sheep. Norbury Lake is close to the historic town of Fort Steele, a fascinating example of turn-of-the-century life in Canada and a real delight to visit. In 1961 the provincial government recognized Fort Steele as being of historical significance, and the reconstruction that started then continues today. A perfect example of a pioneer town, Fort Steele contains some 50 buildings, including an original North West Mounted Police camp, excellent bakery, restaurant, theatre, and museum.

Additional information

Norbury Lake is named after F. Paget Norbury, a magistrate who served in Fort Steele in the late 19th century. This park is the site of the Kootenai Nation's ceremonial grounds. An informative display giving details of their culture is found at Peckhams Lake entrance.

PREMIER LAKE

Location

Long ago, the K'tunaxa Nation camped, hunted, and fished in this area. Today, visitors are attracted to the region for the splendid views. Premier Lake is in the Hughes Range of the Rockies, about 45 kilometres northeast of Kimberley. It is reached by turning off Highway 93/95 at Skookumchuck (a Chinook word meaning "strong or turbulent water") and travelling 9 kilometres on a paved road and 5 kilometres on a gravel road. (Watch for logging trucks, which frequently travel along this route.) A gas station, shop, and restaurant are available at Skookumchuck.

Facilities

Set amongst Douglas fir, western larch, cottonwood, and aspen trees are 57 campsites, suitable for all vehicles and some with tent pads. Facilities are the basics (pump water, fire pit, picnic tables, pit toilets). The park is wheelchair accessible. An unusual, manually operated solar-heated shower is available here; plastic shower bags are supplied by the park. Some sites are adjacent to a bubbling creek.

Recreational activities

Five lakes—Premier, Canuck, Yankee, Cats Eyes, and Quart—exist in this 662-hectare park, which has gained a reputation as a good spot to fish for eastern brook trout and Gerrard rainbow trout. A short walk from the campground there is a spawning and viewing area together with an interpretive display to explain enhancement procedures, including how eggs are collected for the Kootenay Trout Hatchery. Forty percent of rainbow trout eggs required for the provincial egg hatchery system come from here and are distributed to over 350 lakes and streams in the province. There is a boat launch and swimming is available. The park also contains a number of trails that cover a variety of distances and take between 20 minutes and two hours to complete. For children, an adventure playground is found at the entrance to the campground.

Additional information

The area is rich in wildlife—watch for elk roaming on the cleared hills near the highway. Premier Lake is yet another B.C. provincial park located in spectacular, breathtaking scenery. It is a little off the beaten track and offers a very adult camping experience.

Rosebery

Location

Rosebery campground is undoubtedly one of the better campgrounds dedicated primarily to one-night stops. The scenery here is lovely: visitors can gaze across Slocan Lake to the majestic Valhalla mountains. The park is situated on Highway 6, 6 kilometres south of Rosebery between Nakusp and New Denver, where services are available.

Facilities

Campers can take their pick of 33 large, private, shady camping spots suitable for every type of recreational vehicle. Some overlook the rushing Wilson Creek, while others are closer to the road (although at night the road is not busy). There is no sani-station or access for the disabled, and the facilities are basic (pit toilets, water, fire pit, and picnic tables).

Recreational activities

There are few activities to pursue in the park itself. Wilson Creek runs through the park and has a short trail leading along its edge. Fishing for rainbow trout is possible. By crossing nearby Slocan Lake you can explore and hike Valhalla Park. There are a number of private golf courses in the area. New Denver is a delightful place to wander around, and a number of lovely coffee shops have recently sprung up to entice tourists to linger. This turn-of-the-century community has some wonderful buildings that are currently being restored to their former glory.

Additional information

Located directly across Slocan Lake from Rosebery Provincial Park is Valhalla Park. This is a region of dramatic and diverse wilderness that includes lakes, alpine meadows, and the impressive New Denver glacier. With limited road access it offers 50,000 hectares of beautiful, unspoiled land to explore. Observant sailors heading toward Valhalla can spot pictographs painted by the forefathers of the Arrowhead First Nations on the western shoreline of Slocan Lake.

SUMMIT LAKE

Location

Although this relatively small, eight-hectare provincial park was established in 1964, it only opened as a campground in 2001, making it one of B.C.'s newest provincial park campgrounds. Situated at the southwestern corner of Summit Lake, it is one of only two campgrounds in the Slocan Valley (Rosebery is the other) and therefore a much-needed addition to the area. It can be found on Highway 6 between New Denver and Nakusp. The nearest services are at Nakusp, 18 kilometres north.

Facilities

The campground has 36 vehicle-accessible sites. Some are quite closely packed together, but a number have wonderful views of the lake and are set in a lightly forested area of hemlock and cedar. There are flush and pit toilets, water, and fire pits, as well as a picnic shelter with a wood stove. Reservations are not accepted. Although the campground is quite near the road, noise is not much of a problem, as traffic is not heavy.

Recreational activities

For my family the biggest attraction here was skimming stones on the fantastically calm waters of Summit Lake. The lake has 100 metres of pebbly beach and is quite warm and attractive for swimming (we visited in September 2003 and did not go in). There is a small trail that meanders from the day-use area to the campground. The campground has a boat launch, and canoeing and kayaking are popular pastimes. Fishing is also reputed to be good, as the lake is stocked with over 10,000 rainbow trout annually—do you ever wonder whose job it is to count them—and the local fly-fishing championships are held here. New Denver and Nakusp are pleasant places to wander through and stop for coffee in, and to the north of Nakusp you'll find the wonderful Nakusp Hot Springs.

Additional information

This park could easily have been named Toad Provincial Park. It houses an important breeding ground and migration habitat for western toads. Information boards in the park describe these primarily nocturnal creatures. In the fall, thousands of toads emerge from the lake and head for the adjacent forest to hibernate. Other wildlife includes eagles, kingfishers, hawks, bears, and mountain goats. Summit Lake is a delightful addition to the campgrounds of the province, and one of the better roadside ones.

SYRINGA

Location

Syringa Provincial Park is on a creek on the eastern side of Lower Arrow Lake, below the Norns Range of the Columbia Mountains. The lake, on the Columbia River, resulted from the construction of the Keenleyside Dam. The campground is reached by turning off Highway 3A just north of Castlegar and travelling 19 kilometres on a paved road. All services are available in Castlegar, while a nearby marina and store offer more limited supplies.

Facilities

Sixty-one large, private spots, some overlooking the water and others adjacent to a grassy meadow, are available in a forest of red cedar, western hemlock, and ponderosa pine. In addition to all the basic facilities, Syringa Creek has a sani-station, flush and pit toilets, and wheelchair access. Reservations are accepted.

Recreational activities

Syringa boasts a fantastic rocky beach from which to view the Columbia Mountains and Monashee Range. All forms of water activity are possible, including swimming, boating, water-skiing (the park provides the only public boat launch in the area, but be warned—the waters can be rough when there is a wind), and fishing for Dolly Varden and rainbow trout. For those who prefer non-water-based pursuits, a number of trails lead from the park for walking and mountain biking. (The 2.7-kilometre Yellow Pine Trail is a particularly pleasant 45-minute interpretive trail.) There is an adventure playground and a beautiful grassy area by the beach that's perfect for ball games. When I stayed here, I got chatting with Jackie, the volunteer campground host who for the previous three years had spent three months at Syringa giving help and advice to campers while her husband was employed as the parks facilitator, collecting fees and undertaking maintenance. She told me that the mosquitoes were never a problem here, as the wind tends to keep them away—information well worth having.

Additional information

The park is named after the syringa, or mock orange, a regional, white-flowered shrub that blooms in early spring. Nearby Castlegar is rich in Doukhobor history; a heritage museum near the airport details this culture and is worth a visit. Although the paved road ends at the park, an unpaved road carries on to an area known as Deer Park, where there is an attractive waterfall.

Wasa Lake

Location

This gem of a campground, one of the largest in the region, provides a comprehensive range of facilities and activities. The campground lies on the northern end of Wasa Lake, a glacier-formed kettle lake, reputed to be one of the warmest in the east Kootenays, if not the province. (Both Osoyoos and Christina also claim this distinction.) The views from the Wasa Lake campground are staggering, with the Rocky Mountains to the east and the Purcells to the west. Wasa Lake Provincial Park is situated 40 kilometres north of Cranbrook on Highway 93/95. The community of Wasa, a kilometre away, has stores, a gas station, restaurants, laundry facilities, a neighbourhood pub, and a good ice cream parlour.

Facilities

This campground can accommodate every type of recreational vehicle in 104 well-appointed camping spots set among pine and aspen trees. There are flush and pit toilets and a sani-station but no showers. The campground is wheelchair accessible and reservations are accepted.

Recreational activities

The lake supplies a wealth of recreational activities with four excellent beaches providing access to warm waters. There is a boat launch, and fishing for largemouth bass is a favourite pursuit. A self-guided nature trail that takes about an hour (2 kilometres) gives details of the flora and fauna of the area. A 33-kilometre mountain-bike trail leads from Wasa Lake to Lazy Lake (BC Parks has a leaflet, which is also available on its web site, describing the details of this trail). There is also an adventure playground. In addition to the recreational activities provided in the park itself, the historic town of Fort Steele is only 18 kilometres to the south; likewise, the Bavarian community of Kimberley, Canada's highest city, is within easy reach. Here visitors can marvel at the world's largest operating cuckoo clock, stop at gingerbread-fronted stores, or play a round of golf.

Additional information

Each year on the Sunday of the August long weekend, a sand-sculpture contest is held on Camper's Beach, the main beach on the lake. The park contains a variety of vegetation, including an area of endangered grasslands. A few years ago Wasa had a bad reputation for mosquitoes, which arrived the second week of July and stayed until the end of August (like most of the tourists). This problem has been curtailed by helicopter spraying, paid for by the taxes of the local community. The local population is keen to preserve Wasa as a family camping location. A few years ago they constructed the Wasa Lions Way—an 8-kilometre walking/cycling/rollerblading trail. A BC Parks representative informed me that two grandmothers in Wasa had recently purchased rollerblades—so go check out the rolling grannies.

Kekuli Bay Park is on the west side of Kalamalka Lake.

Kids enjoy the playground at Kekuli Bay.

Kayaking, canoeing, and swimming are popular pastimes at Kekuli Bay.

The pier and picnic area at Lac Le Jeune are designed for easy wheelchair access. (Heritage Collection photo)

Boating, fishing, and water-skiing are among the activities enjoyed at Lac la Hache park.

The fishing's good at Premier Lake.

Spectacular Helmcken Falls is just one of the many attractions in Wells Gray park.

The long and the short of it: A small camper stands next to a large moose at Clearwater campground in Wells Gray.

In one of B.C.'s most spectacular parks, beautiful Mount Robson is reflected in the still waters of this alpine lake.

Nancy Greene Provincial Park (BC Parks photo).

Monck Provincial Park is an ideal family vacation spot.

Yoho National Park, a UNESCO World Heritage Site, is often compared to the Swiss Alps.

Fishing for dinner at Meziadin Lake.

Walking around Barkerville's graveyard is like stepping back in time to the gold-rush days.

The campground at Bull Canyon park is in a beautiful setting by the Chilcotin River. (Heritage Collection photo)

The clear aquamarine water of Boya Lake is unlike that of most other lakes in the province. (BC Parks photo)

Beaver ponds can be seen in Eskers Provincial Park, a short distance from Crooked River Provincial Park.

The Telkwa and Buckley rivers meet at Telkwa, close to Tyhee Provincial Park.

Hiking, boating, fishing, and wildlife viewing are popular activities in Muncho Lake Provincial Park, but the water's too cold for swimming.

Whiteswan Lake

Location

Driving to Whiteswan Lake can be an adventure in itself. The gravel road is frequented by huge logging trucks, and in places it narrows to one lane, necessitating excellent driving skills. The journey is well worth the effort. This provincial park is located on a plateau in the Kootenay Range of the Rocky Mountains east of Canal Flats, which has a store and restaurant. Both Alces and Whiteswan lakes are contained in the almost-2,000-hectare park, which has some fantastic views of the surrounding mountains. The campground is reached by turning off Highway 93/95 and travelling along Whiteswan Lake Road (gravel) for 18 kilometres. The nearest comprehensive services are at Invermere.

Facilities

The park has four campgrounds, providing 114 spaces in total. Alces Lake has a sani-station and is reached after travelling 21 kilometres from the main highway. Packrat Point is 24 kilometres from the highway, Inlet Creek a further 4 kilometres, and Home Basin is the most distant at 33 kilometres from the highway. Home Basin and Alces Lake have lakeside camping and are my personal preferences. There are also wilderness campsites in the park. In addition to all the basic amenities (water, fire pit, picnic tables, pit toilets), the park is wheelchair accessible.

Recreational activities

One of the main attractions of this location is the undeveloped Lussier Hot Springs, near the park's western boundary. The hot springs flow from the mountainside into a series of pools and, unlike the ones at Radium, Ainsworth, and Fairmont, are unspoiled by commercial development. Both Whiteswan and Alces lakes provide plenty of swimming opportunities, with a beach at the north end of Whiteswan Lake. The two lakes are among the most productive fisheries in the East Kootenays, and in May and June rainbow trout can be seen spawning in Inlet and Outlet creeks. Boat launches are available at Packrat Point and Home Basin (electric motors only on Alces Lake). An 8-kilometre hiking trail takes walkers from Alces Lake to Home Basin, and there are opportunities for viewing wildlife such as golden eagles, bald eagles, mountain goats, bighorn sheep, and moose. (*Alces* is Latin for "moose.")

Additional information

This is an area rich in history. It has been used by the K'tunaxa (Kootenai) Nation for more than 5,000 years. In the 1800s and 1900s, trappers and prospectors worked the region, and today logging is the prime industry—a fact you will be well aware of if you encounter a logging truck on your journey to this beautiful, away-from-it-all camping location. It's a huge park not oriented toward families but great for anglers.

Yʌʜᴋ

Location

This nine-hectare park can be found in a quiet, uncommercialized area of B.C., on the banks of the Moyie River. It is close to the United States border and the state of Idaho. Situated on Highway 3/95 at Yahk, 39 kilometres east of Creston, Yahk Provincial Park is very much an overnight camping or picnic spot. Services can be found in Moyie, Yahk, or Creston, or at a gas station just south of the campground.

Facilities

There are 26 campsites here, set amidst a forest of Douglas fir, lodgepole pine, and ponderosa pine. The basic amenities are found (cooking pit, picnic table, water, pit toilets). The park is located close to both the railway line and road, so traffic noise may be disturbing to some. It is wheelchair accessible and can accommodate every size of recreational vehicle.

Recreational activities

Yahk is primarily for one-night campers or for brief rest stops, and there is not a great deal to do here besides fish in the Moyie River for Dolly Varden. As you travel down Highway 3/95 following the Moyie River, moose and mule deer can be seen feeding, so keep your eyes peeled. The day-use area is an ideal picnic spot.

Additional information

Yahk was once a major supplier of railway ties to the Canadian Pacific Railway, an industry that still exists but has been in steady decline since the 1940s. Today, Yahk has a population of almost 200. Set on a hillside overlooking the lake, the pretty community of Moyie to the south has some interesting buildings. Moyie owes its development to silver-lead mining and at one time was the richest mine of this type in the province.

YOHO NATIONAL

Location

Yoho is thought to be the word used by the Kootenai people to express awe, and visitors certainly have this emotion in Yoho, Canada's second oldest national park. Designated by UNESCO as a World Heritage Site and often compared to the Swiss Alps, Yoho has spectacular lakes, mountains, icefields, alpine meadows, glaciers, and waterfalls. The park is found on the Trans-Canada Highway between Golden and Lake Louise. The small community of Field, which is in the park, offers services. A lovely restaurant/coffeehouse that also sells camping supplies is located near the Kicking Horse campground.

Facilities

Over 300 camping spots are available from which campers can access the delights of Yoho. The three main vehicle/tent campgrounds are Kicking Horse, in a lightly forested area 5 kilometres east of Field (86 spots), Chancellor Peak, 5 kilometres from the western park boundary (58 spots), and Hoodoo Creek, 7 kilometres from the western boundary (106 spots). Showers, flush toilets, and a sani-station are available at Kicking Horse, which also has overflow camping, an outdoor interpretive theatre, and a play area for children. Hoodoo is densely wooded and peaceful; it has flush toilets and a sani-station but no showers. Chancellor Peak provides only the basic camping facilities but has great views and is on the Kicking Horse River. In addition, walk-in campsites a short distance from the car park are available at Takakkaw Falls (35 spots). Monarch, with 46 spots, is the most recent addition. A number of primitive camping facilities also exist in the park. Park-use permits are required for overnight camping, and in 2003 a $6.00 charge was made for firewood. Kicking Horse is open from mid-May to mid-October, Chancellor Peak from late May to mid-September, and the others from late June until early September.

Recreational activities

Visitors to Yoho should make their first stop at the Yoho Park Information Centre located at the junction of Highway 1 and the access road into Field. Detailed maps of the vicinity can be obtained here. In a park of this size (131,300 hectares), internationally recognized for its beauty, there is a multitude of things to do, including canoeing (canoes can be rented on Emerald Lake), rafting, fishing, mountain biking, mountaineering, and, of course, hiking. Fantastic hiking opportunities abound; choose between short interpretive trails or hikes that last for days. When I stayed, I hiked the Iceline Trail, which takes you to glaciers, alpine meadows, forests, and mountains among some of the best scenery in the world. It is impossible to recommend this trail too highly. While driving to the start of this hike we also saw a grizzly bear. The Iceline Trail (and others) has views of Takakkaw Falls, which at 254 metres is one of the highest waterfalls in North America. *Takakkaw* is a Cree word meaning "magnificent." A short 10-minute walk to these falls is also well worth undertaking.

Additional information

Yoho National Park was established in 1911. Yoho owes its development to the Canadian National Railway workers who managed to push the tracks through Kicking Horse Pass and build the first company hotel in Field. Climbers, tourists, and artists came to the hotel and recognized the overpowering beauty of the area. In 1886 Mount Steven Reserve was set aside, and in 1911 it was renamed Yoho.

Lac la Hache.

Bowron Lake.

CARIBOO
CHILCOTIN COAST

Steeped in the history of the gold rush and covering an area of over 100,000 square kilometres, the Cariboo region includes campgrounds situated off Highway 97 north of Cache Creek to Prince George. This section of road is known as the Gold Rush Trail after the pioneers who travelled it in search of the precious metal. Today, many buildings and historical markers recount the days of this original wagon road built in 1860. The Cariboo region also includes campgrounds found on minor roads off this major route and incorporates an area characterized by rolling hills, grasslands, over 8,000 lakes, and numerous rivers stretching from the foothills of the Rockies to the Pacific coast. Recently the area has become known for its many guest ranches and for being "cowboy country," so go and ride 'em, cowboy!

Try your luck panning for gold in Barkerville Provincial Park.

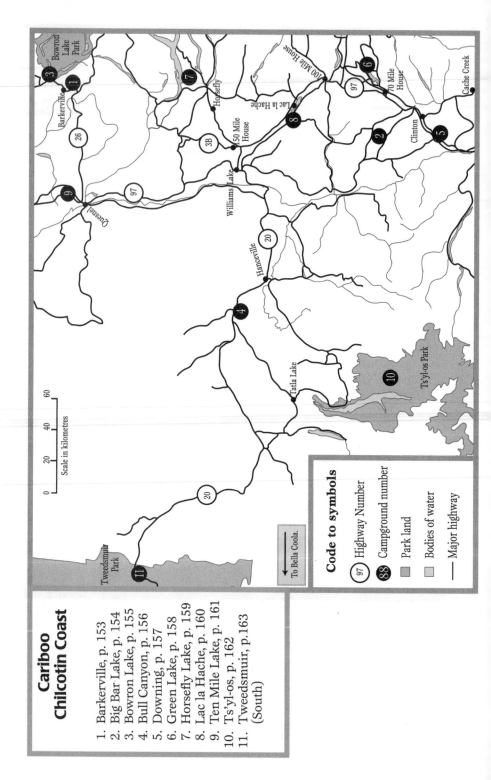

Cariboo Chilcotin Coast

1. Barkerville, p. 153
2. Big Bar Lake, p. 154
3. Bowron Lake, p. 155
4. Bull Canyon, p. 156
5. Downing, p. 157
6. Green Lake, p. 158
7. Horsefly Lake, p. 159
8. Lac la Hache, p. 160
9. Ten Mile Lake, p. 161
10. Ts'yl-os, p. 162
11. Tweedsmuir, p.163 (South)

Code to symbols

97   Highway Number

88   Campground number

   Park land

   Bodies of water

——   Major highway

Scale in kilometres

0   20   40   60

To Bella Coola.

BARKERVILLE

Location

For those wanting to visit the historic gold-rush town of Barkerville, this provincial park is an excellent base. Barkerville was once the largest town west of Chicago and north of San Francisco. The park is situated 89 kilometres east of Quesnel off a paved and scenic road (Highway 26) and within a few kilometres of Wells, where a comprehensive range of services can be found.

Facilities

There are 170 campsites at three locations within this provincial park. The two campgrounds nearest to the historic town are Lowhee, with 87 quite open and sparsely treed sites, and Government Hill, with 25 very open, small, functional sites that offer little privacy. A sani-station, showers, and flush toilets are available at Lowhee. I prefer the third campground, Forest Rose, with 56 sites that are larger and more private. There are a number of pull-through spots, and this location also has showers and flush toilets. All the campgrounds are wheelchair accessible. Reservations are accepted at Lowhee campground

Recreational activities

Although there are a few walking and hiking trails in the area and fish can be caught in the nearby rivers and lakes, the main draw is the reconstructed and faithfully restored 1870s gold-rush town. Barkerville houses over 40 pre-1900 buildings and provides an active interpretive program that successfully conveys the life of a gold-rush pioneer. Actors dressed in period costume wander the streets and interact with visitors, providing thousands of people every year with an enjoyable experience of a bygone era.

Additional information

BC Parks manages the three campgrounds in the area, but not the town of Barkerville. Although this provincial park is not the most beautiful B.C. has to offer, it provides easy access to an important element of the province's history. While staying here it is possible to try your luck at panning for gold. The journey from Highway 97 is scenic and there are a number of historical markers with information about the region's rich past. The nearby town of Wells has many buildings that date back to the early part of the century, and many are being slowly restored, making Wells an interesting community to explore.

Big Bar Lake

Location

The people who once walked the land around Big Bar Lake were Native hunters, cowboys, cattle rustlers, and gold prospectors. According to local legends, their ghosts can often be seen and heard, so be attentive when you stay here. Big Bar Lake is on the southern edge of the Fraser Plateau, a landscape formed millions of years ago by debris left by glaciers. Evidence of the ice age can be seen at the west of the lake, where gravel eskers remain; much of the topography owes its development to this geological period. To reach Big Bar Lake, drive 8 kilometres north of Clinton on Highway 97 and then take a gravel road west for 34 kilometres to the park itself. The nearest services can be found at 70 Mile House.

Facilities

The park has two campgrounds with a total of 46 spots. Fifteen sites are on the lakeshore, and the remaining ones are located in the forest above the lake. There is no sani-station and facilities are basic (fire pit, picnic tables, water, pit toilets).

Recreational activities

A naturalist's delight, the area is characterized by forests of lodgepole pine and spruce. It's an excellent habitat for wildlife, including mule deer, black bear, cougar, lynx, marmots, and snowshoe hares. Easy access to the lake means boating, swimming, and fishing are possible, and the lake is stocked annually with rainbow trout. A 2-kilometre trail provides excellent waterfowl and birdwatching, facilitated by a water control structure that was built by Ducks Unlimited to encourage nesting. Longer hikes are also possible. There is a children's playground in the day-use area.

Additional information

Big Bar Lake Park covers 332 hectares. This area of rolling hills was originally settled by the Salish First Nation. Today, it's known as ranch country, and trail rides can be arranged through the numerous guest ranches located in the area. These ranches operate year-round and also offer riding lessons, pack trips, gold-panning excursions, and skiing. The fact that snowshoe hares are found around Big Bar Lake should forewarn you that even early in the season, beautiful, warm days can develop into clear, cold nights. So act like a cowboy and remember the longjohns if you'll be camping under canvas.

Bowron Lake

Location

This world-renowned park's famous Bowron Lake canoe circuit covers over 116 kilometres around 11 different lakes, an excursion that takes seven to ten days. The campground is located 113 kilometres east of Quesnel, 18 kilometres past the end of Highway 26 on a gravel road. Two commercial resorts on Bowron Lake offer a selection of services, including food and camping supplies, while a full range can be found in Wells, 23 kilometres away.

Facilities

Twenty-five wooded, secluded campsites suitable for vehicles and tents are located near the park entrance. Facilities are basic (picnic tables, fire pit, water, and pit toilets), and reservations are accepted. Anyone planning to canoe the circuit can reserve by phoning 1-800-435-5622. There are 103 wilderness/walk-in sites in this park of 123,117 hectares.

Recreational activities

Near the campground it is possible to swim, canoe, and fish for Dolly Varden, rainbow trout, and lake char. Boat and canoe rentals are available nearby. Wildlife includes moose, deer, caribou, black and grizzly bears, and coyotes. There are bald and golden eagles, ospreys, and hawks, as well as a wealth of waterfowl and songbirds. The visitor centre has an informative video of the park that is well worth watching.

Additional information

To be able to fully appreciate the beauty of Bowron Lake Provincial Park, you should spend a week or more here. The park's reputation grows annually, both within North America and Europe; consequently, it is becoming increasingly difficult to get a reservation. Advance planning is required if you want to canoe the circuit. For those who just want to visit the area, it may be easier to stay at Barkerville. Wells is a neat little community where canoe-rental companies also operate, delivering canoes and kayaks to Bowron Lake for those interested in paddling the circuit or even spending a day paddling and enjoying the beauty of the area. This campground is a delight to stay in even if you're not a canoeing enthusiast.

Bull Canyon

Location

The campground at Bull Canyon Provincial Park is in a particularly beautiful setting on the Fraser Plateau by the Chilcotin River and is an excellent overnight stop for those travelling between Williams Lake and Bella Coola. This pleasantly treed 123-hectare park is found 6 kilometres west of Alexis Creek on Highway 20. The nearest full range of services is at Williams Lake, 122 kilometres away, but gas and basic food items can be purchased at Alexis Creek.

Facilities

Twenty basic campsites are located in an open camping area overlooking the Chilcotin River. Facilities are rudimentary (water, fire pit, picnic tables, pit toilets). There is no sani-station and water is obtained from a pump.

Recreational activities

The river is suitable for fishing, canoeing, and kayaking, as are the lakes in the area. There is good birdwatching and wildlife viewing, and a wonderful array of wildflowers can be found here at certain times of the year. In the winter, however, this region experiences very cold temperatures, sometimes as low as minus 50 degrees Celsius.

Additional information

While staying at another provincial park, I met a retired gentleman from Germany who had been holidaying by RV in B.C. for the past 10 years and claimed to have travelled on every road other than Highway 20; the year I talked with him, he was going to undertake that journey. One of the more pleasant aspects of staying in B.C. provincial parks is having the opportunity to meet people from all over the world, who often give advice on travelling in the province, including which campgrounds are their favourites. Bull Canyon was given provincial-park status in 1993. The Chilcotin River in the park is designated Class II, which means special fishing restrictions apply. Archaeological sites exist in the park.

DOWNING

Location

The scenery at this campground is quite lovely. Mount Bowman, which can be seen to the north, is, at 2,243 metres, the highest mountain in the Marble Range. Downing Park almost completely encircles Kelly Lake and is located 18 kilometres southwest of Clinton off Highway 97 on a paved road. Services are available at the quaint town of Clinton and include restaurants, post office, grocery store, pub, bakery, gas, and an excellent ice cream store.

Facilities

There are 18 campsites on an open grassy area with views of the lake. There is no sani-station, wheelchair accessibility is limited, and facilities are restricted to the basics (fire pit, picnic tables, water, pit toilets).

Recreational activities

Recreational activities include fishing for rainbow trout, hiking, sunbathing on the small beach, and swimming. There is no public boat launch. The nearby community of Clinton has a small museum and excellent ice cream bar and is a pleasant place to while away a few hours. It also boasts the largest log building in B.C., which is a hotel, pub, and restaurant. It offers a really good breakfast and is a pleasant place to play pool in the evening should you decide to escape from the tent for a while.

Additional information

Downing Park, which covers approximately 100 hectares, was donated by C. S. Downing in 1970, and his family still owns the adjoining property. BC Rail runs along one side of the lake, so you may be lulled to sleep by the sound of trains. If you don't have time to stay here, this site is an ideal spot to rest, picnic, and bathe and is particularly inviting to travellers who have taken the unpaved road between Pavilion, north of Lillooet, to Clinton. Drivers should be warned that the unpaved road between Downing Park and Pavilion is at times very steep and has hairpin bends that can be nerve-wracking. Pavilion has a beautiful little church well worth a photograph. The park is located on the land of the Shuswap First Nation.

GREEN LAKE

Location

The Green Lake area was recognized as bountiful by Canada's indigenous population many years ago; today, campers of every age continue to appreciate its bounty. Green Lake Provincial Park is situated among groves of aspen and lodgepole pine, 15 kilometres northeast of 70 Mile House off a paved road, adjacent to the 14-kilometre lake from which it takes its name. Three campgrounds are available on both sides of the lake. Information about the exact location of the campgrounds is available at the road junction 10 kilometres east of 70 Mile House. Services are available at 70 Mile House, and a store and restaurant are located at Emerald Bay.

Facilities

Each of Green Lake's three campgrounds has something different to offer. The most popular, Arrowhead, is relatively small and has 16 spots, all situated on the beachfront. (Probably the best family swimming is to be found here.) The second camping area is Emerald Bay. Like Arrowhead, Emerald Bay is situated on North Green Lake Road, but it has 51 sites, several of them on the water's edge. Sunset View campground has 54 sites and is on South Green Lake Road. It is usually the last campground to fill up. All spots are relatively private and situated amongst aspen trees. There is limited access for the disabled and a sani-station. Reservations are available at Sunset View and Emerald Bay campgrounds.

Recreational activities

Boredom should not be a problem here, as there are numerous activities to entertain every age group. The lake has moderately good fishing for rainbow trout and is restocked annually. There is a boat launch at Sunset View and water-skiing is allowed, but boats and skiers should keep well away from the swimming areas. There are children's playgrounds at both Emerald Bay and Sunset View and hiking trails leading from the park. The shallow west area of the lake attracts numerous waterfowl and migratory birds and is a magnet for ornithologists. Horseshoe pits are located at each campground, but you have to bring your own horseshoes.

Additional information

Green Lake is 14 kilometres long and averages 1.5 kilometres in width. It has minimum outflow, which enables a high buildup of algae and other microorganisms. This, along with the composition of the water itself, gives the lake its greenish tinge. BC Parks suggests using the park in the spring, when large rainbow trout spawning in the creeks attract large numbers of bald eagles, and in the fall, when the aspens turn fantastic shades of red and orange, each occurrence being quite beautiful for those with an appreciative eye (or a camera at hand).

HORSEFLY LAKE

Location

Horsefly Lake is a delightful 148-hectare park set amongst an assortment of trees including western hemlock, red cedar, various types of spruce, and subalpine fir. It is accessed by turning off Highway 97 at 150 Mile House and travelling 52 kilometres on paved road to Horsefly, then 13 kilometres along a good gravel road. Services at Horsefly include a café, grocery store, and gas station.

Facilities

The campground has 23 private sites in a coniferous forest and six walk-in sites. There is no sani-station and just the basic facilities (pit toilets, water, picnic tables, fire pit). Recently, coin-operated showers and laundry facilities were installed.

Recreational activities

Trails lead to Viewland Mountain and Eureka Park; details on these are available at the information board at the park entrance. Anglers visit the park to fish for rainbow trout in Horsefly Lake and in the smaller adjacent lakes. Canoeing and boating are possible, and there is a boat launch. The beach has a change room for swimmers. Just outside the community of Horsefly there are spawning channels, with a system of dikes for walking and viewing. The best viewing is in mid-September when the sockeye are spawning. A 1-kilometre trail to a lookout is a pleasant stroll. There is also a horseshoe pit and basketball hoop.

Additional information

This area was once a centre for gold mining. The first gold in the Cariboo was discovered here in 1859, and even today some people are drawn to the area in search of gold. Horsefly was originally called Harpers Camp after one of the early settlers, but was renamed by later pioneers when they discovered one of the area's drawbacks. Seriously, don't be put off by the name. Recent information supplied by the park's administration notes there are actually few biting flies in the park, and when I visited in June 2002, there were none (there were also no other campers). The park covers a considerable area, most of which is semi-wilderness and inaccessible to the visitor.

Lac la Hache

Location
Lac la Hache means "axe lake," and numerous stories have been advanced to explain how this name came to be. According to one, the name is based on the shape of the lake; another story holds that it gained its name when a trapper lost his axe through the frozen lake when trying to reach into the water. To local Native people, the lake is known as *Kumatakwa*, which means "chief" or "queen of the waters." Whatever name you prefer, this is a wonderful provincial park. It's situated 12 kilometres north of the community of Lac la Hache on Highway 97. Services can be found in Lac la Hache, and there is a small store opposite the campground, which has been open whenever I have visited or driven past, even out of season and in the most inclement weather.

Facilities
The facilities here are good and include 83 campsites, flush toilets, tap water, and a sani-station. All sites are large, relatively private, and set in open Douglas fir and aspen woodlands. Some sites are close to the road, however, and it is possible there to hear the traffic from busy Highway 97. You can reserve campsites at this park, but when I visited in August 2004, spaces were readily available.

Recreational activities
Small trails lead around the vicinity and allow you to see and walk remnants of the historic Cariboo Wagon Road. There is an adventure playground and a self-guided interpretive trail. The lake is popular for water-skiing, boating (there is a boat launch), and fishing. Rainbow trout, kokanee, and burbot can be caught. There is a pebbly beach and excellent swimming to be had in weed-free water. A change house and showers are located near the beach. (Be aware that the campground is across the road from the lake and that vehicles can and do travel at high speeds along this stretch of highway.) Three kilometres north of the campground is the Cariboo Nature Park, which is an excellent location for birdwatching. Lac la Hache also claims to be B.C.'s longest town. Unfortunately, with the exception of some small cafés and restaurants, I find there is little in town to attract the visitor.

Additional information
I am sentimentally attached to this park, as it was the first B.C. provincial park I ever stayed in. That time, and on the rare occasions I have had the opportunity to visit again, I have been impressed by the friendly and informative camp hosts. The lack of other provincial parks on Highway 97 coupled with this one's good family facilities make it a popular location. The small store is a magnet for children walking to and from the lake, and during the early evening pop and candy seem to be the store's most popular wares. Swimmer's itch can be a problem here in July and August—so be sure to shower after swimming—as can the dreaded mosquito.

Ten Mile Lake

Location

Looking for somewhere to camp with the children? Then look no further than Ten Mile Lake. Situated in an area of pine and aspen forest 11 kilometres north of Quesnel on Highway 97, this large campground is popular with both RVers and tenters, and it is particularly appealing for those with little ones to entertain. Services are available in Quesnel, and a small store in the park sells chips, pop, ice cream, bread, milk, etc.

Facilities

Excellent facilities exist at this location and include a sani-station, flush toilets, a pressure water system, showers (coin operated, a dollar for five minutes), and access for the disabled. There are two campgrounds offering 142 spaces. One is near the lakeshore and the other (which has slightly larger spots) is set among pine trees. There are a number of pull-through sites and reservations are accepted.

Recreational activities

As is common among the larger provincial parks, a variety of leisure pursuits for both old and young are available, but Ten Mile Lake is particularly attractive for those with children. A gently sloping beach gives swimmers easy access to the lake. There is a boat launch, and fishers can cast their lines for rainbow trout. An extensive 10-kilometre network of trails leads explorers through mixed forest; the trail to a huge beaver dam and lodge is only half a kilometre long, and well worth the effort. Mountain bikes can be ridden on a number of trails. Ducks Unlimited has placed nesting boxes in the area to encourage avian wildlife. For entertainment, there is a children's play area and horseshoe pits. When I visited the park, I discovered musical "jam sessions" taking place in the pavilion. Park hosts who welcome campers, answer questions, and give advice are available at this park.

Additional information

At the start of the 1900s, Ten Mile Lake was a milepost for the Pacific Great Eastern Railway, evidence of which can still be seen in the day-use area. This campground is a delight, as there are numerous activities within the park itself as well as in the immediate vicinity. The town of Quesnel, named after Jules Maurice Quesnelle, a member of Simon Fraser's exploration party, is only a short distance away. It is rich in pioneer gold-rush history and has a museum, historical markers, and, for those less interested in the past, a couple of golf courses. Ten Mile Lake is heavily used in winter for cross-country skiing and other outdoor activities. When we stayed here in 2004, we met Gord, the wonderful park administrator who told me that in summer, he works from 5:30 a.m. to 11:00 p.m. Keep it up, Gord, campers like me really appreciate your efforts!

Ts'yl-os

Location

Do not expect to explore much of Ts'yl-os (pronounced 'Sigh-loss') when you visit, as this provincial park, approximately 200 kilometres from Williams Lake, is roughly the size of Prince Edward Island (233,240 hectares) and for the most part is a vast undeveloped wilderness. There are huge mountains, glaciers, clear blue lakes, waterfalls, and meadows, many of which are completely inaccessible. Ts'yl-os is accessed either from Highway 20 at Hanceville by driving 150 kilometres of rough gravel road, or at Tatla Lake (which is the only option for those without a four-wheel-drive vehicle) for a 60-kilometre drive on another, although slightly better, rough gravel road. BC Parks actually recommends using four-wheel-drive vehicles in the park. Limited services are available at Tatla Lake.

Facilities

There are 15 campsites at the Nu Chugh Beniz site on the east side of the lake and eight at the Gwa Da Ts'ih at the north end. Both sites have water and pit toilets. BC Parks informed me that Gwa Da Ts'ih may be closed during the salmon season because of the threat of bears (mid-August to mid-September). Reservations aren't accepted, and despite its away-from-it-all location, the campgrounds do get full.

Recreational activities

The most popular recreational activity is fishing for lake and rainbow trout and Dolly Varden in the 50-kilometre-long Chilko Lake, which is the largest natural high-elevation freshwater lake in North America. Other activities include hiking and wildlife viewing. BC Parks does not recommend canoeing, as the lake is frequently prone to rough conditions. For those who really want to get a feel of the place, a five-day hiking trail leads through the Yohetta Valley, Spectrum Pass, and Tchaikazan Valley. (To make arrangements to undertake this route, contact Ts'yl-os Park Lodge and Adventures at 1-800-487-9567.) There are also horseback riding opportunities.

Additional Information

The park takes its name from the mountain, Mount Tatlow, which stands over 3,000 metres high. Legend tells how a man, his wife, and six children watch over the people of the Tsilhqot'in Nation and intervene when necessary. A number of private lodges operate in the area for those who want to experience the park in relative luxury.

TWEEDSMUIR (SOUTH)

Location

It is not just people who are attracted to this area. In salmon-spawning season, grizzly bears can often be seen fishing in the numerous streams that flow through Tweedsmuir, so be careful. Tweedsmuir, the largest park in the province, is named after the 15th Governor General of Canada, John Buchan, Baron Tweedsmuir of Elsfield, who travelled in the area in 1937 and was impressed by its beauty. The park is divided into north and south regions; only the south is accessible by road. This southern section is accessible from Highway 20 on the Williams Lake to Bella Coola road, 51 kilometres from Bella Coola, where services are found. Services such as gas, food, accommodation, restaurants, and canoe rentals can be obtained close to the park itself.

Facilities

There are two campgrounds accessible from Highway 20. Atnarko has 28 sites set amidst a grove of old-growth Douglas fir, 28 kilometres from the eastern entrance of the park. Fisheries Pool campground, located near to Stuie, 44 kilometres from the park's eastern entrance, has 14 high-density open sites. Facilities include a sani-station, picnic tables, fire pit, pump water, and pit toilets.

Recreational activities

As one would expect in a provincial park of this size, there is a wealth of things to see and do. The park is home to a wide variety of wildlife, including deer, moose, caribou, black and grizzly bears, wolf, and cougar. Rainbow trout, cutthroat trout, and Dolly Varden are found in the park's many lakes and streams, while the Atnarko and Dean rivers are spawning grounds for trout and salmon. Water sports including swimming (although the water is very cold), canoeing, and kayaking are possible. The area is known as one of B.C.'s most outstanding for alpine hiking, and numerous trails take backpacking enthusiasts into the spectacular mountain scenery. Rustic wilderness campsites exist along these trails. For the less energetic, a number of less arduous day hikes are also available. The park is also popular for horseback riding.

Additional information

With some superb scenery and varied terrain, the South Tweedsmuir area definitely is worthy of more than an overnight stop. The area is a real delight for those who enjoy backcountry exploration. Details of all the facilities and activities available can be obtained from the park's headquarters near the Atnarko River campground.

Naikoon Provincial Park on the Queen Charlotte Islands is a photographer's paradise.

Dress warmly when strolling the windswept beaches at Naikoon.

NORTHERN B.C.

Famous for excellent fishing and big game, the Northern B.C. region stretches from the Canadian Rockies to the Pacific Ocean and incorporates mountain ranges, deep valleys, majestic fjords, glaciers, dense forests, lakes, and rivers. In addition to its natural beauty, it is an area rich in First Nations history and culture. Although there are not a lot of large settlements, excellent wildlife viewing opportunities compensate for the lack of people, and travellers are blessed with an open road. Even at the peak of summer it is not unusual to drive for 30 minutes without seeing another vehicle.

The region includes campgrounds accessible from the minor roads leading off the Trans-Canada/Yellowhead Highway (Route 16) and from the highway itself west of McBride, all the way to and including the Queen Charlotte Islands. This region also encompasses Route 37, a gravel and paved road that goes from Kitimat to the road's junction with the Alaska Highway and into the Yukon. The area incorporates Highway 97 north of Prince George all the way to Dawson Creek and beyond, following the Alaska Highway up to the Yukon border. It also includes Highway 29 from Fort St. John to Tumbler Ridge and Highway 2. Go—travel and enjoy a region of B.C. that feels like it has been created with only you in mind.

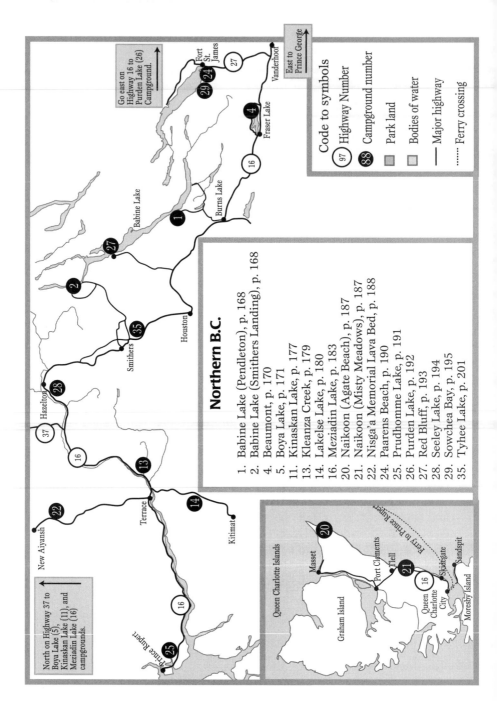

Go east on Highway 16 to Purden Lake (26) Campground. →

East to Prince George

Code to symbols

- 97 Highway Number
- 88 Campground number
- ▨ Park land
- ☐ Bodies of water
- —— Major highway
- ······ Ferry crossing

Northern B.C.

1. Babine Lake (Pendleton), p. 168
2. Babine Lake (Smithers Landing), p. 168
4. Beaumont, p. 170
5. Boya Lake, p. 171
11. Kinaskan Lake, p. 177
13. Kleanza Creek, p. 179
14. Lakelse Lake, p. 180
16. Meziadin Lake, p. 183
20. Naikoon (Agate Beach), p. 187
21. Naikoon (Misty Meadows), p. 187
22. Nisga'a Memorial Lava Bed, p. 188
24. Paarens Beach, p. 190
25. Prudhomme Lake, p. 191
26. Purden Lake, p. 192
27. Red Bluff, p. 193
28. Seeley Lake, p. 194
29. Sowchea Bay, p. 195
35. Tyhee Lake, p. 201

North on Highway 37 to Boya Lake (5), Kinaskan Lake (11), and Meziadin Lake (16) campgrounds. ←

Queen Charlotte Islands

Ferry to Prince Rupert

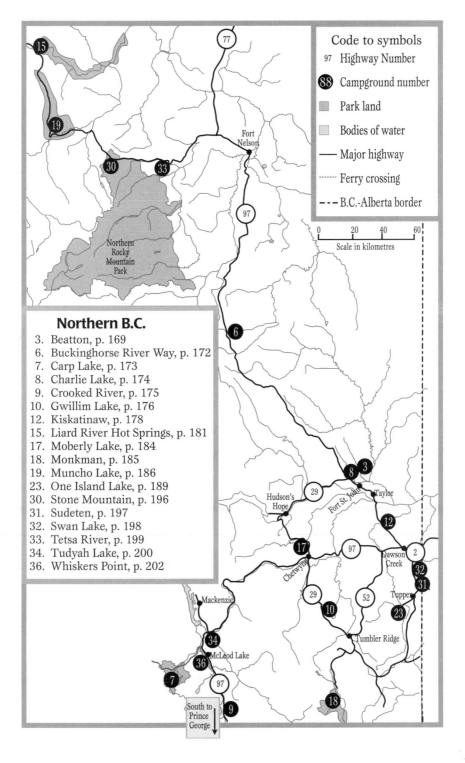

BABINE LAKE

Location

Campers who choose to stay on the banks of the longest natural lake in B.C. have the choice of three campgrounds. Two are in Babine Lake Provincial Park, while the third is in Red Bluff Provincial Park (described later). Babine Lake's two campgrounds are Pendleton Bay at the southern end of the lake and Smithers Landing to the north. To reach Pendleton Bay, turn off Highway 16 at Burns Lake and travel 35 kilometres on a gravel road. To reach Smithers Landing, turn off Highway 16 at Smithers and travel 35 kilometres north on a gravel road.

Facilities

The two camping locations provide 22 sites, 12 at Pendleton Bay, 10 at Smithers Landing. Facilities are rudimentary and consist of pit toilets, water access, picnic tables, and fire pits. Pendleton Bay also has group camping provisions.

Recreational activities

Both campgrounds have boat launches, and Babine Lake provides angling opportunities for rainbow trout and char. Because of the park's somewhat remote location, Babine Lake campers have an opportunity to see a wide array of wildlife, including moose and bear. Swimming and sailing can also be enjoyed here.

Additional information

The distance to these campgrounds and their limited facilities dissuade some people from coming to Babine Lake. But if you can undertake the drive, the scenery and tranquility are very rewarding. Bears frequent the area, so you must take all the necessary precautions for storing food (see Introduction). The community of Burns Lake, originally called Burnt Lake after a nearby fire, now serves as the major retail source of fishing equipment and supplies. Numerous commercial resorts that have been gradually developing in the area offer fishing, canoeing, horseback riding, and skiing excursions. The town of Smithers is larger and a little more geared toward tourists. It has a delightful main street to wander along that has restaurants, stores specializing in merchandise for enjoying the outdoors (including rainwear), and gift shops. The two campgrounds on Babine Lake are ideal for those who want to get away from it all and fish. If you prefer other recreational pursuits, you should try somewhere else.

BEATTON

Location

For the angler, Beatton Provincial Park boasts the best fishing for walleye in British Columbia. For those who do not fish, Beatton is a lovely camping retreat that has been enjoyed by campers for decades. Established on September 14, 1934, this is one of B.C.'s oldest provincial parks. Beatton is located 13 kilometres northwest of Fort St. John off Highway 97 on a paved road access. Limited services can be found on Highway 97, but a more comprehensive range is available at Fort St. John.

Facilities

Thirty-seven campsites are found here on the eastern side of Charlie Lake, set among poplar and spruce trees. Some spots are on the lakeside; all are large and very private. There is no sani-station, and facilities are restricted to the basics (fire pit, water, pit toilets, picnic tables). The park is wheelchair accessible and reservations are accepted.

Recreational activities

Aspen-lined trails lead from the campground to a 300-metre beach on the banks of Charlie Lake. Although it is possible to swim, the high algae content of the lake may make it unappealing. There is good fishing for northern pike and walleye. A boat launch is available, and hikers will enjoy the 15 kilometres of walking trails. Cycling is allowed, and there are 12 kilometres of cross-country ski trails available to mountain bikers in the summer months. In addition to over 40 species of birds and waterfowl, moose, mule, and white-tailed deer can be seen in the park. Beatton Provincial Park also has an adventure playground in the day-use area, a horseshoe pit, and a baseball field.

Additional information

The 440-hectare park is popular in both summer and winter. BC Parks produces literature on the winter recreational pursuits available at Beatton. During the colder months, visitors can go tobogganing, cross-country skiing, ice fishing for walleye and northern pike, or snowshoeing. The park provides "warm-up huts" (for someone from the south of the province, these conjure wonderful images). The site is relatively close to Charlie Lake park, and although both offer similar facilities, I prefer Beatton.

BEAUMONT

Location

This provincial park is located on Fraser Lake, west of Vanderhoof, 134 kilometres from Prince George on Highway 16. Early people named the area "Natleh" and used trails in this area to trade with the people of neighbouring settlements. During the last century, fur traders used the same trails. The remains of Fort Fraser, which was established by Simon Fraser in 1806, are situated within the park. Food, gas, and accommodation are available just a few kilometres away at Fort Fraser to the west of the park, or Fraser Lake to the east.

Facilities

There are 49 large campsites at this location. Some are quite open and exposed and others are situated amongst trees. The park has a sani-station, flush toilets, and facilities for the disabled. A number of campsites are available for reservation.

Recreational activities

A range of recreational activities is available, including swimming in a designated swimming area (a change house is located close to the beach), sunbathing, boating, and fishing for kokanee, char, burbot, rainbow trout, and sturgeon. Boaters should be aware that strong winds can easily transform the generally calm waters of Fraser Lake and cause a serious hazard. There are hiking trails, a children's play area, a volleyball net, and horseshoe pits. Information on the park's notice board informs campers that bears, wolves, and moose inhabit the area.

Additional information

The campground is surrounded by the Hazelton, Skeena, and Omineca mountains and is set amidst an abundance of willow, poplar, birch, spruce, and aspen trees. The site was originally chosen by early pioneers for its commanding view and because of the breezes that kept mosquitoes at bay. When I visited in late August, there were no signs of the dreaded bug; other campers, however, may tell a different story. Beaumont is an ideal location to stop for a picnic or take a stroll. The play area and beach make it particularly attractive for parents who have young children to entertain, with sandy shores and clear waters adjacent to a grassy picnic area. This campground never feels busy or crowded—an ideal place for every age group.

Boya Lake

Location
A stunningly beautiful sight awaits the camper who heads for Boya Lake. The lake is remarkable for its clarity and aquamarine colour, the result of light being reflected from the lake bottom, which is composed of silt and shell fragments. In this regard Boya is quite unlike the lakes found in many other B.C. provincial parks, and it is a wonderful lake to photograph. Boya Lake Provincial Park is situated 150 kilometres north of Dease Lake and 34 kilometres from the Cassiar–Alaska Highway junction, which is where the nearest services are located. Two kilometres of gravel road (rudimentary, when we visited in 2004) east of Highway 37 lead to the campground itself, which sits adjacent to Boya Lake and affords truly spectacular views of the Cassiar Mountains.

Facilities
The campground has 45 spaces of a variety of shapes and sizes. Some are close to the lake, some are just for tents, and most are private and set amongst black and white spruce trees. There is no sani-station and only basic facilities (picnic tables, pit toilets, water, fire pit).

Recreational activities
Because the lake is so clear, fishing here is not good for the serious angler, although my children had a ball catching small toe-biters. Fishing for grayling can be enjoyed a short distance away, in Dease River. A small, 1.5-kilometre lakeside trail is home to a multitude of songbirds and waterfowl attracted to the area by its topography, vegetation, and mild climate. Moose and beaver are found in the park, as are mountain goats and caribou. The lake is ideal for boating and swimming (although it's somewhat cold), and photographers will enjoy the mix of spectacular scenery and plant life. In 2004 a small children's play area (not built to code) had been constructed by the park administrators.

Additional information
The quietest campground on Route 37, Boya Lake also seems to have been personally cared for. For example, a box where campers can deposit and select reading material is placed at the entrance. I love these personal touches; they make camping special. In 2004 the four-day weather forecast was available on the campground notice board—again, a lovely touch. The main draw of this campground, though, is still the crystal-clear lake and stunning views. Boya Lake is a gorgeous place to camp.

Buckinghorse River Wayside

Location

Buckinghorse River Way campground is oriented very much toward overnighters travelling the Alaska Highway. When I stayed, I recognized a number of vehicles that I had passed or that had passed me during the course of the day. The campground is located 200 kilometres northwest of Fort St. John at Mile 173 of the highway. A restaurant and gas station are conveniently situated near the campground.

Facilities

There are 33 spots, all with a view of the river. They are quite closely positioned with no interspersed vegetation and have little privacy; the better ones are toward the end of the campground. Because the campsite is set a short distance away from the highway, noise is not a problem. All the basic amenities are provided (fire pit, water, pit toilets, picnic tables).

Recreational activities

This campground is primarily for travellers en route to other destinations, so there are limited recreational activities. The river provides an opportunity to fish for Arctic grayling, and if you take a short walk downstream you can find areas in which to swim. As is the case in many provincial parks in the north, it is possible to spend hours stargazing. The sky seems bigger in this area of the world. Peaceful evenings with only the noise of flowing waters and a crackling fire provide the ideal setting for this astronomical pursuit.

Additional information

BC Parks warns that both black bears and grizzly bears inhabit the area. Caution must be exercised. During the winter months, moose graze here. For those who do not wish to cook their own breakfast or dinner, there is a restaurant conveniently located across the road from the campground. Although the camping spots are close to each other, when I stayed (early September), there were only 10 spots taken, so it did not feel crowded. Buckinghorse River is one of the better roadside campgrounds.

CARP LAKE

Location

Why not camp on top of the world? At an elevation of 841 metres, Carp Lake is a picturesque island-dotted lake covering 19,000 hectares of the Nechako Plateau. It can be reached by turning off Highway 97 at McLeod Lake (where the nearest services can be found) and travelling along a gravel road for 32 kilometres. This gravel road is single lane and not particularly good in places. There are a number of tight corners, and the route is not suitable for cars or trailers during the spring breakup period.

Facilities

There are two campgrounds to choose from. The main one, Carp Lake, is situated at Kettle Bay and has 90 large sites that can accommodate most recreational vehicles. War Lake campground at the east end of War Lake has just 12 sites, and these are not suitable for larger vehicles. Wilderness camping is possible on three of the islands in Carp Lake. There is a sani-station, no wheelchair access, and the facilities are the basic ones found in parks of this type (fire pit, water, pit toilets, picnic tables).

Recreational activities

Visitors do not lack for something to do here. Two sandy beaches are located along the beach trail, a 20- and a 40-minute walk from the main campground. A boat launch is available, and powerboating and canoeing can be enjoyed on the lake. Fishing is good. Rainbow trout, burbot, and northern squawfish are plentiful in the lake, and a short trail leading to McLeod River takes anglers to an ideal fly-fishing spot. There are numerous trails for those who wish to hike or mountain bike. One of these trails follows a section of a route used long ago by the Carrier Nation between Fort McLeod and Fort Stewart. Wildlife viewing is good, and moose are often seen at the lake, especially at dawn and dusk. There is a playground and horseshoe pit.

Additional information

In his journal of 1806, Simon Fraser wrote of the Carrier people who visited the area to catch large quantities of fish similar to carp. The park is still a magnet for those who enjoy fishing. The summertime temperature at Carp Lake can be cool, averaging 12 to 18 degrees Celsius in July, and can drop considerably at night, so be sure to bring enough warm clothing.

CHARLIE LAKE

Location

Naturalists love this area for the chance of seeing a wide variety of wildlife, including white-tail and mule deer, black bear, beaver, moose, and an array of waterfowl. It is easy to see why this campground situated on the southwestern shore of Charlie Lake in the broad valley of the Peace River is popular with both locals and visitors. It is conveniently located 11 kilometres north of Fort St. John on the Alaska Highway at its junction with Highway 29. All services can be found at Fort St. John, while more limited facilities are available closer to the campground on Highway 97.

Facilities

The 58-site campground is set amongst a heavily treed deciduous forest of aspen, birch, alder, lodgepole pine, and spruce on the southwestern shore of the 13-kilometre Charlie Lake. A few sites are located close to the road, but most are not. The well-appointed sites are large and suitable for every type of recreational vehicle. Some have grassy areas for tents. The park is wheelchair accessible, has a sani-station, and accepts reservations.

Recreational activities

Fishing in summer and winter is popular here; northern pike and walleye inhabit the lake. BC Parks calls Charlie Lake the walleye "hot spot" of the province (what a claim to fame!). A 2-kilometre trail leads from the campground to the lake, where there is a boat launch. You can swim in the lake, although the high algae content of the water may put you off. The campground has a play area for children and a horseshoe pit. For those who choose activities away from the campground, an 18-hole golf course and country club can be found at Mile 54 of the Alaska Highway.

Additional information

Archaeological research in the area has revealed Aboriginal habitation dating back 10,000 years. If you succeed in obtaining a campsite away from the road, Charlie Lake is a delightful place to camp. A variety of berries grows in the vicinity, but remember, picking the vegetation in B.C. parks is prohibited.

CROOKED RIVER

Location

There are two kinds of campgrounds: those geared for overnight camping and those where you want to spend time relaxing and overdosing on B.C.'s wonderful scenery. Crooked River falls into the second category. This delightful spot is found in the Fraser Basin amid a forest of lodgepole pine interspersed with alder, birch, aspen, and spruce. It is situated 70 kilometres north of Prince George on Highway 97. The nearby community of Bear Lake provides accommodation, gas, and food (try the Grizzly Inn for a good breakfast).

Facilities

There are 90 spots of various sizes here. A tarmac approach road gives way to a gravel road upon entering the camping area. As with all B.C. provincial park campgrounds, a map at the entrance to the park illustrates where the largest sites are and where the pull-throughs are located. Some sites overlook the lake, and trees provide privacy and shade. There is a sani-station as well as flush and pit toilets and showers. The campground is accessible by wheelchair, and reservations are accepted. During the peak summer months, campers register at a booth upon entering the park.

Recreational activities

The park is on Bear Lake, which has two good sandy beaches ideal for children. Youngsters will also enjoy the adventure playground, volleyball net, and horseshoe pits. Fishing is not confined to Bear Lake. Nearby Squaw and Hart lakes and the river yield opportunities to catch rainbow and brook trout, Dolly Varden, Arctic grayling, and whitefish. There are a number of trails that take about an hour to complete, as well as longer hikes. The trail around Squaw Lake is great for viewing wildlife and birds—so the park information states. The Crooked River Trail follows the same route that early Canadian explorers such as Simon Fraser and Alexander Mackenzie took in the 19th century. It is possible to canoe and kayak, and boats can be rented in the park. With powerboats prohibited, paddlers are assured of a tranquil visit, as are windsurfers. Ornithologists may be rewarded by sightings of bald eagles and ospreys.

Additional information

BC Parks literature states that Crooked River was originally established to protect the area's attractive lakes and surrounding landscape. I stayed at this location in June one year and got completely bitten from head to toe by mosquitoes, despite the fact that I dressed in layers of clothing and stood over the fire pit. This experience tainted my opinion of the park, although I have not had the same problem on subsequent visits. Crooked River is a beautifully maintained campground that can be perfect if you choose a mosquito-free time.

Gwillim Lake

Location

Gwillim Lake is definitely a place to include on your camping itinerary. It is found in a stunning location in the Rocky Mountain foothills, with breathtaking mountain views, at an elevation of 765 metres and with 25 kilometres of shoreline. The park is located on Highway 29, a 40-minute drive from Chetwynd to the north and Tumbler Ridge to the south. Services are available in both of these centres.

Facilities

All the basic amenities found within B.C. parks are available at this 49-space park (fire pit, water, pit toilets, picnic tables), which is partially wheelchair accessible. The campsites are located in an area lightly forested with pines; many have commanding views of the lake and the Rocky Mountains. There are also numerous walk-in camping spots. No sani-station is provided.

Recreational activities

A perfectly wonderful time can be had here just reading, relaxing, and enjoying the beauty of B.C. Other leisure pursuits include fishing for a variety of fish. Arctic grayling, northern pike, Dolly Varden, burbot, and mountain whitefish can be caught, although anglers should be warned that the deep blue waters of the lake do not yield fantastic fish populations. Gwillim Lake has a boat launch and hiking trails, and the area is very good for observing wildlife, particularly deer and moose, which are most often spotted in the early morning. There is an adventure playground in the middle of the campground.

Additional information

This park provides some panoramic views of the Rocky Mountains. Above the northwestern shore, an open meadow creates a viewpoint of the western part of the lake. The park is beautiful to visit in the fall when the colours are spectacular, but it really is a gem of a location any time of the year. The town of Chetwynd is basically a forestry community with a relatively small population (3,000), yet it boasts a museum, a railway museum, and a trapper's cabin—all open to the public. The town also displays a number of interesting chainsaw sculptures by B.C. artists.

KINASKAN LAKE

Location

For those who have bounced along the gravel section of Highway 37, Kinaskan Lake is a gift from the gods. Set in the south Stikine Plateau and Iskut River Valley between the Skeena and Coast mountains is a remote lakeside campground. One hundred and eight kilometres north of the campground is the community of Dease Lake, the "jade capital of the world," which offers amenities such as gas, propane, food, lodging, and a huge SuperValu store that has everything the camper needs. More limited amenities are available at Iskut, approximately 40 minutes north of Kinaskan Lake.

Facilities

The campground is situated in a desirable location on the lake itself, and a large number of the 50 campsites are on the water's edge. The sites, which are quite large and surrounded by trees, afford more privacy than those of Kinaskan Lake's nearest competitor, Meziadin Lake, a three-hour drive away. There is no sani-station. Only the basic amenities exist (picnic tables, pit toilets, water, fire pit) but the views are wonderful.

Recreational activities

Lake fishing for rainbow trout here is reputed to be excellent. There is a boat launch, and swimming is possible, although the lake is prone to high winds and waves that can develop quite suddenly. This is the provincial park closest to Mount Edziza Park, which covers over 230,000 hectares. Mount Edziza Park and recreational area was established to conserve some spectacular volcanic landscapes, including lava flows, cinder fields, and basalt plateaus. The Mowdade Trail leads from Kinaskan Lake to the Coffee Crater area of Mount Edziza Park.

Additional information

This area also offers beautiful scenery and is a welcome rest for those who have endured the gravel section of Route 37. It was established in 1987, and its remote location makes it a magnet for fishermen, moose, black and grizzly bears, wolves, coyotes, mink, goats, and Stone sheep. Staying here lets campers see the B.C. featured in the tourist literature. I have only stopped to picnic here, which is a great pity, because it is a stunning location (if a little cool). There is little for children to do here, so I don't think I will be experiencing this campground fully for quite a few years.

KISKATINAW

Location

Kiskatinaw is located on the old Alaska Highway. Nearby, aromatic cottonwood trees on the edge of the river exude a delicate perfume in the summer (a delight for most people except those with allergies). Primarily used as an overnight camping spot, this 58-hectare provincial park is located on the northern Great Plains, 28 kilometres north of Dawson Creek. A 5-kilometre paved access road leads to the campground. Services can be found at Dawson Creek to the south or Taylor to the north.

Facilities

The camping facilities here are basic and include 28 spots secluded in groves of poplar and spruce. Pit toilets, water, fire pits, and picnic tables are all provided. There is no sani-station or access for the disabled.

Recreational activities

There are limited swimming possibilities, but tubing and wading are available, and the campground has swings, a sandbox, and a horseshoe pit. An archaeological site is also located in the park. From the campground you can walk to the scenic deep-walled canyon of the Kiskatinaw River and view the historic curved wooden bridge that was developed for the original Alaska Highway in 1942. The bridge was built in just nine months by a Canadian construction company and was the first curved wooden bridge built in Canada. It is 190 feet with a banked nine-degree curve to conform to the bend of the highway, and is the only curved, banked trestle bridge remainng in western Canada.

Additional information

The town of Dawson Creek was established in 1931 when the Northern Alberta Railway Line was extended to the area. It flourished in 1942 when American soldiers and engineers arrived to build the Alaska Highway. Dawson Creek is now home to the Mile Zero Post, a 3-metre-high marker that identifies mile zero of the Alaska Highway. The Dawson Creek Station Museum gives information on the construction of this famous road. Many tourists visit Dawson Creek to have their photographs taken at Mile Zero before heading north to the Yukon and Alaska.

KLEANZA CREEK

Location
At the beginning of the 20th century, the area in which this park is now situated was inhabited by gold seekers. Some years later, in 1934, a 180-gram nugget of gold was taken from the creek, and there may be some more gold left. This wonderful, peaceful campground is situated 19 kilometres east of Terrace on Highway 16, where all amenities can be found.

Facilities
The 32 large campsites in Kleanza Creek Provincial Park receive privacy and shade from the tall fir trees. Many sites overlook the clear bubbling waters of the creek itself—a calming sound to lull you to sleep. Facilities are basic (pit toilets, water, picnic tables, fire pit); there is limited wheelchair access and no sani-station. The area is great for a picnic stop even if you do not have a chance to camp.

Recreational activities
There is an exquisite, relaxing ambience here. Leisure pursuits include a 1-kilometre trail leading up to a viewpoint above the creek. There is also a smaller trail that runs alongside the creek. If you look hard, the remains of the Cassiar Hydraulic Mining Company's operations can be seen above the canyon. Pink salmon are often observed in the creek during the fall, and there is limited fishing potential. Swimming is possible in cool pools. The campground has a basketball hoop, horseshoe pit, and checkerboards. If it happens to be raining, visit Mount Layton Hot Pools or the Heritage Park Museum in Terrace.

Additional information
Kleanza means "gold" in the Tsimshian people's language. Maybe it is because I visited this park during good weather, but the campground lives in my memory as serene and quite beautiful. Even if you are not intending to stay the night, Kleanza Creek is a perfect place to stop and relax, for BC Parks has conveniently placed benches that face the tumbling creek. The only note of caution is that bears occasionally pass through the area. A highly recommended and exquisite place to camp.

Lakelse Lake

Location

For campers who crave hot springs and camping, this is the place to be. Lakelse Lake Provincial Park is just 3 kilometres from Mount Layton Hot Springs, and given the comprehensive range of facilities the park offers, it is a very attractive campsite for all ages. Set amidst majestic old-growth forest and located 24 kilometres south of Terrace on Highway 37, the park provides a beautiful haven for travellers. Services are available either in Terrace or in Kitimat, 33 kilometres to the south.

Facilities

Within a forest of cedar, hemlock, and Sitka spruce are 156 large, well-organized, and well-maintained campsites (gravel), catering to every type of recreational vehicle. A full range of facilities exists here, including a sani-station, flush toilets, and showers. There are facilities for the disabled, and reservations are accepted.

Recreational activities

The lake offers excellent canoeing, sailing, and water-skiing, and there is a paved boat launch. There are wonderful, golden, sandy beaches, picnic shelters, and a children's playground. A 45-minute interpretive trail that leads through the park allows closer exploration of the old-growth forest. In the lake and in the nearby Skeena and Kitimat rivers, anglers can catch steelhead, rainbow trout, Dolly Varden, and all five species of Pacific salmon. In August, hundreds of sockeye salmon can be seen in Williams Creek at the end of the park. The adjacent Mount Layton Hot Springs Resort has waterslides and mineral pools, as well as a café and pub. The resort offers a dollar off the admission price to those staying at Lakelse Lake Provincial Park. The town of Kitimat is a 30-minute drive away. Here, visitors can undertake a variety of activities, including tours of a salmon hatchery.

Additional information

Lakelse really is a delight to visit for the wide array of activities it provides both within the confines of its boundary and in the larger vicinity. It is easy to spend an entire day at the hot springs, and children (and some adults) will be entertained for hours on the waterslides and in the play areas. The older generation will also appreciate the therapeutic waters of the springs, which are open well into the evening. I spent a wonderful Wednesday evening in mid-September being one of just six people enjoying the hot springs. After our dip, we played darts and shuffleboard in the pub over food and drinks. Returning to the uncrowded campground at 10:00 p.m., I was met at the gate by a BC Parks representative ready to collect my camping fee and ensure that I was having a good time. (I felt rather like a teenager whose father has waited up for her to return home.)

Liard River Hot Springs

Location

For any B.C. parks enthusiast, Liard River Hot Springs must be one of the biggest jewels in the crown. It certainly ranks as one of the top B.C. parks for me. The only disadvantage this beautiful park has is that it is the most northerly in B.C. and therefore is not easily accessible to most of the people in the province. Those who do travel this far on the Alaska Highway will be amply rewarded for their efforts. Liard River Hot Springs is situated at Mile 496 of the highway, 20 kilometres north of Muncho Lake, and is the second-largest hot springs in Canada (after Banff). A restaurant and small shop are located across the road from the park itself; more comprehensive services can be found at Muncho Lake.

Facilities

At Liard Hot Springs there are 42 large, well-appointed, totally private campsites set among trees and suitable for every type of recreational vehicle. There is no sani-station. The park is wheelchair accessible. Facilities are restricted to the basic ones (fire pit, water, pit toilets, picnic tables). Reservations are accepted. There are no showers ... but here they aren't needed!

Recreational activities

The biggest attraction to this park is, of course, the hot springs, which have been beautifully maintained in their natural setting. A boardwalk takes campers from the campground to two bathing pools, one an 8- and the other

a 12-minute walk from the campground. Both have change rooms. At the larger Alpha pool, bathers can choose which area of the water to sit in and which temperature to endure (from an almost unbearable 53 degrees, where the waters emerge, to a far more comfortable heat). The smaller Beta circular pool is at a constant temperature (approximately 42 degrees). It is possible to swim here. In addition to these two mineral pools, a variety of fauna and flora unique to the region can be seen. More than 100 bird species visit the park. Moose and black bear also live here, and BC Parks literature states that over 28 species of mammals and 250 species of boreal forest plants are found here. A hanging garden at certain times of the year displays this vegetation, which is loved by photographers. There is a children's play area and horseshoe pit.

Additional information

The hot springs have been enjoyed by travellers for centuries. Many hundreds of years ago the Kaska people bathed here, and in 1835 the waters were charted by Robert Campbell, a Hudson's Bay Company factor. In 1942, the American army stationed in the area to build the Alaska Highway constructed the first boardwalk to the pools. I have extremely affectionate memories of the one time I was lucky enough to stay here. We went to the hot pools at 7:00 a.m., before most people were up. A thunderstorm was passing, and we sat in the hot waters watching the lightning as the cold rain fell into the warm pools. After this therapeutic experience, we took our clean, glowing bodies for breakfast in the funky little restaurant across the road from the campground—perfect start to the day. Liard River Hot Springs is well worth a visit, and unlike many of the commercially developed hot springs in the south of the province, it remains in a totally natural environment. This is one of my favourite provincial parks; however, in 1997 two people were killed here following a bear attack and the park received some negative publicity. Such incidents are rare but remind us of the potential hazards in camping outdoors. Liard River is one of the few provincial parks that stays open throughout the year.

MEZIADIN LAKE

Location

Ever seen a live bear trap? When I visited Meziadin Lake, a trap was kept at the park, although I was informed by the BC Parks attendant that it had not been used for a while. Meziadin Lake Provincial Park is in the Nass Basin and rewards the visitor with excellent views of the Coast Mountains. As you travel north from Highway 16, this is the first of three provincial park campgrounds on Route 37. It is just south of Meziadin Junction, the turnoff for Stewart, which has a shop, café, gas, and tourist information. A wider range of services can be found in Stewart, 50 kilometres away.

Facilities

The park has 60 open gravel campsites with little privacy; a few are situated on the lakeshore. There is no sani-station, and because of the prevalence of bears in the area, garbage has to be stored in a concrete structure on the site. All eating, cooking, and drinking utensils must be kept in a vehicle day and night. There is limited access for the disabled, and facilities are basic (picnic tables, fire pit, water, and pit toilets), but the views of the lake are breathtaking.

Recreational activities

Recreational pursuits include fishing for rainbow trout and Dolly Varden in the lake, swimming, and boating. Nearby at the Meziadin River, there is a salmon-counting fence. The road to Stewart provides a breathtaking view of more than 20 glaciers, including Bear Glacier, which comes right down to the road itself. Stewart and Hyder are early gold- and silver-mining communities located 65 kilometres from the campground. There are a number of pleasant cafés and restaurants in Stewart itself.

Additional information

This campground seems to be the busiest on Route 37 and is a popular place for those interested in fishing. Bears are particularly prevalent during the salmon-spawning season, so visiting Hyder at this time of year provides the best chance of seeing both black and grizzly bears. We spent an unforgettable three hours in Hyder watching grizzly bears fish salmon out of the stream, rip them apart, and devour them. It is an image I will never forget. When we got back to our tent at 8:00 p.m., it was dark and raining heavily. A couple in the neighbouring RV took pity on us and invited us in for the remains of their chicken stew and alcohol. We retired to our tent two very happy campers, and when we awoke the next morning our benefactors had already gone. We stayed again in August 2004, swam in the lake with a beaver, had brilliant weather, and saw grizzly and black bears. A truly wonderful location.

Moberly Lake

Location

This campground is well maintained and a real delight to stay in, but at certain times of the year watch out for black bears, which feed on the abundant berries growing in the area. Positioned in the valley of the Moberly River on the south shore of the lake, between the foothills of the Rocky Mountains and the northern Great Plains, Moberly Lake Provincial Park is reached by turning off Highway 29, 24 kilometres northeast of Chetwynd, and taking a good gravel road 3 kilometres. All services are available at Chetwynd, and more limited ones are at Moberly Lake, 11 kilometres from the campground.

Facilities

One hundred and nine large, private camping spots set in a forest of mature white spruce and aspen make this a desirable destination. Streams flow through the campground and a few sites overlook the lake. Grassy sites are available, and there is ample space for the longest RV. The park is accessible for the disabled. There is a sani-station and reservations are accepted.

Recreational activities

A number of activities can be undertaken both within the park itself and in the wider area. The park has a boat launch, and it is possible to fish for Dolly Varden, whitefish, and char. A developed beach and changing facilities make swimming a delight. There are a number of walks and trails. A children's play area has been built near the lake. A wealth of bird life can be observed in the area, including bald eagles, American kestrels, belted kingfishers, and common loons. In addition, two power dams are easily accessible. The W.A.C. Bennett Dam, one of the largest earth-filled dams in the world, houses a visitor centre with interpretive programs and a restaurant, and Peace Canyon Dam is also well worth a visit. Golfing is available nearby.

Additional information

Moberly Lake was named after Henry Moberly, a trader and trapper working for the Hudson's Bay Company, who settled on the shores of the lake in the mid-1800s. It has special significance to the Dunne-za First Nations, who knew it as "the lake that you could depend on" because it was a consistent food source. They also believed it had a hole in its bottom (or no bottom at all) and that a mythical creature lived in the lake—so be careful when you go swimming ...

Monkman

Location
Monkman Provincial Park is a wonderland of waterfalls and scenic lakes surrounded by the Hart Range of the central Rocky Mountains. Accessing it requires travelling 60 kilometres south from Tumbler Ridge on a gravel road, a trip that may deter some visitors. Services are located at Tumbler Ridge. The park was established in 1981; 22,000 hectares were added in 1999 to take in the Upper Fontiniko Creek Valley and Limestone Lakes area, which contains an area of old-growth spruce and unique geological forms.

Facilities
Forty-two camping spots are found here, a number of them less than 50 metres from the Murray River. All accommodate every type of recreational vehicle, and some have specific areas for tents. Backcountry campsites are also available. In addition to the basic amenities (water, picnic tables, pit toilets, fire pit), the park is wheelchair accessible.

Recreational activities
Among the biggest attractions here are the hiking trails. A short trail leads to the spectacular 60-metre Kinuseo Falls, where a viewing platform ensures excellent photographic opportunities. A 7-kilometre (one way) trail leads to the Murray River, where a suspension bridge can be crossed, taking hikers along the Mount Head Trail into the park's backcountry. This route follows the original one of the Monkman Pass Highway (see below). Powerboats can be launched on the Pine and Murray rivers, and below the falls the Murray River can be canoed. Fishing in the lakes and rivers yields trout, char, grayling, and whitefish. The campground has a playground and horseshoe pit.

Additional information
In 1922, Alex Monkman, a fur trader, farmer, and visionary, dreamed of creating a route to link the farms of the Peace River to Hansard (northeast of Prince George). In 1936 he formed the Monkman Pass Highway Association, and a year later work started. Unfortunately the project was plagued by a lack of funds, and in 1939, with the outbreak of the Second World War, all work ceased. Today the Monkman Lake Trail follows much of the original highway, while the pass bears the name of the pioneer whose dream was never realized. The area is very rich in wildlife, including grizzly and black bears, mountain goats, moose, and caribou.

Muncho Lake

Location

When travelling to or from Muncho Lake, stop near kilometre 650 (mile 474) of the Alaska Highway and look for Stone sheep licking the mineral rocks. The best time for viewing is at dawn or dusk in the late spring and early fall. Muncho Lake is an area of parkland covering over 200,000 hectares in the Terminal and Muskwa ranges of the Rocky Mountains, an area noted not only for its wildlife but also for its classic Rocky Mountain features, such as folded and vaulted rock and alluvial fans. Like many provincial parks along the route, it owes its existence to the Alaska Highway and is situated at Mile 422 of the Alaska Highway, 250 kilometres west of Fort Nelson. Services such as gas, restaurants, and small shops are located, quite unusually, in the park itself at Muncho Lake.

Facilities

Thirty campsites are positioned in two campgrounds on the shores of Muncho Lake. The more northerly campground, MacDonald, has 15 spots that are quite close to the road and provide little privacy. Strawberry Flats (my preference) is the more southerly location, with 15 spots that are more private, some on the waterfront. There is no sani-station, and facilities are basic in both campgrounds (fire pit, water, pit toilets, picnic tables).

Recreational activities

Muncho Lake, 12 kilometres long and over 2 kilometres wide in places, is typical Canadian Rocky Mountain scenery and offers endless photo opportunities. The 90-kilometre drive through the park itself on the Alaska Highway is often described as the most scenic stretch of the road. From here, campers can take hiking trails, go boating (there is a boat launch at MacDonald campground), and fish for trout, Arctic grayling, Dolly Varden, and whitefish. The park is also noted for its wildlife, including black bears, Stone sheep, mountain goats, caribou, deer, and wolf. The lake tends to be cold in the summer, so it is not a popular swimming location.

Additional information

Muncho Lake takes its name from the Kaskan language; it means "big lake." The jade-green colour comes from copper oxides leached in from the surrounding bedrock, coupled with the refraction of sunlight on sediments brought into the lake by glacial meltwater. The scenery here is spectacular, but the weather can be quite cool and windy.

NAIKOON

Location

Naikoon is a photographer's paradise: the atmospheric conditions and the variety of plants and wildlife yield fantastic photographic opportunities. The only provincial park with camping facilities on the Queen Charlotte Islands, Naikoon is found on Graham Island, the most northerly of the Charlottes. *Naikoon* means "long nose" and is derived from the Haida name *Nai-kun*. There are two campground facilities: Misty Meadows is located near Tlell, 42 kilometres north of Skidegate on Highway 16; Agate Beach is 26 kilometres northeast of Masset on a secondary road. Services are available in the communities of Port Clements, Tlell, Masset, and Queen Charlotte City.

Facilities

The 32 vehicle and 11 tent sites at Agate Beach are close to the ocean and somewhat exposed; in contrast, the 30 vehicle and 10 tent sites at Misty Meadows are situated under pine trees. Misty Meadows is my preference, as it is less exposed. When I was here, each campsite had a hanging basket full of flowers at its entrance—a wonderful touch. Neither site has sani-stations or flush toilets. There is limited access for the disabled at Agate Beach. Wilderness camping is permitted throughout the park, and three wilderness shelters are located along East Beach near the mouths of the Cape Ball and Oeanda rivers and at Fife Point.

Recreational activities

Numerous recreational activities can be enjoyed at this park, and visitors frequently spend a week or more. Trail details are available at the information board at the campground entrance. There are more than 60 kilometres of beach to explore, and it is possible to dig for clams and to swim. Coho salmon and steelhead can be caught in the Tlell River, and opportunities to see wildlife abound. The Tow Hill Ecological Reserve and Rose Spit Ecological Reserve have been established in the park to protect the flora and fauna. It is illegal to camp, fish, hunt, or use motorized vehicles in these ecological reserves.

Additional information

The Queen Charlottes, renowned for overcast skies and frequent fogs, are often referred to as "the misty islands." Campers should come well prepared for cold, damp conditions, even if they're planning to visit in July and stay in a vehicle. If you wear the correct gear, you can enjoy walking along deserted, windswept beaches, and there are excellent opportunities to see an assortment of sea mammals and birds—the Charlottes boast the second-highest eagle population in the world.

Nisga'a Memorial Lava Bed

Location
North of Terrace, you can camp adjacent to Canada's most recent volcanic eruption, which experts believe took place in the mid-1800s. The 17,683-hectare park is reached by turning off Highway 16 at Terrace, travelling 55 kilometres north, then driving another 55 kilometres of gravel road. There is a visitor centre and information kiosk at the entrance to the park. Full services can be found at Terrace; grocery stores, restaurants, and gas stations are in the four local Nisga'a villages. Watch for logging trucks, especially if you're driving the road on a weekday.

Facilities
This campground was established in 2000 beside Vetter Creek and has 16 vehicle/tent spaces. Features include flush and pit toilets, wheelchair accessibility, and picnic tables.

Recreational activities
This provincial park is jointly managed by BC Parks and the Nisga'a Tribal Council. The Council has established a visitor centre to illustrate its traditional culture, display aspects of the Nisga'a lifestyle, and to arrange tours of the volcano (a 2-kilometre guided walk is offered on weekends and on Wednesdays in the summer). In addition to seeing spectacular lava beds, you can sail here and fish for salmon and trout. There are two boat launches and limited hiking trails. Swimming is also possible at Lava Lake. More information on the park is available at the visitor centre in Terrace.

Additional information
It is believed the Tseax Cone erupted in 1775, destroying two Nisga'a villages and killing as many as 2,000 people. The lava flow rerouted the Nass River and dammed other waterways. Visitors now see a sparsely vegetated lava plain that stretches over 10 kilometres. Be warned: Walking on the lava beds, although fascinating, is hard on the feet, so be sure you have appropriate footwear. This is another fascinating and unique area of B.C. to visit.

One Island Lake

Location

I have not had the opportunity to visit this park, but all of the people I spoke to who know the area stressed the cleanliness of the lake's water (as does the literature on the park). Somewhat off the beaten track, this 62-hectare provincial park does not have the advantage of being a conveniently situated roadside campground for one night's stop, but it will guarantee a very quiet night's rest. One Island Lake Provincial Park is situated 72 kilometres south of Dawson Creek in the foothills of the Rockies. Turn off Highway 2 at Tupper, where services are available, and take an unpaved road 33 kilometres to the campground.

Facilities

There are 30 campsites available on the southeastern shore of the lake, some overlooking the lake. Services are limited to the basics (water, fire pit, picnic table, pit toilets).

Recreational activities

It is possible to swim, fish, and boat from this campground. There is a boat launch, and the fishing for rainbow and brook trout is reputed to be excellent, with fish reaching over two kilograms in size. The lake is stocked annually. This area is popular with residents of Dawson Creek in both winter and summer. There is a small playground, should you have children, or the urge to stop fishing and play yourself.

Additional information

The first settlers of Tupper were Sudetens (Czechoslovakians from the Czech/Polish border) who wanted to escape Hitler and who settled here in the 1930s. Information from BC Parks states that the park is representative of the Kiskatinaw Plateau ecosystem and that moose, white- and mule-tailed deer, and beaver are found here. BC Parks also implies there is little to do here other than fish. For those who do not like travelling on gravel roads, Swan Lake is a nearby alternative.

PAARENS BEACH

Location

Watch the sun go down and the stars come out from this lovely campground on the warm southern shores of Stuart Lake, one of the largest lakes in the province, amidst the Nechako Plateau Hills. It's a little less than two hours from Prince George on Highway 27. Approximately 15 minutes away by car is the historic town of Fort St. James, which has all amenities.

Facilities

The campground contains 36 sites; six are close to the water's edge. With a few exceptions, the sites are large, private, and partly wooded. There is a sani-station and pit toilets. Reservations are accepted.

Recreational activities

The site boasts a large sandy beach, and BC Parks has made the location ideal for families by providing a change house, picnic tables, play area for children complete with a large grassy area perfect for ball games, and a picnic shelter. Campers can fish for rainbow trout and lake char, and there is a concrete boat launch. Stuart Lake is also an ideal location for sailing and windsurfing, but users must be cautious because sudden strong winds can easily develop on this large lake. The National Historic Park at Fort St. James provides an account of pioneer life in the reconstructed Hudson's Bay Trading Post and is well worth a visit. Guides dressed in period costume give accounts and anecdotes of the lives of the early settlers. For the more energetic, the Mount Pope trail just north of the community takes hikers on a two- to four-hour hike (one way) up to the top of Mount Pope, where there are spectacular views of Stuart Lake.

Additional information

Swimmer's itch can be a problem here at certain times of the year. The site is very close to Sowchea Bay, where there are comparable facilities, and it is easy to travel between the two to determine which one provides the best camping location for your needs. Stuart Lake is part of the Stuart–Takla chain of lakes, which includes Stuart Lake (one of the largest in the province at 70 kilometres), Trembleur Lake, and Takla Lake (almost 90 kilometres long). With so much water, this is a fisher's nirvana.

PRUDHOMME LAKE

Location

Twenty kilometres east of Prince Rupert is the small coniferous-forested campground of Prudhomme Lake. Access from Highway 16 is immediate, and all amenities are available in Prince Rupert. By staying here, campers can enjoy the best of two provincial parks. Diane Lake Provincial Park is just 1 kilometre away, accessed by a 2.5-kilometre gravel road off Highway 16.

Facilities

Prudhomme Lake Provincial Park offers 24 spacious campsites adjacent to the lakefront. Large RVs may have difficulty accessing some of these spots. There is no sani-station or access for the disabled, and facilities are basic (picnic tables, pit toilets, pump, water, fire pit). Noise from passing traffic is easily audible, although the road is not that busy, especially at night.

Recreational activities

Although the activities at Prudhomme Lake are limited to fishing for steelhead, rainbow trout, and Dolly Varden, Diane Lake has a day-use area for swimming, canoeing, and sunbathing. From Diane Lake Park it is possible to take a trail that meanders through the coastal rain forest to Diane Creek Falls, or to fish in the creeks that run through the park. Prudhomme Lake is the provincial park campground closest to the town of Prince Rupert. There you can find many leisure activities, including the Museum of Northern B.C., a railway museum, a self-guided walking tour, and an 18-hole golf course. In the nearby community of Port Edward, you can visit one of the B.C. coast's oldest fishing canneries, which is being restored, and learn how commercial fishing developed in this area. This historical site is well worth a visit, although whenever I have visited, it has seemed in desperate need of a large cash injection to carry on the restoration process. Hopefully, cash will be forthcoming, as the cannery is a unique piece of B.C. history. Well worth a visit.

Additional information

In August and September it is possible to see salmon spawning in Diane Creek, and black-tailed deer also inhabit this area. From Prince Rupert, air charters to the Khutzeymateen, 45 kilometres north of the city, can be arranged. This area of 445 square kilometres is home to the largest known grizzly bear population on the B.C. coast and one of the largest in the world. I see Prudhomme Lake primarily as a convenient overnight camping location for visiting Prince Rupert.

Purden Lake

Location

Exceptional photographic opportunities can be had at Purden Lake, especially in the early morning as the mist slowly clears over the calm waters of the lake. Situated in the foothills of the Rockies, less than an hour's drive from Prince George on a paved road 2 kilometres off the Yellowhead Highway, this popular campground is regularly used by both Prince George residents and visitors. Services such as gas, propane, and restaurants are conveniently located less than 5 kilometres from the campground itself, although its proximity to Prince George means that with motorized transport, campers are within an hour's reach of every amenity.

Facilities

There are 78 campsites set amongst trees, a sani-station, but no showers or flush toilets. All sites are relatively private, and some sites are specifically set aside for tents. Facilities for the disabled are available.

Recreational activities

Amenities include an adventure playground, horseshoe pit, a sandy beach, and swimming area. Lakeside walking trails offer beautiful views of the surrounding area and make it possible to explore a variety of plant life. There is a concrete boat launch, and water-skiing is permitted on the lake. Anglers can fish for rainbow trout and burbot. The city of Prince George provides a wealth of things to see and do, including the Fraser–Fort George Regional Museum and the University of Northern British Columbia, which affords spectacular views of the surrounding landscape.

Additional information

With its beautiful setting amidst undulating, forested mountains and its easy access to Prince George, Purden Lake is one of the region's most popular parks. Consequently, it is regularly full on weekends, and reservations are not taken. The lakeside is very picturesque and its beauty quite haunting.

Red Bluff

Location

Like Babine Lake Provincial Park, Red Bluff is situated on Babine Lake, the longest natural freshwater lake in British Columbia. So-called because of the dramatic reddish cliffs under which it nestles, the park is a few kilometres south of the community of Granisle, a 45-minute drive on paved road from Highway 16. Granisle was a copper-mining town until the mine closed in 1992.

Facilities

The provincial park has 27 large sites set in woodland; a few overlook the lake, while others are more open and closer to the day-use area. There is an overflow camping area, but no sani-station or flush toilets, and facilities are the basic ones generally found in B.C. parks (picnic tables, fire pit, water, and pit toilets).

Recreational activities

Visitors can engage in numerous pursuits, including fishing (BC Parks information boasts that cutthroat trout weighing up to one kilogram, rainbow trout of up to six kilograms, and char up to 13 kilograms can be caught here), boating (there is a somewhat rudimentary boat launch), swimming, and hiking. A number of small trails provide the opportunity to see wildlife—black bear and moose being particularly abundant—and one trail overlooks the marsh area, where patience may be rewarded by a sighting of elusive birds and waterfowl. At certain times of the year, when the water level is high, the trail can be flooded. The Fulton River Salmon Hatchery just south of the park also deserves a visit for the opportunities it provides to view salmon leaping up a series of channels and to learn about salmon spawning.

Additional information

This area is known for its wildlife, and animals are regularly sighted along the quiet drive from Highway 16 to the park—we saw black bears when we drove here. The lake can become extremely rough, as high winds are easily whipped up in the area. I spent a somewhat uneasy night at this campground listening to the winds high in the trees and wondering which tree was going to crash down on top of me. My fears were totally unfounded.

Seeley Lake

Location

Seeley Lake is nestled amongst the Hazelton Mountains and located on Highway 16 just west of New Hazelton, where services are located. It's a quaint, picturesque campground with fantastic views. Bring your binoculars to this park, as you will be rewarded with sightings of bald eagles, ospreys, kingfishers, and a variety of waterfowl.

Facilities

The campground itself is relatively small, containing only 20 sites. All of them are large, private, and wooded. Approximately half of the sites overlook the lake. There is no sani-station, and only the basic amenities—pit toilets (with information signs posted inside them), water, fire pit, picnic tables.

Recreational activities

The fish that can be caught here include cutthroat and rainbow trout. Swimming is possible, although there is no beach. In May ice can still be found on the lake, so be prepared for a cold dip. A short trail starting at the day-use area leads to a wildlife-viewing platform. Seeley Lake is only a short drive from Old Hazelton, where the K'San have created an authentic reproduction of a Gitksan village, including six longhouses with painted fronts and totem poles, a gift shop, and a carving school. In the summer K'San dancers perform in the early evenings. For those interested in exploring First Nations culture, this campground is also an ideal base from which to travel to see the totem poles of Kispiox, Kitwanga, and Kitwancool.

Additional information

I stopped here early one morning as the mist was rising over the lake and the surrounding snow-topped mountains were just coming into view; the moment was magical. The only downside to the location is that the campsites are quite near the road; light sleepers may want earplugs. Seeley Lake is a lovely picnic spot for those who do not have the time to camp.

SOWCHEA BAY

Location

This region is full of historical accounts of early European settlers and is an educational and relaxing recreational destination. Sowchea Bay is a five-minute drive from Paarens Beach Provincial Park, 70 kilometres from the Yellowhead Highway. Its location and the recreational facilities it provides are similar to those available at Paarens Beach. Campers can easily travel between the two to decide which campground to choose. The nearest community is Fort St. James, 20 kilometres away.

Facilities

This is a particularly attractive campground with 30 sites. The advantage Sowchea Bay has over its nearby neighbour, Paarens Beach, is that all sites here are located on the water's edge. The sites are quite large, relatively private, and set amongst trees. There is no sani-station. Unlike Paarens Beach, Sowchea Bay campground does not accept reservations.

Recreational activities

Recreational activities are similar to Paarens Beach (but there are no day-use picnic facilities). They include fishing for rainbow trout, lake char, burbot, and kokanee in Stuart Lake; swimming, sunbathing, sailing, and boating (there is a boat launch at the site). In addition, the nearby community of Fort St. James provides historical interest as well as a nine-hole golf course with views of Stuart Lake.

Additional information

Although Paarens Beach seems to be the more popular site—perhaps because it has a day-use area and accepts reservations—I prefer Sowchea Bay. With all sites on the beach, it is an ideal place to watch the sun set while taking a stroll along the shoreline. The views are quite spectacular, and on a clear night the stargazing from this vantage point is awe-inspiring. Caution must be exercised by those who plan to windsurf or sail on the lake, as it is prone to high winds and waves. Swimmer's itch may also be a problem here.

Stone Mountain

Location
High in the breathtaking Rocky Mountain scenery at Mile 373 of the Alaska Highway, 130 kilometres west of Fort Nelson, is the Stone Mountain Provincial Park. This campground may be regarded as either bleak or beautiful, depending on the weather and your personal camping preferences. Full services are available at Fort Nelson, while gas and food can be obtained a few kilometres from the park.

Facilities
Stone Mountain campground is situated at the end of Summit Lake. The 28 campsites are very exposed and close to the road. They all overlook the lake to varying degrees but have little privacy, as there are no trees or vegetation. The facilities are basic (fire pit, picnic table, pit toilets, water).

Recreational activities
The area is known for five hiking and backcountry exploration trails, accessed from the campground. These trails take up to a week to complete and let you appreciate the full beauty of this area of the Rocky Mountains. Summit Lake has a boat launch. Fishing for trout and whitefish in the lake and for Arctic grayling and Dolly Varden in MacDonald Creek can be attempted. The fishing is not fantastic, however, as the waters are too cold to yield high fish populations. Mountaineering, horseback riding, photography, and wildlife observation are popular activities here.

Additional information
This campground, located on the highest part of the Alaska Highway (1,267 metres), is exposed to very cold winds. The scenery, characterized by steep, bare mountain slopes, is quite beautiful, and the location provides easy access into the backcountry. The park features erosion pillars and hoodoos, plus subalpine lakes and waterfalls. One of the primary attractions of the area is the abundant wildlife, but visitors have to be patient in order to see the hundreds of mountain caribou, Stone sheep, moose, mule deer, black and grizzly bear, lynx, wolverine, beaver, and elk that live in the region.

SUDETEN

Location

This provincial park should really be in Alberta, as the landscape of this five-hectare site is more typical of that province than of B.C. Situated on a prairie close to the Alberta border, the park is just south of Tomslake on Highway 2, 32 kilometres southeast of Dawson Creek, the nearest town with services.

Facilities

The exact number of camping spots available here seems to change from year to year. Information from BC Parks for 1997 said there were 12 spaces, in 1996 there were none, and in 2003 there were 14 spaces. Facilities include drinking water, six pit toilets, picnic tables, and fire pits. The campground is sandwiched between the old road and the new Highway 2, so expect traffic noise.

Recreational activities

This is primarily a roadside campground that boasts little in the way of entertainment. I have not stayed here, and when I spoke to a BC Parks representative for the Peace River Region, he said there was really no reason to stop at Sudeten and advised travellers to use Swan Lake instead, which has a boat launch, swimming, fishing, and hiking possibilities and is not adjacent to the road.

Additional information

The campground is named after a region in former Czechoslovakia that was the birthplace of the park's benefactor, Henriette Herold. The word Sudeten derives from the Sudetes, a mountain range on the Polish–Czechoslovakian border. As already noted, I have not visited this park, and when I tried to obtain information about it I got the impression that it did not rank high on anyone's list of campgrounds to stay in. With Swan Lake only 3 kilometres south, my advice has to be to stop here only if you have to.

SWAN LAKE

Location

Swan Lake is probably the B.C. provincial park closest to the Alberta border and has a colourful history spanning 50 years. The park is found 35 kilometres southeast of Dawson Creek on Highway 2, just north of Tupper, which has basic services. A 1-kilometre gravel road leads to the campground. A comprehensive range of services is available at Dawson Creek.

Facilities

Situated on the lakeside are 42 campsites catering to every type of recreational vehicle. There is no sani-station, limited access for the disabled, and facilities are restricted to the basic ones found in B.C. parks (fire pit, water, picnic tables, pit toilets).

Recreational activities

Water-oriented activities are favoured at this location and include swimming from an excellent beach, fishing for northern pike, walleye, and perch, and boating on the 5-kilometre Swan Lake. The park has a boat launch, and water-skiing and powerboats are permitted. Hikes around the lake can be taken from the campground. A large grassy area attracts day trippers and picnic parties, and there is an adventure playground for children as well as horseshoe pits and a baseball diamond. The vast number of waterfowl and migratory birds in the area makes this location attractive to the birding community.

Additional information

This 67-hectare park was established on June 19, 1918, making it B.C.'s third-oldest provincial park. It has a long record of hosting local social events and has been popular with residents of Dawson Creek for over 50 years. For those who are visiting the area for the first time, the town of Dawson Creek has an interesting pioneer village open during the summer months. It's worth a visit. Dawson Creek marks the start of the Alaska Highway: Mile 0. The lake itself has an average depth of two metres and is only three metres at its deepest point.

Tetsa River

Location

If you crave fishing and tranquility, this provincial park is for you. In the foothills of the Rocky Mountains at the meeting of the Tetsa River and Mill Creek, 100 kilometres west of Fort Nelson, is Tetsa River Provincial Park. The site is reached by travelling for a kilometre along a gravel road off Highway 97. The nearest full range of services can be found at Fort Nelson.

Facilities

Twenty-five large, private campsites are available at this park. Approximately half overlook the water and many have grassed areas ideal for tents. All offer privacy and are set amid a poplar forest. There is no sani-station and only partial wheelchair accessibility. Facilities are confined to the basics (fire pit, water, pit toilets, picnic tables).

Recreational activities

The main leisure pursuit at this 115-hectare campground is fishing. Because the Tetsa River flows into the Arctic drainage system, fishing for Arctic grayling can be very rewarding in the spring and fall. It is also possible to take short strolls up and down the water's edge on a pebble beach to explore the potential of other fishing locations. Observing wildlife is also possible, as moose, elk, white-tailed deer, and mule deer all frequent the park, as do black and grizzly bears.

Additional information

Tetsa River is one of the better B.C. parks geared primarily to overnight camping along the Alaska Highway because it offers private, treed camping accommodation away from the main road. If you manage to stay in a site overlooking the river and enjoy fishing, this is a very quiet, beautiful location. When I visited, there were several people horseback riding in the area. The nearest large town is Fort Nelson. It is home of the Japanese-owned Canadian Chopstick Manufacturing Company Limited, the world's largest chopstick manufacturer, producing 9 million pairs daily. The town also has a small museum close to the visitor centre, which features information on the construction of the Alaska Highway.

TUDYAH LAKE

Location

A 56-hectare lakeside campground with a creek running through it awaits the weary traveller here. Tudyah Lake is 9 kilometres north of McLeod Lake on Highway 97, and 157 kilometres from Prince George. Situated at the southern end of Tudyah Lake in the Rocky Mountains between the Hart Range and the Nechako Plateau, it is close to the junction of Highway 97 and Highway 39. The nearest services at McLeod Lake.

Facilities

Primarily used for overnight stays, this campground has a somewhat unusual feel to it because the 36 sites are set in an open grassy meadow, creating a pleasant, pastoral atmosphere. The spots are far enough apart to ensure privacy. There is no sani-station or access for the disabled, but the park includes all the basic amenities (fire pit, water, pit toilets, picnic tables).

Recreational activities

It is possible to swim (be aware of a sharp drop-off), kayak, canoe, and fish at Tudyah Lake and nearby Parsnip River. Anglers will enjoy fishing for rainbow trout, Dolly Varden, and whitefish. There is a large group-camping facility and day-use area with horseshoe pit. The town of Mackenzie, 30 minutes away, has a nine-hole golf course and a recreation centre, and is on the banks of Williston Lake, a prime fishing spot.

Additional information

The community of Mackenzie is at the south end of Williston Lake, a huge artificial reservoir that supplies water to the hydroelectric plant at Hudson's Hope. The town is named after Alexander Mackenzie, the first white person to reach Canada's Pacific coast by land. The town of Mackenzie was built in 1965 in an area of wilderness as a centre for pulp, paper, and lumber manufacturing. It has a museum and is home to the world's largest tree crusher, seen on Mackenzie Boulevard, but it has little architecturally to recommend it.

TYHEE LAKE

Location

Children adore Tyhee Lake for the beach; anglers love it for the fish; birdwatchers are attracted to the abundant bird life. But for me, Tyhee Lake's biggest attraction is its friendly atmosphere. While it is the convention in B.C. parks to say hello and pass the time of day with other campers, when I stayed at Tyhee everyone I met was happy and communicative. Consequently, Tyhee Lake lives in my memory as being the "very friendly provincial park." This family-oriented campground is a 15-minute drive east of Smithers on Highway 16 near the quaint settlement of Telkwa in the Buckley River Valley. All amenities are therefore available within a few kilometres of the park itself.

Facilities

This is a large and well-maintained campground set amidst an aspen forest on the side of Tyhee (Maclure) Lake. There are 59 campsites—a few with views over the lake—accommodating every kind of recreational vehicle as well as tents. In addition to all the usual facilities found in a provincial park, Tyhee Lake has a sani-station, flush toilets, and showers, making it one of the more expensive parks in which to stay. Reservations are accepted.

Recreational activities

A beautiful 200-metre beach provides access for swimming; there is a boat launch, and water-skiing is permitted on the lake. Horseshoes and volleyball are also available, as is a play area for children. Fish found in the lake include cutthroat and stocked rainbow trout, while smaller anglers can go for minnows and sticklebacks. An interpretive trail has been developed around the campground, and there is a marsh-viewing platform where you may see loons, rednecked grebes, ruffed grouse, and beavers. In addition, the communities of Smithers and Telkwa are pleasant places to visit. Smithers houses a wildlife museum that displays a variety of big game animals, and Telkwa dates back to the 1860s. Both are lovely places to wander around in and they have good restaurants if you're getting bored of camping fodder.

Additional information

The large, well-kept, day-use area and the park's proximity to the Yellowhead Highway make this an ideal picnic spot if you do not have time to spend the night. But with the many activities available here, Tyhee Lake is a perfect place for family camping, and visitors usually spend more than one night. For me, the only downsides of Tyhee were the jet-skiers who dominated the lake in the early evening hours when I last stayed, and the Canada Goose droppings on the grass.

WHISKERS POINT

Location

Rich in Aboriginal and pioneer history and situated on a sand spit jutting out into McLeod Lake, Whiskers Point is an extremely agreeable location. The campground is 130 kilometres north of Prince George on Highway 97, and about 10 kilometres south of McLeod Lake, where gas, food, and lodging are available.

Facilities

Sixty-nine large, secluded sites set in a mature forest of spruce and pine are available. A number of the campsites overlook the lake or are near Whiskers Creek, which runs through the campground. There is a sani-station, flush and pit toilets, and access for the disabled. Reservations are not accepted.

Recreational activities

McLeod Lake provides a wealth of opportunity for the water enthusiast. There is a good beach and excellent swimming; a concrete boat launch has been built, and windsurfing, canoeing, kayaking, and fishing for Dolly Varden and rainbow trout are all possible. (A note of caution: The lake is subject to suddenly changing conditions, and strong winds can easily transform the calm water.) For younger ones, a children's play area, horseshoes, and volleyball are available, and there's also a 20-minute nature trail. The area is rich in bird and animal life.

Additional information

I have visited Whiskers Point but have not spent a night here. All the literature on this area stresses the beauty of the sunsets visible from the park, which have been described as "spectacular," "magnificent," and "breathtaking" in various publications. The community of McLeod Lake, 10 kilometres north of the campground, was first established in 1805 by Simon Fraser (Fort McLeod) and was the first trading post and first European settlement west of the Rocky Mountains at the time. Although the Hart Highway (Highway 97) was developed in the 20th century, the local Sekani people had a system of trails developed in this region long before the Europeans came. You will not be disappointed in your decision to stay here.

CAMPING TOURS

This chapter provides suggestions for one-, two-, and three-week camping excursions that start in the Lower Mainland and are designed for individuals travelling in a vehicle. The itineraries can easily be amended to accommodate personal preferences or alternative starting points. They act only as a recommendation for those who may not be too sure where they want to journey.

The following pages offer brief synopses of the roads on which it is necessary to travel for each of the recommended tours. These routes should be reviewed in conjunction with a detailed map of the province. A good map is required for anyone planning to camp and travel in B.C. An excellent resource is the *British Columbia Recreational Atlas*. It provides comprehensive, detailed coverage of all the major and minor routes as well as data on places, area boundaries, trails, elevations, lakes, and parks. The fact that it is an 8- by-11-inch bound mapbook and not a four- by four-foot paper map makes it easy to read in the car (and to keep in one piece). In addition, Tourism British Columbia sells the *Road Map and Parks Guide*, which lists all provincial parks. Both of these publications are readily available at tourist information offices, and the *British Columbia Recreational Atlas* is carried in most bookstores.

For those who may be uncomfortable travelling without a reservation, each of the one-, two-, and three-week tours has a "fully reserved" option whereby it is possible to book all camping spots in advance. Anyone planning to vacation in the popular peak months of July and August without reserving ahead must be prepared to encounter some full campgrounds and to plan alternative options.

7-Day Tours

Trip 1: A Little Taste of the Province

Although this route may appear to involve a lot of driving, for those who like this pastime it provides a good introduction to the province, a taste of some of the best scenery, and an introduction to lovely provincial parks. It is a circular tour whereby you travel north to Highway 97, east on the Yellowhead Highway, south on Highway 93, then west on Highway 3.

Day 1 Lac la Hache	Day 5 Moyie Lake
Day 2 Mount Robson	Day 6 Kettle River
Day 3 Mount Robson	Day 7 Manning
Day 4 Kootenay National	

Trip 2: Fully Reserved

This itinerary gives campers the security of knowing they have accommodation in some of the most popular campgrounds in the province. It also includes campgrounds on B.C.'s mainland, Vancouver Island, and the Gulf Islands, making for wonderful ferry trips and minimal driving. After staying at Alice Lake, travel south on the Sea to Sky Highway to Horseshoe Bay and take the ferry to Vancouver Island. From there it is just a short drive north on Highway 19 to Rathtrevor. After Rathtrevor, head south on Highway 19 to Goldstream. To reach Montague Harbour, take a ferry from Swartz Bay to Galiano Island.

Day 1 Alice Lake	Day 5 Goldstream
Day 2 Alice Lake	Day 6 Montague Harbour
Day 3 Rathtrevor	Day 7 Montague Harbour
Day 4 Rathtrevor	

Swim in weed-free water at Lac la Hache Provincial Park.

Trip 3: Vancouver Island and Gulf Island Hopping

Like Trip 2, this route has some fantastic ferry rides through breathtaking scenery. Montague Harbour on Galiano Island is reached by ferry from Tsawwassen. Ruckle Provincial Park is on Saltspring Island, and ferries regularly leave from Galiano for Saltspring. From Saltspring, take a ferry to Swartz Bay; from here, the Island Highway leads to Goldstream and Bamberton. French Beach is located south of Victoria on Highway 14.

Day 1	Montague Harbour	Day 5	Goldstream
Day 2	Montague Harbour	Day 6	Bamberton
Day 3	Ruckle	Day 7	French Beach
Day 4	Ruckle		

Trip 4: Circle Tour

This easy-to-complete circular excursion takes campers to some of the less popular camping spots that are easily accessible from Vancouver. It involves driving north on the lovely Sea to Sky Highway, Highway 99, then (after a brief diversion off Route 99 to access Birkenhead) continuing along this scenic road until it joins Highway 97 just north of Cache Creek. At Cache Creek, take Highway 97C south to Kentucky-Alleyne. From this campground, travel south on Highway 5A to Highway 3, which leads through Manning Park and back to Vancouver.

Day 1	Nairn Falls	Day 5	Manning
Day 2	Birkenhead	Day 6	Manning
Day 3	Birkenhead	Day 7	Emory Creek
Day 4	Kentucky-Alleyne		

Kentucky-Alleyne Provincial Park is great for a weekend getaway.

Trip 5: The Hiker's Dream

This trip is designed for driving one day and hiking the next. To reach Wells Gray, take the Coquihalla toll road (Highway 5) to Kamloops and then head north on Highway 5. After Wells Gray, continue north on Highway 5 until it joins the Yellowhead Highway (Route 16). After Mount Robson take the fantastic Glacier Highway (Highway 93) south until it meets Highway 1. (Pray for good weather, as the views along this road are some of the best in the province.) Travelling west on Highway 1 leads to Yoho. From Yoho it is possible to drive back to Vancouver in a day. For those who want a less hurried route, take Highway 1 as far as Kamloops, then Highway 97 until it reaches Highway 99, and return to Vancouver on Highway 99.

Day 1	Wells Gray	Day 5	Yoho National
Day 2	Wells Gray	Day 6	Yoho National
Day 3	Mount Robson	Day 7	Marble Canyon
Day 4	Mount Robson		

The spectacular beauty of Mount Robson Provincial Park draws outdoor enthusiasts from all over the world.

14-Day Tours

Trip 1: A Bigger Taste of the Province

Two weeks is a good length of time in which to tour the province. On the first day of this itinerary, there is little driving involved, as campers head out of Vancouver on Highway 7 to nearby Golden Ears. After camping here, continue on Highway 7 to the junction with Highway 3, then take Highway 3 through Manning. After Manning, travel north to Kamloops. A number of routes are available, and my advice to those who have time is to take 5A. From Kamloops take Route 5 north until it joins the Yellowhead Highway. Travel east on the Yellowhead until you get to Highway 93, which can be taken all the way south to Kootenay National Park and beyond, where it meets Route 95. From Jimsmith Lake, follow Highway 3, then 3A to Crawford Bay and the longest free ferry ride in the world over Kootenay Lake, where Highway 31 leads to Kootenay Lake Provincial Park. Travel south from Kootenay Lake on Highway 3A and take a slow drive along Route 3 back to Vancouver.

Day 1	Golden Ears		Day 8	Mount Robson
Day 2	Manning		Day 9	Kootenay National
Day 3	Manning		Day 10	Kootenay National
Day 4	Paul Lake		Day 11	Jimsmith Lake
Day 5	Wells Gray		Day 12	Kootenay Lake
Day 6	Wells Gray		Day 13	Kootenay Lake
Day 7	Mount Robson		Day 14	Haynes Point

Wells Gray is one of the best provincial parks in B.C.

Trip 2: Fully Reserved

This excursion uses campgrounds that accept reservations. It is also recommended for families (who may want to cut out the northern excursion to Mount Robson). Travel along Route 7 to Highway 3 and continue east on this road until it meets Highway 97. At this juncture you will adopt a northward direction as the road leads toward Highway 1, dividing into highways 97, 97A, and 97B. All these roads lead in the direction of Shuswap Lake. After staying at Shuswap Lake, drive west on Highway 1 to Kamloops, then take Route 5 north to the Yellowhead Highway and the stunningly beautiful Mount Robson Park. Retrace your steps to Kamloops and follow Highway 5A south to Princeton and the nearby Otter Lake Provincial Park. The return journey to Vancouver leads you back on Highway 3.

Day 1	Golden Ears	Day 8	Shuswap Lake
Day 2	Golden Ears	Day 9	Shuswap Lake
Day 3	Manning	Day 10	Shuswap Lake
Day 4	Manning	Day 11	Mount Robson
Day 5	Okanagan Lake	Day 12	Mount Robson
Day 6	Okanagan Lake	Day 13	Mount Robson
Day 7	Okanagan Lake	Day 14	Otter Lake

Trip 3: Vancouver Island and Gulf Island Hopping

On this lovely relaxed excursion you will be able to explore the camping highlights of Vancouver Island and the Gulf Islands. Montague Harbour on Galiano Island is reached by ferry from Tsawwassen. Ruckle Provincial Park is on Saltspring Island, and ferries regularly leave from Galiano for Saltspring. From Saltspring, a ferry is needed to reach South Pender Island, the last Gulf Island on the tour. Travel from South Pender Island to Vancouver Island's Swartz Bay by ferry. At Swartz Bay the Island Highway (Route 1) leads south to Victoria. Take Highway 14 from Victoria to French Beach. From here the return journey north starts, taking the Island Highway as far as Parksville. At Parksville head west on Highway 4, which meanders across Vancouver Island to Pacific Rim National Park (the road from Port Alberni to the coast is particularly lovely). Return along this road to the Island Highway and continue north until reaching Campbell River. Highway 28 just north of this town leads into Strathcona Park. Return to the Lower Mainland by ferry from Nanaimo.

Day 1	Montague Harbour	Day 8	Bamberton
Day 2	Montague Harbour	Day 9	Pacific Rim National
Day 3	Ruckle	Day 10	Pacific Rim National
Day 4	Ruckle	Day 11	Miracle Beach
Day 5	Prior Centennial	Day 12	Strathcona
Day 6	French Beach	Day 13	Strathcona
Day 7	Goldstream	Day 14	Strathcona

The small town of Coalmont, near Otter Lake Provincial Park, sprang to life during the gold rush.

Trip 4: Fruit and Freedom–The Okanagan and the Kootenays

This tour offers the best of both worlds, as the somewhat more populated Okanagan is visited in conjunction with the calm, quiet Kootenays. The quickest way to reach Bear Creek, the first provincial park campground on the itinerary, is to take Highway 1 out of Vancouver, then the Coquihalla Highway ($10.00 toll road) to Merritt. Turn east on Highway 97C toward Kelowna. Alternatively, do not use the Coquihalla and instead take Highway 3 through Manning Park to Princeton, then Highway 5A north to Highway 97. From Bear Creek drive north to Vernon, then take Highway 6 east to reach Mabel Lake. After staying here, continue on Route 6 until the turnoff for Highway 31A; this leads to Highway 31 and, by travelling north, to Kootenay Lake Provincial Park. From Kootenay Lake, travel south on Highway 31 and take Highway 3A to find Kokanee Creek. A short drive south on this road leads to Champion Lakes. Continue the journey back to Vancouver on Route 3, stopping at Otter Lake and Manning or any other campgrounds that look appealing.

Day 1	Bear Creek	Day 8	Kootenay Lake
Day 2	Bear Creek	Day 9	Kokanee Creek
Day 3	Mabel Lake	Day 10	Champion Lakes
Day 4	Mabel Lake	Day 11	Otter Lake
Day 5	Rosebery	Day 12	Otter Lake
Day 6	Kootenay Lake	Day 13	Manning
Day 7	Kootenay Lake	Day 14	Manning

Trip 5: Rocky Mountains and the National Parks

It is easily possible to visit all the "big" parks in a two-week period, but a few long days in the car are required. This tour has been designed to compensate for these long travelling times with two- or three-night stays in some of the largest and most spectacular parks in the province. To take this excursion, leave Vancouver on Highway 1, then take the Coquihalla toll road ($10.00) north to Kamloops. Just north of Kamloops is Paul Lake Provincial Park. The following day, take Route 1 east to Glacier, and a few days later proceed the few kilometres to Yoho. From Yoho, Route 1 east leads to Lake Louise. From here, head south on Highway 93 to Kootenay National Park. Continue on Route 93, which eventually becomes Route 95 and joins Route 3. Route 3 travels across the bottom of the province and leads back to Vancouver.

Day 1	Paul Lake	Day 8	Kootenay National
Day 2	Glacier National	Day 9	Kootenay National
Day 3	Glacier National	Day 10	Kootenay National
Day 4	Glacier National	Day 11	Moyie Lake
Day 5	Yoho National	Day 12	Kettle River
Day 6	Yoho National	Day 13	Manning
Day 7	Yoho National	Day 14	Manning

Beautiful Manning Provincial Park is a hiker's paradise.

21-Day Tours

Trip 1: A Huge Taste of the Province

If travelling hundreds of kilometres a day across remote regions of the province is a pleasurable notion for you, then this trip will be a dream. I undertook it in 19 days, which required a lot of driving—over 6,500 kilometres. It is not an itinerary for those who suffer from motion sickness. Leave Vancouver on the Sea to Sky Highway and travel north on what I believe to be one of the best roads in the world. When the road joins Highway 97, head north. This is the Gold Rush Trail. After stopping at Lac la Hache and turning east just north of Quesnel on Highway 26 to visit Barkerville, return to Highway 97 and proceed north to Prince George. From here, turn west on the Yellowhead Highway (Highway 16). At Terrace, take Highway 97 south to Lakelse, after which you should be prepared to travel north on this highway as far as the Alaska Highway. (Be warned that sections of Highway 37 between Dease Lake and Meziadin Junction are unpaved.) Upon reaching the Alaska Highway, head south as far as Dawson Creek, then drive Route 97 south to Prince George. At Prince George, travel east on the Yellowhead Highway to Mount Robson, then head south on Highway 5 to Kamloops. At Kamloops you can choose between returning to Vancouver via the fast Coquihalla toll road or on Route 1 through the Fraser Canyon.

Day	1	Lac la Hache
Day	2	Barkerville
Day	3	Barkerville
Day	4	Sowchea Bay
Day	5	Sowchea Bay
Day	6	Tyhee Lake
Day	7	Lakelse Lake
Day	8	Lakelse Lake
Day	9	Meziadin Lake
Day	10	Boya Lake
Day	11	Liard River
Day	12	Liard River
Day	13	Buckinghorse
Day	14	Gwillim Lake
Day	15	Bear Lake
Day	16	Bear Lake
Day	17	Mount Robson
Day	18	Mount Robson
Day	19	Wells Gray
Day	20	Wells Gray
Day	21	Emory Creek

Magnificent falls tumble down a canyon in Wells Gray Provincial Park.

Trip 2: Fully Reserved

Many of the campgrounds in this itinerary are ideal for families and those who require more comfort when camping (for example, flush toilets, showers, and nearby stores). To reach the first campground, leave Vancouver on Highway 1, then take Highway 3, which meanders through Manning Park. Carry on travelling east along this road until you reach Osoyoos, then head north on Highway 97. After staying at Ellison, continue the journey north on Highway 97 until you reach the junction with Highway 1. At this stage, head west as far as Kamloops, then north on Highway 5 to the Yellowhead Highway and Mount Robson. After Mount Robson take the Yellowhead Highway west to Prince George, then travel north on Highway 97 as far as Crooked River. On the next stage of the journey, take Route 97 south as far as the turn for Highway 99, just north of Cache Creek. You will spend the final days of your camping tour driving the wonderful Highway 99 back to Vancouver.

Day 1	Manning	Day 12	Crooked River
Day 2	Manning	Day 13	Crooked River
Day 3	Manning	Day 14	Barkerville
Day 4	Okanagan Lake	Day 15	Barkerville
Day 5	Okanagan Lake	Day 16	Green Lake
Day 6	Okanagan Lake	Day 17	Green Lake
Day 7	Ellison	Day 18	Green Lake
Day 8	Ellison	Day 19	Alice Lake
Day 9	Mount Robson	Day 20	Alice Lake
Day 10	Mount Robson	Day 21	Porteau Cove
Day 11	Mount Robson		

Trip 3: Vancouver Island, Gulf Islands, and the Sunshine Coast

An easy-to-complete excursion featuring beautiful drives and numerous ferry rides, this route follows the same one detailed in the 14-day Vancouver Island and Gulf Island Hopping. However, upon leaving Strathcona Provincial Park, travellers extend their tour by taking the ferry from Courtenay to Powell River on the Sunshine Coast. From here, drive south on Highway 101. To end the journey, take the ferry back to Horseshoe Bay.

Day 1	Montague Harbour	Day 12	Pacific Rim National
Day 2	Montague Harbour	Day 13	Pacific Rim National
Day 3	Ruckle	Day 14	Miracle Beach
Day 4	Ruckle	Day 15	Strathcona
Day 5	Prior Centennial	Day 16	Strathcona
Day 6	Goldstream	Day 17	Strathcona
Day 7	Goldstream	Day 18	Saltery Bay
Day 8	Bamberton	Day 19	Saltery Bay
Day 9	Rathtrevor	Day 20	Porpoise Cove
Day 10	Rathtrevor	Day 21	Porpoise Cove
Day 11	Pacific Rim National		

Trip 4: Gold Rush Trail and the Queen Charlotte Islands

The drawback of this trip is that the same roads have to be travelled on the outbound and the return journeys. However, the scenery en route to the Queen Charlotte Islands more than compensates. From Vancouver, go north via highways 99 and 97 as far as Prince George, then follow the Yellowhead Highway west to Prince Rupert, where a six-hour ferry ride connects you to the Queen Charlottes. Retrace the same route back until just north of Cache Creek, where you can continue on the Gold Rush Trail south (Highway 1) down the Fraser Canyon all the way to Hope.

Day 1 Lac la Hache
Day 2 Sowchea
Day 3 Sowchea
Day 4 Tyhee Lake
Day 5 Lakelse Lake
Day 6 Lakelse Lake
Day 7 Lakelse Lake
Day 8 Prudhomme Lake
Day 9 Naikoon
Day 10 Naikoon
Day 11 Naikoon

Day 12 Naikoon
Day 13 Naikoon
Day 14 Kleanza Creek
Day 15 Beaumont
Day 16 Beaumont
Day 17 Barkerville
Day 18 Barkerville
Day 19 Green Lake
Day 20 Green Lake
Day 21 Emory Creek

Wilderness camping is permitted throughout Naikoon Provincial Park.

Trip 5: The Rockies and the Larger Provincial and National Parks

Designed with the hiker in mind, this itinerary features some of the best parks in the province. On leaving Vancouver, take either Route 1 or the quieter Route 7 to the junction of Highway 3. Travel east on Highway 3 to Castlegar, then take Route 3A to Kokanee Creek. Continue along Route 3A until it rejoins Highway 3, which turns into Highway 95 and leads north into Kootenay National Park. Next, travel north to meet Highway 1, then drive west through Yoho and Glacier national parks as far as Kamloops, where Route 5 leads north to the Yellowhead Highway and Mount Robson. From Mount Robson head west on Route 16 (the Yellowhead Highway) as far as Prince George and then south on Highway 97, back through the Fraser Canyon to Vancouver.

Day	1	Manning	Day	12	Glacier National
Day	2	Manning	Day	13	Glacier National
Day	3	Kokanee Creek	Day	14	Wells Gray
Day	4	Kokanee Creek	Day	15	Wells Gray
Day	5	Moyie Lake	Day	16	Wells Gray
Day	6	Kootenay National	Day	17	Mount Robson
Day	7	Kootenay National	Day	18	Mount Robson
Day	8	Kootenay National	Day	19	Mount Robson
Day	9	Yoho National	Day	20	Ten Mile Lake
Day	10	Yoho National	Day	21	Downing
Day	11	Yoho National			

Camper Rentals

At least 26 RV rental companies detail their equipment offerings and locations at
http://www.travel.bc.ca

Another website to check out is:
http://www.camping.bc.ca

SPECIAL-INTEREST CAMPING RECOMMENDATIONS

Although many campers are content to explore any and every provincial park they find, a number of people have special needs or interests and seek camping facilities that reflect these desires. Following are a few suggestions on campgrounds that accommodate specific passions.

Hiking
Numerous provincial and national parks offer superb hiking. Most offer easier walking but among the best known for varied hikes are the larger parks such as Wells Gray, Manning, Robson, Strathcona, Yoho, Glacier, Kootenay National, Pacific Rim, Garibaldi, and Tweedsmuir. It is easy to spend a week or more at any of these locations and only begin to touch the beauty they offer.

Diving
A number of campgrounds in B.C. offer diving potential, but the most notable ones in the province are Saltery Bay on the Sunshine Coast (home to Canada's first underwater statue), Ellison in the Okanagan (the country's only freshwater dive park), and Porteau Cove, less than one hour's drive from Vancouver.

Canoeing
With an abundance of lakes, the possibilities for canoeing and kayaking are almost limitless. Those who seek serious paddling excursions should consider Champion Lakes, Wells Gray, Bowron Lakes, Okeover Arm (with access to Desolation Sound), and Harrison Lake (Sasquatch Provincial Park). For remote, less-known canoeing adventures, try Moose Valley or Nazko lakes in the Cariboo region of the province. BC Parks offers canoes for rent at a number of provincial parks, including Manning and Golden Ears.

Hot Springs

What better way to relax than in warm mineral pools? Kootenay National Park, Whiteswan Lake, Lakelse, and Liard River all offer this idyllic environment.

Gold Panning

Although the potential to pan for gold exists in many provincial parks, Emory Creek, Barkerville, Kettle River, and the aptly named Goldpan are particularly renowned. (For information on gold panning around Barkerville, read *Goldpanning in the Cariboo* by Jim Lewis and Charles Hart.)

Horseback Riding

Relive that pioneer spirit by exploring B.C. parks on horseback. For those who do not have their own horse, facilities adjacent to South Tweedsmuir, Yoho, Golden Ears, and Manning provincial parks have horses available to ride on specifically designated trails in these parks.

Birdwatching

You can spot wonderful birdlife almost everywhere in B.C., but the parks that are particularly notable include Vaseux Lake, Manning, Kootenay National, Big Bar Lake, Green Lake, Inkaneep, and Naikoon. All are excellent destinations for the ornithologist.

Fishing

All anglers have their own tips for the best fishing location, and BC Parks provides thousands of spots to choose from. Of particular note are Elk Falls, Stake-McConnell Lakes, Stamp Falls, Wells Gray, Charlie Lake, and Kokanee Creek. Numerous books offer advice, including a reasonably priced publication entitled *The Best Fishing Adventures in Southwestern B.C.*, which is packed with useful advice for those planning to fish in this area of the province.

A site by the water is the perfect place for a picnic.

Strathcona Provincial Park is located in a majestic wilderness of old-growth forests.

Island
Island campgrounds are magical, since the neigbouring communities (if any) on these quiet oases are quite distinct from those of the mainland. Montague Harbour, Newcastle Island, Fillongley, Ruckle, and Sidney Spit all provide fantastic camping retreats.

Beach
Tidal beaches are attractive to every age group, but especially to children. The following recommended sites are on Vancouver Island: French Beach, Pacific Rim, Rathtrevor Beach, Miracle Beach, and Sidney Spit. There are also spectacular lakeside beaches to be enjoyed at Gordon Bay, Haynes Point, Okanagan Lake, and Birkenhead.

Family
BC Parks has a number of family-oriented campgrounds that have activities for children, playgrounds, and numerous safe environments to explore. Alice Lake, Kokanee Creek, Rathtrevor Beach, Shuswap Lake, Tyhee, Porpoise Bay, Cultus Lake, Golden Ears, and Wasa are but a few of these fantastic locations.

Useful Information

Web sites
Several informative web sites give details about camping in B.C.
www.travel.bc.ca
www.camping.bc.ca
www.discovercamping.ca
www.canadianrockies.com
www.britishcolumbia.com
www.bcadventure.com
www.spacesfornature.org
www.bcparks.ca
www.gocampingbc.com

The following web sites give details of the various regions of the province:
www.islands.bc.ca
www.coastandmountains.com
www.ThompsonOkanagan.com
www.BCRockies.com
www.LandWithoutLimits.com
www.NorthernBCtravel.com
www.visitcariboo.com
www.totabc.com

For information on RV rentals in B.C., see:
www.travel.bc.ca

Maps
Tourism British Columbia produces a map of the province that details all of the provincial parks and summarizes their facilities. It is available from most tourist offices and bookstores (*Road Map and Parks Guide*, $2.95). *The British Columbia Recreational Atlas*, 4th edition, is an excellent 140-page guide of the province, featuring colour maps scaled at 1 centimetre to 36 kilometres (1 inch to 9.5 miles).

GROUP
CAMPING

I celebrated my 40th birthday in 2001 in a number of different ways, one of which was renting the group campsite at Alice Lake Provincial Park for a weekend party with my friends and their families. Twenty adults and 16 children between the ages of eight months and nine years spent two days—one wonderful and one wet—at this location. We hiked, swam, made trips to Tim Hortons, fished, babysat each others' children, played games, sang, cooked and, of course, drank and told tales into the wee hours. A fantastic, economical time was had by all.

The group-camping facilities at British Columbia provincial parks can be reserved by any group. The minimum fee is roughly the same as if you were to reserve five regular camping sites; above that number, the park administrator will charge an extra fee. A minimum number of nights is often required.

The campgrounds listed below offer group-camping facilities that are generally located a short distance away from the main campground (ideal if you have noisy kids) and usually have their own washrooms, water supplies, and cooking pits. Some parks situate their group-camping section in a large open area, while others provide a more private location.

The B.C. government contracts out the day-to-day operation and administration of BC Parks to private park administrators, who are responsible for booking groups at these facilities. To reserve a group site, contact the park administrator to find out what they offer and how many they can accommodate. Information on group camping can be found at: http://wlapwww.gov.bc.ca/bcparks/reserve/group.htm.

For information on park facility operators, go to:
http:wlapwww.gov.bc.ca/bcparks/operations/pfo_weblist_2004.pdf

The first list that follows is of campgrounds that offer group camping and their administrative areas. The next list provides contact information for each administrative area. Call these administrators to make reservations.

CAMPGROUNDS WITH GROUP FACILITIES

The Islands

Campground	Administrative Area
Loveland Bay	Vancouver Island–North Island
Miracle Beach	Vancouver Island–North Island
Strathcona	Vancouver Island–North Island
Newcastle Island	Vancouver Island–Mid Island
Rathtrevor Beach	Vancouver Island–Mid Island
Sproat Lake	Vancouver Island–Mid Island
Cowichan River	Vancouver Island–South Island
French Beach	Vancouver Island–South Island
Goldstream	Vancouver Island–South Island
Gordon Bay	Vancouver Island–South Island
Montague Harbour	Vancouver Island–South Gulf Islands
Ruckle Park	Vancouver Island–South Gulf Islands
Sidney Spit Marine	Vancouver Island–South Gulf Islands

Vancouver Coast and Mountains

Campground	Administrative Area
Alice Lake	Lower Mainland–Sea to Sky Corridor
Nairn Falls	Lower Mainland–Sea to Sky Corridor
Porpoise Bay	Lower Mainland–Sunshine Coast
Golden Ears	Lower Mainland–Lower Mainland
Cultus Lake	Lower Mainland–Fraser Valley
Sasquatch	Lower Mainland–Fraser Valley
Skagit Valley	Lower Mainland–Fraser Valley

Thompson Okanagan

Campground	Administrative Area
Manning	Okanagan–Manning/Similkameen
Shuswap Lake	Thompson–Shuswap
Paul Lake	Thompson–Kamloops
Conkle Lake	Okanagan–Boundary
Kentucky–Alleyne	Thompson–Merritt
Kettle River	Okanagan–Boundary
Fintry	Okanagan–North Okanagan
Mabel Lake	Okanagan–North Okanagan

B.C. Rockies

Campground	Administrative Area
Mount Robson	Omineca–Mount Robson
Syringa	Kootenay–West & Northwest
Kikomun Creek	Kootenary–East
Kokanee Creek	Kootenay–West & Northwest

Cariboo Chilcotin Coast

Campground	Administrative Area
Green Lake	Cariboo–Cariboo
Barkerville	Cariboo–Cariboo

Northern B.C.

Campground	Administrative Area
Tyhee Lake	Skeena–Smithers/Highway 37
Tudyah Lake	Omineca–Highways 16, 27, & 97

BRITISH COLUMBIA PROVINCIAL PARK ADMINISTRATORS

The Islands

Vancouver Island–North Island and Mid Island Park Facility Operator

Osprey Parks Operations Ltd.
Box 373
Parksville, BC V9G 2G5
Tel: 250-248-9460
Fax: 250-248-4119
Email: opo@telus.net
Web site: www.ospreyparks.com

For Newcastle Island:

Park facility operator: Snuneymuxw First Nation
Tel: 250-754-7893
Fax: 250-754-7894
Email: admin@newcastleisland.ca

Vancouver Island–South Island Park Facility Operator

R.L.C. Enterprize Ltd.
PO Box 272
Malahat, BC V0R 2L0
Tel: 250-474-1336
Fax: 250-478-0376
Email: rlcenterprize@shaw.ca
Web site: www.vislandcamping.com

Vancouver Island–South Gulf Islands Park Facility Operator

K2 Park Services Ltd.
S3 C9
Galiano Island, BC V0N 1P0
Tel: 250-539-2115
Fax: 250-539-2115
Email: K2parks@cablelan.net

Vancouver Coast and Mountains
Lower Mainland–Fraser Valley Park Facility Operator
Gibson Pass Resort
Suite 21, 46244 Airport Road
Chilliwack, BC V2P 1A5
Tel: 604-795-6169
Email: camping@manningpark.com

Lower Mainland–Lower Mainland Park Facility Operator
Gibson Pass Resort Inc.
Suite 21, 46244 Airport Road
Chilliwack, BC V2P 1A5
Tel: 604-795-6169
E-mail: camping@manningpark.com

Lower Mainland–Sea to Sky Corridor Park Facility Operator
Sea to Sky Park Services Ltd.
1700 Mount Seymour Road
North Vancouver, BC V7G 1L3
Tel: 604-986-9371
Email: seatosky@mountseymour.com

Lower Mainland–Sunshine Coast Park Facility Operator
Swens Contracting
Tel: 604-885-3714
Email: swens@uniserve.com

Thompson Okanagan
Okanagan–Boundary Park Facility Operator
Kayola Contracting Ltd.
4611 Towgood Road.
Oyama, BC V4H 2B4
Tel: 250-766-1835
Fax: 250-548-3468
Email: kayola2@telus.net

Okanagan–Manning/Similkameen Park Facility Operator
Gibson Pass Resort Inc.
Tel: 604-795-6169
E-mail: camping@manningpark.com

Okanagan–North Okanagan Park Facility Operator
Quality Recreation Ltd.
1905-28 Crescent
Vernon, BC V1T 1V1
Tel: 250-545-1560 (April–October: 250-260-3590)
Email: quality-recreation@shaw.ca

Thompson–Kamloops Park Facility Operator
Larry Carrell
Brandywine Environmental Management Ltd.
4111 Cameron Rd.
Kamloops, BC V2H 1K9
Tel: 250-554-0720

Thompson–Merritt Park Facility Operator
L. Lemkay and D. Baker
Site 1, Comp 0, Box A, RR1
Naramata, BC V0H 1N0
Tel: 250-315-2771
Email: blparks@telus.net

Thompson–Shuswap Park Facility Operator
PEG Ltd.
Box 24108
Scotch Creek, BC V0E 3L0
Tel: 250-955-0861
Fax: 250-955-0862
Email: peg@mail.ocis.net

B.C. Rockies
Kootenay–East Park Facility Operator
Kootenay Forest Resources
Tel: 250-427-5452
Fax: 250-427-5452

Kootenay–West and North West Park Facility Operator
For Syringa:
West Kootenay Park Management Inc.
Box 2569
Revelstoke, BC V0E 2S0
Tel: 250-837-5734
Fax: 250-837-5764
Email: information@westkootenayparks.com
Web site: www.westkootenayparks.com

For Kokanee Creek:
West Kootenay Park Management Inc.
1224 Stanley Street
Nelson, BC V1L 1P8
Tel: 250-825-4212
Fax: 250-825-4293
Email: information@westkootenayparks.com
Or: kokaneecreek@westkootenayparks.com
Web site: www.westkootenayparks.com

Omineca–Mount Robson Park Facility Operator
Mariah Recreation Management Services
10355 Robson Road
Prince George, BC V2N 5B5
Tel: 250-964-2243
Fax: 250-964-2286
Email:marrec@telus.net

Cariboo Chilcotin Coast
Cariboo Park Facility Operator
G & P Kleenery Ltd.
Box 46
Forest Grove, BC V0K 1M0
Tel: 250-397-2523
Email: gpkleenery@telus.net

For Barkerville:
Hagar Business Services Ltd.
Tel: 250-992-2901
Email: regah@telus.net

Northern British Columbia
Skeena–Smithers/Highway 37 Park Facility Operator
Tel: 250-846-9535
Fax: 250-846-9535

Omineca–Highways 16, 27, & 97 Park Facility Operator
Quartz Contracting
10378 Jutland Road
Prince George, BC V2N 4Y8
Tel: 250-964-3489
Email: northquartz@aol.com

CAMPGROUND COOKING

The secret of campground food is simplicity. If you want to savour the best veal in cream and mushroom sauce, save this desire until you return home; do not attempt it while camping, for disappointment will ensue. Whether the results are stupendous or disastrous, cooking over an open fire is tremendous fun. Appetites increase when you're outdoors, especially after a day of hiking or swimming, and the fun continues if you have a few basic necessities and let everyone join in the cooking.

Following are seven simple, practical, evening meal suggestions designed primarily for the novice camper who will be cooking on a fire pit. Although there are a couple of camp cooking books to guide the enthusiast, I found them far too complicated to be practical, with recommendations that included anchovy-and-tomato-stuffed eggplant and peaches in spiced brandy sauce! These recipes I have difficulty with at home, let alone in the open air. I believe experimentation is the order of the day when cooking outdoors, but I do have a few suggestions on preparations that can be done before leaving home to ensure that cooking over an open fire is relatively problem free.

1. Purchase a large roll of heavy-duty aluminum foil. This will be used frequently and is invaluable.

2. Before leaving home, pack salt, pepper, olive oil, and any herbs and spices you think you will need (plastic film containers make excellent herb jars). Also take a couple of tins of tuna or cooked meat, rice, noodles, and pasta as standbys.

3. Buy bottles of ready-made salad dressing, barbecue sauce, and any other sauces you deem appropriate (e.g. Thai peanut sauce, mustard, mayonnaise, HP sauce, lemon juice) to keep in your camping food box. A

few years ago we found Dragon sauce. It went on everything we put on the fire—I have no idea who made it, what was in it, or whether it was good for us, and I doubt we would have used it at home, but outdoors it tasted great and only cost a dollar.

4. Sachets of salt, pepper, tomato sauce, relish, vinegar, milk, etc., are also useful. The camper with initiative will easily be able to access these items.

5. Purchase ready-made salads in sealed plastic bags, available from large supermarkets. If kept cool, these provide good supplies of fresh vegetables that do not require washing.

6. Metal grills with wooden handles (from old hibachis) are useful for cooking food on the fire pit and ensure that sausages are less likely to fall into the fire. In addition, long toasting forks are mandatory instruments for turning food.

7. Take a pan with a lid for boiling water (without a lid, the water ends up tasting like charcoal and usually has bits of ash floating in it—nutritious but not appetizing). Alternatively, a couple of flasks can be easily replenished with coffee or boiling water at gas stations or cafés when travelling, to be consumed later in the day.

8. Plastic food containers are useful not only for keeping food but also as bowls for marinade or dips. Bring an assortment.

9. Remember to pack newspaper, matches, dish detergent, tea towels, plastic plates, cups, bowls, cutlery, a sharp knife, wet wipes, a can/bottle opener, and plastic bags (for collecting the garbage that has to be disposed of after every meal—do not leave it until the next morning, as this attracts animals).

10. A fire takes awhile to get started, especially if the wood is damp, so be sure you have a few appetizers designed to reduce, not enhance, the appetite. Chips, nachos, bags of pre-washed baby carrots, celery, cauliflower, broccoli, and any fresh vegetables are ideal with ready-made dips (salsa, guacamole, peanut butter, plain yogurt, etc.) purchased from the supermarket.

11. Remember that vegetables last, meat rots, and seafood should be eaten fresh— plan meals accordingly.

12. Pita bread, flour tortillas, and enchiladas keep very well, and even when a bit stale, they come to life once heated over an open fire.

13. Buy wine in a box, as this is easier to transport and unbreakable (it also has the advantage of not disclosing how much has been drunk).

14. Fruit such as bananas (delicious when baked whole on the fire), apples, pears, peaches, and grapes are ideal desserts. If camping in the Okanagan, it is difficult to resist the numerous fruit stands.

15. To round off the evening, don't forget the marshmallows. However, for a really good night's sleep, oblivious to the unfamiliar sounds of the forest, a tot of good malt whiskey just before bedtime is an excellent sleeping potion.

Pack the bikes along; they're great for exploring the province's parks.

A campground cooking spot at Mount Robson Provincial Park looks cosy.

Cooking outdoors is easier then it may seem.

Recipes

Cooking on an open fire requires a bit of trial and error, which is the enjoyable part. Campers soon learn from mistakes and develop their own unique recipes. Here are a few that are easy and appetizing, requiring only the open fire and one pan.

Tortilla Wraps

Flour tortillas	Can of tuna
Cheese	Bacon
Tomatoes	Salad
Mayonnaise	

Flour tortillas keep well and offer easy meal options. Heat them until soft on the grill (2 minutes), then fill with salad, tuna, mayonnaise, cheese, salsa, tomatoes, bacon, or whatever you have available. While they are better warm, if it's raining too hard to start a fire this is a good cold-menu alternative and also offers sustenance for hiking.

Happy Hamburgers

Hamburgers	Bacon
Mushrooms	Buns
Cheese salad	Chips

The easiest meal option: Grill hamburger patties on an open fire along with bacon and mushrooms (cooked whole), then place in a bun (or pita bread) with salad, tomatoes, cheese, etc., and serve with chips—what could be easier?

Steak, Potatoes, and Vegetable Surprise

Steak	Potatoes
Zucchini	Onions
Red and green peppers	Tomatoes
Bacon	Mushrooms

A meal guaranteed not to taste the same twice. Make a concoction of sauces for the steak marinade. Include any or all of the following: red wine, olive oil, mustard, salt, pepper, garlic, mixed herbs, tomato purée/sauce. Soak the steak for as long as possible. Place the steak directly on the grill and baste as required. Wrap the potatoes in foil and place *in* the fire. Use a fork to test for when they are done (30 to 60 minutes depending on how hot the fire is). For the vegetable surprise, take a large piece of foil and layer it with sliced onions, cut peppers, mushrooms, bacon, sliced zucchini, sliced tomatoes, and any other vegetable you may have. Season with garlic and herbs and other appropriate sauces. Fold the foil to create a tight parcel and place on the grill. Turn upside down once. Cook for about 15 minutes. This makes a fantastic "gunge" as the tomatoes disintegrate over the rest of the ingredients and are delicious.

Saucy Sausages in Pita Bread

Sausages   Red peppers
Tomatoes   Pita bread
Salad

Place the sausages on the grill and start to cook. Slice the red pepper and cook by placing directly on the grill. Cook the tomatoes either on the grill or on a piece of foil placed on top of the grill (this option means you lose fewer to the ravages of the fire). When all is cooked, place the pita breads on the grill to warm. Slice the pitas and fill with the sausages, tomatoes, and red peppers. Serve with salad. (N.B. This recipe can be done with bacon instead of sausages and is also an easy breakfast alternative, if you leave out the peppers.)

Campground Chicken with Zucchini and Yams

Chicken pieces   Yams
Zucchini

Marinate the chicken pieces to taste (see steak recipe) and place on the grill. Wrap the yams in foil and place in the fire until soft (20 to 60 minutes). Place the zucchini on the grill and cook until just beginning to turn brown (10 to 15 minutes).

Spare Ribs with Sweet Corn and Noodles

Marinated spare ribs
Sweet corn
Noodles

Place marinated spare ribs directly on the barbecue until cooked. Remove the green leaves from the sweet corn and place on the grill. Cook until tender (15 minutes), turning regularly. Cook the noodles in the pan as directed. (There are many varieties of already-spiced meats in the supermarket, all ideal for convenient campground cooking.)

Salmon Steaks with Spicy Vegetables and Rice

Salmon steaks   Broccoli
Cauliflower   Mushrooms
Peppers   Tomatoes
Rice

Place the salmon steaks on a large piece of foil and season with salt, pepper, lemon juice, and mustard. Place on the grill and turn the fish until cooked. Wash and marinate vegetables such as broccoli, sliced red and green peppers, cauliflower, mushrooms, and tomatoes (see recipe for steak marinade and amend as desired). Place these on the grill to cook. Cook the rice as directed.

Bon appétit!

Facts and Figures on B.C. Parks

- B.C. has the second-largest parks system in Canada, after Canada's national parks.

- In 1960 approximately 3 million visits were made to B.C. Parks. By 2003 this figure had increased over seven times to 23.5 million.

- In 2001 2,639,293 camping parties visited B.C. parks.

- Over 234 parks have facilities for people with disabilities.

- More than 3,000 kilometres of hiking trails are available in B.C. parks.

- The highest concentration of grizzly bears is found in Khutzeymateen Provincial Park (no camping facilities), which is Canada's only grizzly bear sanctuary.

- Tweedsmuir Provincial Park is B.C.'s largest provincial park, covering 974,046 hectares.

- Canada's second-highest waterfall, Della Falls, is found in Strathcona Provincial Park.

- Roderick Haig-Brown Provincial Park has the world's most productive sockeye salmon run.

- Strathcona Park was the first provincial park in B.C., created in 1911.

- Golden Ears is the most popular provincial park with camping facilities in B.C., followed by Manning, Rathtrevor Beach, and Cultus Lake.

- Rathtrevor Beach is the most popular provincial park with camping facilities on Vancouver Island.

- Okanagan Lake is the most popular provincial park campground in the Okanagan.

- Approximately six out of every ten B.C. residents use a provincial park at least once a year.

- As of May 2003, there were 817 provincial parks, recreational areas, and ecological reserves in B.C.

- Twelve percent of B.C.'s land base (more than 11 million hectares) is dedicated park or protected area.

CAMPER NOTES

CAMPER NOTES

CAMPER NOTES

CAMPING
with Kids

The Best Family Campgrounds in British Columbia and Alberta

Jayne Seagrave

Children have "certainly altered my camping life," writes Jayne Seagrave in this latest addition to her popular camping series. She rises to the challenge, however, and with this detailed guide, so will many other camping enthusiasts who feel daunted by the prospect of camping with kids.

Seagrave covers it all, from camping while pregnant to camping with pre-teens. Each entry on her favourite family-oriented, government-owned campgrounds in B.C. and Alberta provides historical, environmental, and recreational information. As always, Seagrave offers first-hand experiences and practical tips on what to bring, what to expect at each campground, how to avoid potential hazards, and the reservation system.

With over 20,000 fans who have bought her camping books and a range of media personnel who have dubbed her their "expert," Jayne may know more about B.C. campgrounds than any other mother in the province.

Recreation/Camping
6 x 9   160 pp
16 pages full colour
1-894384-55-5
$17.95   sc

Great Seashore Books

Fishing with Charlie White

**Charlie White's
103 Fishing Secrets**
5.5 x 8.5   144 pp
1-895811-61-9
$14.95   sc

How to Catch Crabs
5.5 x 8.5   64 pp
1-895811-51-1
$8.95   sc

How to Catch Bottomfish
5.5 x 8.5   128 pp
1-894384-60-1
$15.95   sc

How to Catch Shellfish
5.5 x 8.5   96 pp
1-895811-49-X
$9.95   sc

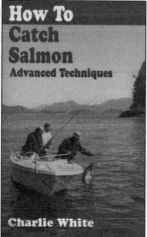

**How to Catch Salmon
Advanced Techniques**
5.5 x 8.5   192 pp
1-894384-64-4
$16.95   sc

Living Off the Sea
5.5 x 8.5   128 pp
1-895811-47-3
$11.95   sc

Visit the Heritage House web site at
www.heritagehouse.ca